*The First Book of*

# Word™ for Windows™ 2

D1477521

*The First Book of*

# Word™ for Windows™ 2

**Sandra E. Eddy and John E. Schnyder**

**SAMS**

*A Division of Prentice Hall Computer Publishing*
*11711 North College, Carmel, Indiana 46032 USA*

*For Elizabeth Eddy*

©1992 by Sams

All rights reserved. No part of this book shall be reproduced, stored in a retrieval system, or transmitted by any means, electronic, mechanical, photocopying, recording, or otherwise, without written permission from the publisher. No patent liability is assumed with respect to the use of the information contained herein. Although every precaution has been taken in the preparation of this book, the publisher and author assume no responsibility for errors or omissions. Neither is any liability assumed for damages resulting from the use of the information contained herein. For information, address Sams, 11711 N. College Ave., Carmel, IN 46032.

International Standard Book Number: 0-672-27389-6
Library of Congress Catalog Card Number: 91-67084

95 94 93 92      8 7 6 5 4

Interpretation of the printing code: the rightmost number of the first series of numbers is the year of the book's printing; the rightmost number of the second series of numbers is the number of the book's printing. For example, a printing code of 92-1 shows that the first printing of the book occurred in 1992.

Screen reproductions in this book were created by means of the program Collage Plus from Inner Media, Inc., Hollis, NH.

*Printed in the United States of America*

**Publisher**
*Richard K. Swadley*

**Associate Publisher**
*Marie Butler-Knight*

**Managing Editor**
*Marjorie Hopper*

**Acquisitions Editor**
*Mary-Terese Cagnina*

**Development Editor**
*Diana Francoeur*

**Manuscript Editor**
*Howard Peirce*

**Production Editor**
*Linda Hawkins*

**Editorial Assistant**
*Hilary Adams*

**Cover Artist**
*Held & Diedrich Design*

**Designer**
*Scott Cook*

**Indexer**
*Susan VandeWalle*

**Production Team**
*Claudia Bell, Michelle Cleary, Keith Davenport, Mark Enochs, Brook
Farling, Dennis Hager, Audra Hershman, Betty Kish, Bob LaRoche, Laurie
Lee, Anne Owen, Juli Pavey, Caroline Roop, Linda Seifert, Lisa Wilson,
Allan Wimmer, Phil Worthington, Christine Young*

*Special thanks to Hilary Adams for ensuring the technical
accuracy of this book.*

vi

# Contents

*Introduction, xi*

vii

1    *The Word for Windows
       Environment, 1*

Starting Word for Windows, 1
The Word Program Window, 5
Understanding Word Menus, 8
Working in Word with a Mouse, 11
Working in Word with the Keyboard, 15
The Toolbar, Ribbon, and Ruler, 19
Getting Help, 20
Reducing Word to an Icon, 21
Quitting Word, 22

2    *Creating Your First Document, 25*

The Document Window, 25
Entering and Viewing Text, 30
Moving Around a Document, 38
About the File Menu, 43
Saving Your Work, 44
Retrieving a Document, 54
Printing a Document, 57

**3   Manipulating Text, 61**

Selecting Text, 62
About the Edit Menu, 68
Moving, Copying, and Deleting Text, 69
The Clipboard versus the Spike, 72
Undoing and Repeating Actions, 77
Finding and Replacing Text, 78

**4   Proofing Your Document, 85**

Checking Your Spelling, 86
Using the Thesaurus, 94
Checking Your Grammar, 96
Document Statistics, 103

**5   Defining Document-wide and Section Formats, 107**

Formatting in Word for Windows, 107
Changing Units of Measure in Word, 109
Document-wide Formatting, 111
Creating Headers and Footers, 124
Creating Page Breaks, 129
Controlling Orphan and Widow Lines, 132
Customizing Page Numbering, 133
Section Formatting, 134

**6   Formatting Paragraphs, 141**

Paragraph Formatting, 141
Enhancing Paragraphs, 159
Using Tabs, 168

**7   Formatting Characters, 175**

Character Formatting, 175
Using Fonts, 189

**8   Advanced Formatting, 205**

Finding and Replacing Formats and Symbols, 206

**viii**

Adding Special Characters, 219
Creating Bulleted and Numbered Lists, 222
Using Multiple Columns in a Document, 225

## 9    *Previewing and Printing Documents, 231*

Defining the Active Printer, 232
Previewing Your Document Before
    Printing, 235
Zooming a Document, 239
Printing Your Document, 240
Troubleshooting Common Printer
    Problems, 246

## 10    *Creating Tables, 249*

Creating Tables, 250
Editing Tables, 258
Formatting Tables, 261
Sorting Items in a Table, 267
Performing Calculations, 269

## 11    *Working with Styles, 273*

Defining a Style by Recording a Paragraph's
    Formats, 274
About the Style Dialog Box, 275
Defining a Style by Using the Format Style
    Command, 277
Basing a New Style on an Existing Style, 278
Specifying the Next Style, 280
Applying Styles, 282
Viewing Style Names in the Document Window, 283
Changing a Style, 284
Deleting and Renaming Styles, 286
Printing a List of Styles, 286

## 12    *Using Word's Advanced Features, 289*

Connecting Glossaries, Macros, Styles, and
    Templates, 290
Using Glossaries to Save Time, 290
Using Macros, 295
Document Templates, 300

ix

**13   Managing Documents, Windows, and the Word Program, 309**

Using the Find File Command, 310
Converting Documents to Different File
    Formats, 313
Manipulating Application and Document
    Windows, 314
Customizing the Toolbar, 319

**14   Creating Form Letters, Labels, and Envelopes, 325**

Creating and Printing Form Letters, 326
Creating and Printing Mailing Labels, 342
Creating and Printing Envelopes, 344

**X   A   Installing Word for Windows, 349**

Before Installing Word for Windows, 349
Installing Word for Windows, 350

**B   Keystroke Shortcuts, 355**

**Index, 361**

# Introduction

## Who This Book Is For

This book is for anyone who wants to start working with Microsoft Word for Windows 2.0 with a minimum of effort. It is designed to cover all basic and intermediate functions of Word for Windows. Every chapter in the book provides you with basic concepts, step-by-step procedures, tips, and shortcuts.

## What Is Word for Windows?

Word for Windows is a sophisticated and extensive but easy-to-use word processor based on the Windows *graphical user interface,* a display format that allows you to select commands, functions, and even other applications by pointing to parts of the screen with the mouse. However, if you do not have a mouse, you can still access every Windows command and feature by using your keyboard.

Selecting commands is easy in Word for Windows. All the commands that you will use are organized under menus—just select the menu and Word displays the commands for that menu. If there is a shortcut key combination for the command, it is displayed next to the command.

After you have used Word for Windows commands to create and edit a document, you can use the built-in spell checker, grammar checker, and thesaurus to proof and refine your document.

Although Word for Windows is extremely complex, it is easy to use. If you hit any roadblocks, you can use its extensive and context-sensitive help facility. *Context-sensitive* means that when you ask for help, Word for Windows displays a help screen related to the command or feature you are trying to use. The help facility also includes an index of topics and a search facility.

## Selecting Menus and Commands

**xii**

Word for Windows allows you to select a command from a menu in one of two ways: by pointing and clicking with the mouse or by typing a key combination from the keyboard. In either case, before you select a command, you must first select a menu.

To select a menu and command with the mouse, simply point to the menu name and click on it with the left mouse button. When you see the list of commands available for that menu, point and click on the command name that you want.

To select a menu and command with the keyboard, first press the Alt key to activate the menu bar and then type the underlined letter in the menu name. When you see the list of commands, type the underlined letter for the command you want. (You do not have to press Alt again.) For example, to select the **File** menu and the **Print** command, press Alt to activate the menu bar and press F to select the **File** menu. Then press P to select the **Print** command. (Note that in this book the underlined letter is boldfaced and the underline is omitted.) We remind you what the key sequence is by showing it in parentheses, for example, "Select the File menu and the Print command (Alt,F,P)."

As a shortcut, we often omit the word *menu* when a menu is immediately followed by a command. For example, "Select the File Print command" means to select the **File** menu and then select the **Print** command.

# Conventions Used in This Book

*The First Book of Word for Windows 2* uses some special conventions and features that make it easier for you to learn Word for Windows. The following sections describe each special convention and feature.

## Terminology

Throughout this book, the term *Word* is interchangeable with *Word for Windows*. When we refer to Word, we mean Microsoft Word for Windows, version 2.0.

If you are told to *select* or *choose* a command, you can use either the mouse or the keyboard to do so.

## Key Commands

Throughout this book, you'll see sets of keystrokes that are entered either in succession or simultaneously. Keystrokes that you enter in succession are separated by commas. The comma means that you press the key and release it before pressing the next key in the command. You do not press the comma. For example, when you see the Alt,F,P command succession, press and release the Alt key, press and release F, and then press and release P. Keystrokes that you enter simultaneously are separated by hyphens (-). The hyphen means that you hold down the first two keys while you are pressing the third one. For example, when you see the Ctrl-Shift-F12 key combination, hold down the Ctrl and Shift keys and press the F12 key while continuing to hold down Ctrl and Shift. (Incidentally, both of the preceding commands enable you to print a document.)

## Typographic Conventions

To make your learning easier, we have incorporated certain typographic conventions. Keys that we want you to press or options we want you to select are shown in color, for example, "Press Enter or select OK."

Text that we want you to type appears in color, in boldfaced computer font, for example, "To start Word for Windows from the DOS prompt, type `winword`." You type `w i n w o r d` and press Enter. If Word for Windows displays text on-screen, it is presented in regular computer font.

When a term is presented to you for the first time, it is displayed in *italics*.

In Word for Windows, you'll see underlined letters in menus, commands, and dialog boxes. The underlined letter is the keyboard key that you press to activate a menu or command. In this book, the letter appears boldfaced rather than underscored. Note that to activate a menu, you must press Alt *and* the keyboard letter.

## *Special Features of This Book*

To help you learn about Word for Windows and to emphasize important points, this book incorporates special features. Each feature has its own distinctive icon to help you identify it.

*Q* Quick Steps are step-by-step instructions summarizing the sequence of tasks needed to perform a common Word for Windows procedure. The left column explains the actions that you perform. The right column explains Word for Windows' response.

 **Tips** provide helpful ideas and advice or give a shortcut for a Word for Windows command. **Notes** provide additional information that is useful to know.

**FYIdeas** give practical, creative ways to use Word for Windows to solve a business problem or perform a task.

 **Cautions** alert you to pitfalls and potential problems.

### *Toolbar Buttons*

Word for Windows' Toolbar is an especially easy-to-use feature that is new to version 2.0. Located above the Ribbon and Ruler, the default Toolbar consists of 22 buttons representing the most frequently used tasks in Word for Windows. To use a Toolbar button, just move the mouse pointer to the appropriate button and press the left mouse button. Word either performs an action or displays a dialog box into which you can enter information needed to perform an action.

In this book, whenever you learn about an action that is represented by a default button on the Toolbar, you'll see the Toolbar button and a short explanation.

# Acknowledgments

**XV**

We had a great deal of help and support from the beginning through the end of this project. We acknowledge the special efforts of Diana Francoeur, Lisa Bucki, Linda Hawkins, and Howard Peirce. Special thanks go to Marie Butler-Knight and Mary-Terese Cagnina. This book wouldn't be as accurate as it is without the extraordinary efforts of Hilary J. Adams.

Thanks to family and friends who provided unending support every step of the way.

A very special thank-you to Indy, Toni, and Bart. They were always there to cheer us up.

# Trademarks

All terms mentioned in this book that are known to be trademarks or service marks are listed below. In addition, terms suspected of being trademarks or service marks have been appropriately capitalized. Sams cannot attest to the accuracy of this information. Use of a term in this book should not be regarded as affecting the validity of any trademark or service mark.

Avery is a registered trademark of Avery International Corporation.

CompuServe is a registered trademark of CompuServe, Inc.

Courier is a registered trademark of Smith-Corona Corporation.

Epson is a registered trademark of Epson America, Inc.

Helvetica and Times Roman are registered trademarks of Linotype AG and/or its subsidiaries.

Hewlett-Packard, HP, and LaserJet are registered trademarks of Hewlett-Packard Company.

Microsoft is a registered trademark and Windows and Toolbar are trademarks of Microsoft Corporation.

WordPerfect is a registered trademark of WordPerfect Corporation.

# The Word for Windows Environment

## In This Chapter

- ► *Starting and exiting Word for Windows*
- ► *Using the mouse and the keyboard*
- ► *Using the Word screen and menus*
- ► *Getting help*

## Starting Word for Windows

Before you start Word for Windows, you'll have to start your computer and make sure that your surge protector and your peripherals, such as your printer, are also switched on.

> **Note:** Before you can use Word for Windows, your computer must have Windows and Word for Windows installed. Unless both of these programs are installed on your computer, Word will not work. For Word for Windows installation instructions, see Appendix A.

There are several ways to start Word for Windows. You can start the program from within Windows or from DOS, and you can use the mouse or the keyboard. The following Quick Steps provide three methods of starting Word for Windows.

 **Using the Keyboard to Start Word from Within Windows**

1. If you have not started Windows, at the DOS prompt, type **win** and press Enter.

   Windows displays a series of screens.

2. Press Alt.

   Word places a highlight on the second line of the window.

3. Press F, the underlined letter in the **F**ile command.

   Windows highlights the word **File** and opens the **F**ile menu (see Figure 1.1).

4. Press R, the underlined letter in the **R**un command.

   Windows opens the Run dialog box, shown in Figure 1.2). A *dialog box* is a small box into which you enter or add information in order to complete an action.

**2**

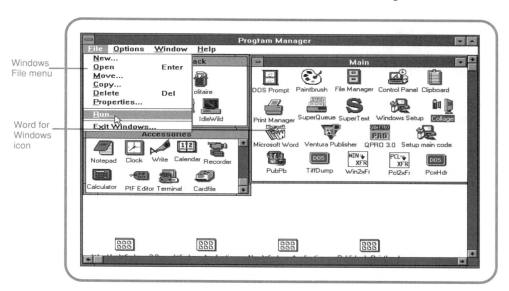

*Figure 1.1   The open Program Manager window showing the File menu.*

**5.** On the Command Line in the dialog box, type **winword**. Press Enter.

Word starts and displays its opening screen (see Figure 1.3). ☐

Select OK or press Enter to complete the action. The heavy border indicates that this is the default.

Select Cancel to escape from the dialog box. The action is not completed, and you return to the previous window.

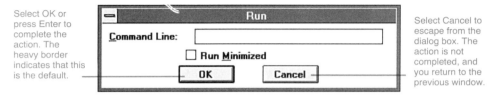

*Figure 1.2   The Run dialog box showing the command line. Type* **winword** *in the Command Line box to start Word for Windows.*

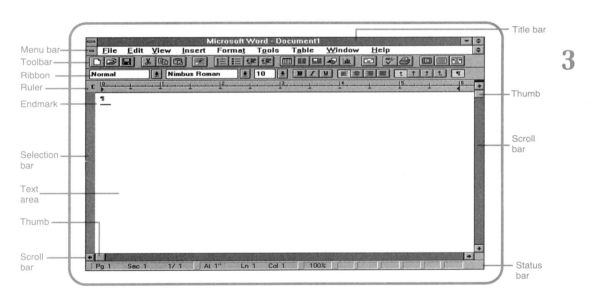

*Figure 1.3   The opening screen of Word for Windows.*

3

> ✎ **Tip:** Whenever you see a button (like OK) surrounded by a heavy black border, this is the default choice. To quickly accept the default choice, press Enter.

## *Q* Using the Mouse to Start Word from Within Windows

1. With Windows already started, find the Word icon on the Windows screen, move the mouse pointer to it, and then *double-click* by pressing the left mouse button twice in succession. (The secret to double-clicking is to click twice rhythmically, rather than too rapidly.)

The mouse pointer temporarily turns into an hourglass, indicating that the computer is processing and you must wait. Then Word starts and displays its opening screen, shown in Figure 1.3.

☐

**4**

 **Tip:** If you have trouble double-clicking, move the mouse pointer to the Word for Windows icon and *click* (press and release the mouse button once). Then you can either press Enter or point to the File command and click; then point to the Open command and click. Note that you can change clicking speed in the Windows Control Panel.

## *Q* Starting Word from the DOS Prompt

1. From the DOS prompt (usually C:\), type **cd\winword** and press Enter. (If you installed Word 2.0 in a directory other than \winword, change to that directory instead.)

DOS changes to the directory \winword.

2. Type **winword** and press Enter.

Windows opens; then Word starts automatically, first displaying its introductory screen and then its opening screen (see Figure 1.3).☐

**Tip:** You can also start Word from within Windows by pressing the arrow keys to highlight the Word for Windows icon in the active window. Then press Enter.

# The Word Program Window

When Word for Windows starts, its display covers the entire computer screen. Any window this large is called a *full screen* or a *maximized* window. Figure 1.3 shows a maximized window and all of its components. Before you create your first document, it is important to learn about the parts of the Word screen—what each component does and how it works. These components are shown in Figures 1.4 through 1.9.

▶ *Title bar*—This long, horizontal rectangle at the top of the screen displays the program name followed by the name, if any has been defined, of the current document. If the document is unnamed, Word names it DOCUMENT*n*, where *n* indicates a number that increases by 1 with each new unnamed document. (See Figure 1.4.) The Title bar includes these components:

*Application Control menu*—Click on this box to open a menu, listing commands that manipulate the current program.

*Minimize button*—Click on this small button to reduce the program to an icon—perhaps to run another program while Word is active without taking up screen space.

*Maximize/Restore button* (Word)—Click on this to switch between a Word text area that encompasses the entire screen and a smaller text area. Notice that the appearance of this button changes depending on the size of the text area. See also the Maximize button.

**5**

Application Control menu    Program name  Document name        Minimize button    Maximize/
                                                                                  Restore button
                                                                                  (Word)

*Figure 1.4    The Title bar, showing the program name and the document name.*

▶ *Menu bar*—This long, horizontal rectangle beneath the Title bar displays the main Word commands. Point to a word on the Menu bar and click, and a menu of commands is displayed, as shown in Figure 1.5. The Menu bar includes the following:

*Document Control menu*—This box contains commands that manipulate the current document.

*Maximize/Restore button* (document)—Click on this button to open a document window within the Word window. To restore the Word window to its previous full size, click on the button to the right of the document name in the document window.

Document Control menu                    Maximize/Restore button (document)

File   Edit   View   Insert   Format   Tools   Table   Window   Help

*Figure 1.5   The Menu bar, which displays Word's main commands, also includes the Document Control menu and another Maximize/Restore button.*

▶ *Toolbar*—This series of buttons, shown in Figure 1.6, provides the Word commands that you use most often. The inside back cover of this book shows an exploded view of all 22 of the Toolbar's default buttons, and Chapter 13 explains how you can customize the Toolbar.

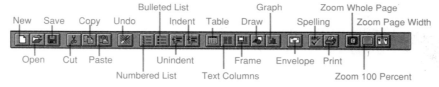

Bulleted List          Graph          Zoom Whole Page
New   Save   Copy   Undo   Indent   Table   Draw   Spelling   Zoom Page Width

Open   Cut   Paste   Unindent   Frame   Envelope   Print
Numbered List   Text Columns   Zoom 100 Percent

*Figure 1.6   The Toolbar shows the default buttons with which Word starts. You can customize the buttons on the Toolbar.*

▶ *Ribbon*—This long rectangle is used to control the appearance and size of text, as well as character and paragraph formatting. Its features are shown in Figure 1.7.

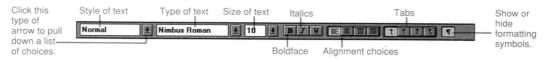

Click this type of arrow to pull down a list of choices.   Style of text   Type of text   Size of text   Italics   Tabs   Show or hide formatting symbols.

Normal   Nimbus Roman   10   B I U   Boldface   Alignment choices

*Figure 1.7   The Ribbon displays the current appearance of the paragraph and the current type and size of the text.*

▶ *Ruler*—This rectangle (shown in Figure 1.8) displays the current margin and tab settings. Use the Ruler to change these settings, to determine paragraph indentation (if any), and to widen or narrow columns of text.

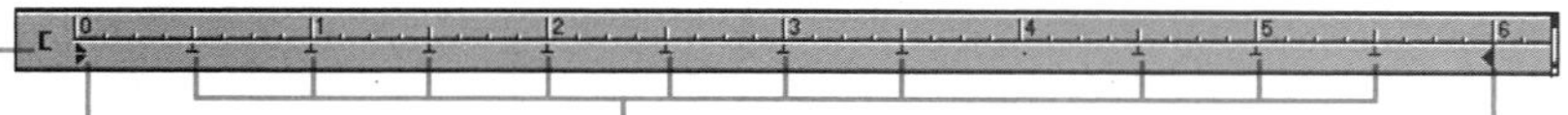

Margin scale symbol

Indent scale symbol        Tab positions        Right margin

*Figure 1.8   The Ruler displays and defines margins and tab positions.*

▶ *Text area*—This area, shown in Figure 1.3, displays your document as you work. The vertical blinking line is the *insertion point*, which shows the location of the next character that you type. If you have not typed anything in the text area, the *endmark*, the horizontal line that marks the end of the document, is located below and to the right of the insertion point. The *selection bar,* from which you can select a line of text in the current document, is an invisible vertical area near the left margin.

▶ *Scroll bar*—There are two types of scroll bars—the vertical bar at the far right of the text area and the horizontal bar at the bottom of the text area (see Figure 1.3). The arrows at the ends of the scroll bar and the *thumb* (the little box within the scroll bar) allow you to move around the document in the text area. The thumb also indicates your current location in a document. You'll learn about moving around a document in Chapter 2.

▶ *Status bar*—This area, shown in Figure 1.9, actually contains three types of information. The left section shows the page location: current page number, section number (explained in Chapter 5), and current page number versus the total number of pages in the document. The middle section is the location of the insertion point. The first number is the distance from the top edge of the page to the insertion point in inches. The second number is the number of the line on which the insertion point is located. The third number is the column, or characters counted from the left margin, where the insertion point is located. The right section shows the magnification level of the text on-screen. This section also displays indicators of certain Word features or modes that are active. For example, if you press the Caps Lock key, the word CAPS appears in the second box from the left.

Sometimes the Status bar also displays messages. If you open a command menu, the Status bar changes in order to show a description of each of the commands.

7

Page number — This indicates the first page of a one-page document.

| Pg 1 | Sec 1 | 1/ 1 | At 1" | Ln 1 | Col 1 | 100% | | This area displays indicators. |

Section number — The insertion point is located here on the page. — The level of magnification

*Figure 1.9    The Status bar contains information related to the current document and also displays messages.*

# Understanding Word Menus

All Word menus are found in the Menu bar (shown in Figure 1.5), which is divided into menus containing related commands, submenus, and dialog boxes. Word's menus are known as *pull-down menus,* which means that after you select a command from the Menu bar, a menu opens or "pulls down" from the Menu bar. (Figure 1.10 shows an example of a pull-down menu.) Once Word opens a pull-down menu, you can select a command by clicking on it, or you can close the menu by clicking anywhere outside the menu. To select a command using the keyboard, press the letter that is underlined. To close a pull-down menu using the keyboard, press the Esc key.

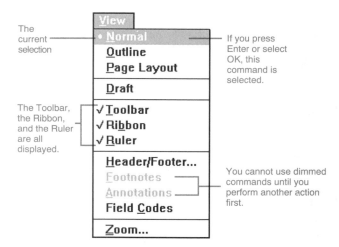

The current selection —— • Normal ——— If you press Enter or select OK, this command is selected.

The Toolbar, the Ribbon, and the Ruler are all displayed. —— √ Toolbar / Ribbon / Ruler

You cannot use dimmed commands until you perform another action first.

*Figure 1.10    An example of a pull-down menu.*

The menus are:

*File*—These commands manage documents. Use this menu to save, create, retrieve, and print documents.

*Edit*—These commands manipulate text. You can copy, cut, and paste text; or you can search for and/or replace text. Use the Undo command to erase the last editing change or go to a specific place in the document.

*View*—These commands control how your document appears on-screen. You can show your document in Draft, Outline, or Page Layout mode. You can also hide or reveal the Toolbar, Ribbon, and/or Ruler on-screen. You can also use this menu to add *footnotes* (additional information that enhances, but is not part of, your document), *annotations* (reviewers' comments), and *field codes* (codes that signal Word to retrieve chunks of information found within the current document, in another document, from an application, or even from your computer system) to your document.

*Insert*—These commands allow you to insert other documents, files, special symbols, and more into your document. You can also use this menu to create a table of contents or an index.

*Format*—These commands control the appearance of characters and paragraphs in your document. Use this menu to set tabs, apply styles, and change the number of columns.

*Tools*—These commands provide miscellaneous features. You can check spelling and grammar, find synonyms, hyphenate words in your document, work with macros, create envelopes, and so on.

*Table*—These commands control tables and columns in your document.

*Window*—These commands let you determine how your current document is viewed on-screen. In addition, you can use this menu to open and arrange multiple windows.

*Help*—These commands offer you immediate help with the program.

Here are some additional facts about the commands in menus:

▶ Related items on a menu are grouped together and separated from other groups of items with a horizontal line.

9

▶ If a command looks dimmed or grayed, you cannot use it at this time. You may have to use another command first before you can use this command.

▶ If a command is preceded by a check mark, the command can be turned on or off. For example, in the **V**iew menu, the **To**olbar command is turned on (will be displayed on-screen) when a check mark is next to it and turned off (will not display on-screen) when there is no check mark next to it.

▶ If a command is preceded by a dot, the command function is the current selection. For example, in the **V**iew menu, either **O**utline or **P**age Layout is the current setting. When one function is selected, the other function cannot be selected.

▶ If a command is followed by an *ellipsis* (three consecutive periods), you will have to enter or select some choices in a dialog box. Figure 1.11 shows a typical dialog box and its different parts.

**10**

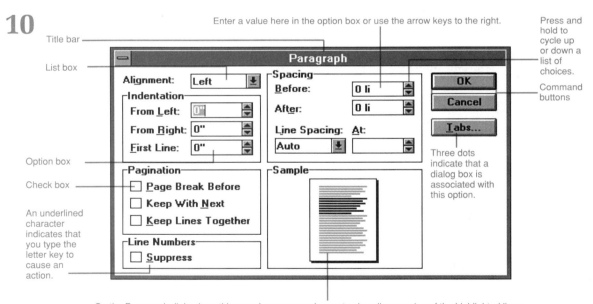

On the Paragraph dialog box, this sample page can change to show line spacing of the highlighted lines.

*Figure 1.11    Use a dialog box to enter text or change a setting. When you have finished using the dialog box, select the appropriate buttons (OK, Cancel, Close, depending on what you want to do).*

You can give commands and move around in Word for Windows using either the mouse or the keyboard. The mouse is easier to use because you can issue commands just by moving the mouse pointer to a certain area of the screen and clicking a mouse button. If you are a beginner, the best way to build your knowledge of Word is by using the mouse. After you have used Word for a while, you will learn keyboard shortcuts and will probably issue commands with a combination of the mouse and the keyboard.

 **Note:** Throughout this book, instructions for selecting a command from a menu are given as follows:

Select *Menu name Command* (**File New**, for example) where *Menu name* represents the name of a pull-down menu on the Menu bar (File) and *Command* is the name of a command on the pull-down menu (New).

**11**

# Working in Word with a Mouse

A *mouse* is an input device that you use by sliding it around on a desktop or other flat surface. As you move the mouse, a mouse pointer moves around on-screen.

The mouse pointer assumes different shapes, depending on where it is on the Word screen. Some of the most common shapes follow:

► When the pointer is located in the text area, it looks like an I-beam.

 **Tip:** Do not confuse the I-beam of the mouse pointer with the insertion point.

► On a window border, the pointer is a two-headed arrow. You can use this type of pointer to change the size of the window—horizontally, vertically, or both (when you move the pointer to a corner of the window).

▶ Outside the text area, the pointer is an arrow that points
diagonally to the left (see Figure 1.12). Use this arrow to
point to parts of the window and click the mouse button
once or twice to cause an action. You can point to *icons*,
which are small illustrations of the programs or components
to be run or activated, or *buttons*, which are small boxes
usually containing pictures that remind you of the action to
be taken or the format to be changed. You can also point to
commands to open menus from which you can choose other
commands.

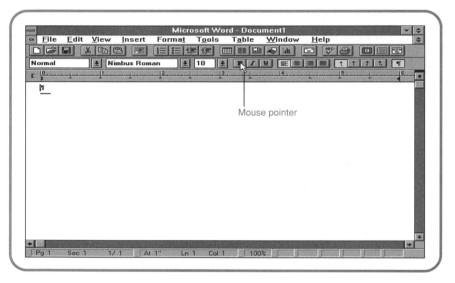

*Figure 1.12    This mouse pointer points to buttons, icons,
and commands that you click on to cause an action.*

▶ When the pointer (pointing diagonally to the right) is in the
selection bar in the left margin, you can highlight an entire
line of text at once. See Figure 1.13.

▶ When Word is executing a command, the mouse pointer
looks like an hourglass. This signals that you have to wait to
execute the next command or take the next action.

Throughout this book, you will learn about specific actions you
take by moving the mouse and then pressing a mouse button. Unless
otherwise mentioned, use the left mouse button. These mouse
actions are described in Table 1.1.

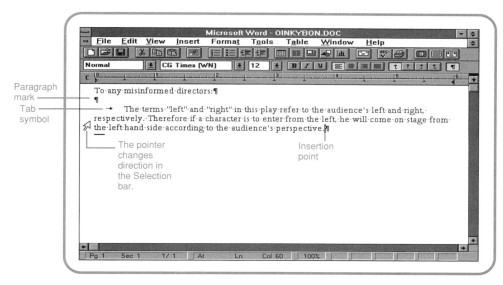

Paragraph mark
Tab symbol

The pointer changes direction in the Selection bar.

Insertion point

*Figure 1.13    From the selection bar, you can highlight a line of text.*

**13**

*Table 1.1    Mouse actions.*

| Action | Description |
|--------|-------------|
| Point | Move the mouse so that the mouse pointer is located where you want it on the screen. |
| Click | Quickly press and release the mouse button once. |
| Double-click | Quickly press and release the mouse button twice. |
| Drag | Press and hold the mouse button down while moving the mouse. |

The following Quick Steps show you how to use a mouse to access Word menus.

 **Selecting Menus and Commands with the Mouse**

1. On the Menu bar, click on the title of the menu that you want to use.

   Word opens the menu and displays all the available choices.

2. Click on the name of the desired command.

   Word either performs an action or gives you more choices.

3. Click on the OK button to perform the action or click on the Cancel button to take no action. If the Cancel button has changed to a Close button, take no further action (some actions, which cannot be reversed, may have already occurred).

Word returns you to the place in your document from which you started the command.

□

**Tip:** You can quickly access many Word commands by clicking on the appropriate Toolbar button. See the inside back cover of this book for a description of all the Toolbar buttons.

14

## Using the Mouse with Dialog Boxes

Often, selecting a command causes Word to display a dialog box. The dialog box can itself contain other types of boxes or it can contain buttons, as shown earlier in Figure 1.11. The mouse is the easiest way to use a dialog box and its associated boxes and buttons. The following list describes the various components of a dialog box and explains how to use the mouse with each component:

*Text boxes*—Boxes in which you enter text, such as a file name. To enter text, place the mouse pointer in the text box and click the left mouse button to move the insertion point to the text box. Type and edit your text just as you would in a document window.

*List boxes*—A type of text box. Either type a value in a list box or, for a drop-down list box, select the list arrow (the underlined down arrow) at the right side of the box to reveal a list from which you can choose. To close a drop-down list box without selecting it, click on the list arrow again.

*Option boxes*—Boxes into which you can either type a value or select the up or down arrow located at the right side of the box in order to increment or decrement, respectively, the value shown in the box.

*Radio buttons*—Small buttons that look like circles. When a group of options is preceded by radio buttons, you can select only one button, or option, from the group. Radio buttons work similarly to buttons in a car radio: you can push only one button at a time and you can select only one station at a time. To select a radio button, move the mouse pointer to the radio button and click with the left mouse button. A large black dot will appear in the button, indicating that the option is turned on.

*Check boxes*—Small square boxes that display an x when a feature is turned on and that are blank when a feature is turned off. When a group of options is preceded by check boxes, you can select several options from this group. For each option that you wish to select, move the mouse pointer to the check box and click with the left mouse button.

*Command buttons*—Rectangular-shaped buttons that can be selected only separately. There are three command buttons that you will see most often: OK, Cancel, and Close. Table 1.2 describes each button. Some dialog boxes contain other command buttons, which will be described as they occur. To select a command button, move the mouse pointer to the command button and click with the left mouse button.

**15**

*Table 1.2   Word's buttons.*

| Button | Description |
| --- | --- |
| OK | Close a dialog box after completing the command. |
| Cancel | Close a dialog box before completing the command. All settings return to their prior state. |
| Close | Close a dialog box before completing the command. All settings that you have changed remain changed. |

# Working in Word with the Keyboard

If you don't have a mouse or are not comfortable using it, you can execute commands in Word by using just the keyboard. However, if you have a mouse, you'll probably find that you use a combination of the mouse and the keyboard.

Word has many commands; you activate them by pressing single keys, *key combinations* (pressing two or three keys simultaneously), and *key successions* (pressing two or three keys one after another). In this book, key combinations are shown as two or three keys, each separated by a hyphen (-); and key successions are shown as two or three keys, each separated by a comma (,). For example, the key combination used to save a file is Shift-F12, and the key succession used to open the File menu is Alt,F.

If you plan to use the keyboard to access menus, look at the Menu bar for a moment. Notice that each menu in it has an underlined letter. Most of the time, the first letter in the menu is underlined. However, because Word has some menus and commands starting with the same letter (for example, **F**ile and Format), sometimes a letter within the word is underlined instead.

 **Note:** Word accepts either uppercase or lowercase letters.

The following Quick Steps show how to select menus and commands with the keyboard.

 **Selecting Menus and Commands with the Keyboard**

1. To select a menu, press and release the Alt key (because this is a key succession, you don't have to hold down the Alt key). Then press the underlined letter for the menu that you want. For example, to select the menu **F**ile, press F.

   Word opens the menu and displays more choices with more underlined letters.

2. To select a command from the menu, press the underlined letter in the command that you want to use.

   Word either performs an action or gives you more choices.

3. When you have finished using the command and associated dialog boxes, press Enter to complete the command or press Esc to cancel the command or close the menu.

Word returns you to the place in your document from which you started the command.

□

When you open a menu, some commands have key combinations or successions displayed to the right. For example, if you use the Exit command, you'll see:

```
Alt+F4
```

In this case, this combination is just another method of exiting Word. Press the Alt key and the F4 key simultaneously to exit. As you view other menus, you'll notice that some (but not all) commands have key combinations or successions.

17

> **Tip:** You can also press Alt to move the cursor to the Menu bar. Then press any combination of arrow keys to open menus and to select commands. You can leave the Menu bar by pressing the Alt key again or by clicking anywhere outside the Menu bar.

## Using the Keyboard with Dialog Boxes

Although the mouse is usually the easiest way to move around in a dialog box, you can use the keyboard, too. Table 1.3 describes the keys commonly used with dialog boxes. In general, to use the keyboard with a dialog box, press Tab to move from upper left to lower right through the options or press Shift-Tab to move in the opposite direction. To close a list and move to the next entry, press Tab or Shift-Tab. To clear an entry, press the Backspace key.

A dialog box can itself contain other types of boxes or it can contain buttons, as shown earlier in Figure 1.11. The following list describes the various components of a dialog box and explains how to use the keyboard with them.

> **Tip:** To quickly select one check box from a list of check boxes, press the underlined letter for that box.

*Text boxes*—Boxes in which you enter text, such as a file name. Press Shift (or Shift-Tab) to move to the text box. Then type and edit your text just as you would in a document window. To exit a text box and move to the next text box, press Tab and then press the underlined letter of the box you wish to move to.

*List boxes*—A type of text box. Either type a value in the list box or select the list arrow (the underlined down arrow located at the right side of the box) by pressing any combination of arrow keys, Alt-↓ or Alt-↑. When a list of choices is revealed and your choice is highlighted, either move to the next option in the dialog box or press Enter.

18

*Option boxes*—Boxes into which you can either type a value or select the up or down arrow located at the right side of the box in order to increment or decrement, respectively, the value shown in the box. Press any combination of arrow keys to cycle through the valid values for this option. When your choice is highlighted, either move to the next option in the dialog box or press Enter.

*Radio buttons*—Small buttons that look like circles. When a group of options is preceded by radio buttons, you can select only one button, or option, from the group. Radio buttons work similarly to buttons in a car radio: you can push only one button at a time and you can select only one station at a time. To select a radio button, press any combination of arrow keys. When your choice is highlighted, either move to the next option in the dialog box or press Enter.

*Check boxes*—Small square boxes that display an X when a feature is turned on and that are blank when a feature is turned off. When a group of options is preceded by check boxes, you can select several options from this group. For each option that you wish to select, press the underlined letter. Press the same letter to clear the box. When you have made your choice, either move to the next option in the dialog box or press Enter.

*Command buttons*—Rectangular-shaped buttons that can be selected only separately. There are three command buttons that you will see most often: OK, Cancel, and Close. Table 1.2 describes each button. Some dialog boxes contain other command buttons, which will be described as they occur. To select the default command button (usually OK), press Enter. To select another button, if a letter is underlined on the button, type that letter. Otherwise, press Tab or Shift-Tab until the button is selected; then press Enter.

*Table 1.3   Commonly used keys, key combinations, and key successions.*

| Key | Description |
| --- | --- |
| Enter | Indicates that a command is complete. Pressing Enter is equivalent to clicking on OK. |
| Tab | Moves to the next field, box, button, or option. |
| Shift-Tab | Moves to the previous field, box, button, or option. |
| ↑ | Moves one item up a list or up one line of text. Increases the value of a measurement. |
| ↓ | Moves one item down a list or down one line of text. Decreases the value of a measurement. |
| Alt-↓ or Alt-↑ | Opens a selected drop-down list box. If an option on a list is highlighted, selects it. If an option on a list is not highlighted, cancels the display of the list. |

**19**

# The Toolbar, Ribbon, and Ruler

The Toolbar, Ribbon, and Ruler provide shortcuts for using Word quickly and efficiently. You can use the default settings or create your own.

The Toolbar is an easy way to use Word's most common commands. Just click on the appropriate button, and Word takes it from there. The inside back cover of this book shows an exploded view of all 22 Toolbar buttons. You can customize the Toolbar so that you can easily access the commands you use most often. For information on customizing the Toolbar, see Chapter 13.

Word's Ribbon and Ruler provide easy access to some commonly used formatting features. The Ribbon has commands that affect the way text appears in your document. Using the Ribbon, you can change the appearance and size of text, and you can format and enhance text characters. You'll learn more about using the components of the Ribbon in Chapters 6 and 7.

The Ruler controls the overall appearance of the document. You can set the alignment of paragraphs, adjust line spacing, change tab positions, and even load different document styles.

# Getting Help

Word has a very useful on-line help facility, which you can access in the following ways:

▶ Press F1 from any screen to display the main menu of the help facility. Then either click on a button or press the underlined letter:

*Index*—Select this option to view the index of help information for Word.

*Back*—Select this option to return to the previous topic.

*Browse*—Select one of these options to view the prior or next topic in this specific group of topics.

*Search*—Select this option to view information about a topic that you select from a list. You can either type the first few letters of a topic or select it from a list.

▶ Remember that if a button looks dim, it is not currently available. In addition, you can use the mouse or the keyboard to select green, underlined text in order to see specific information about that text. To use the mouse, move the mouse pointer to the green, underlined text and either click on it or hold down the mouse button, depending on the amount of available information. To use the keyboard, press the Tab key to move to the next green, underlined text (Shift-Tab to move back to the prior green, underlined text). Press Enter when you find a topic.

▶ Press Shift-F1 from any screen to display a large question mark next to the mouse pointer. Move the mouse pointer to the command, button, or particular area of the screen; then click. Word displays information related to your selection.

**20**

► Click on Help or press Alt,H to open the **Help** menu. Then you can select from the Help Index, Getting Started, Learning Word, WordPerfect Help, or About categories. For information about Getting Started and Learning Word, see the next section.

The Word Help window operates in about the same way as the main Word screen. For example, there is a scroll bar on the right side of the screen.

To leave the help facility, back up screen by screen (either click on Back or press B) until Back is dimmed. Then select File Exit. You can also use **F**ile E**x**it to exit quickly from any help screen.

### *Using the On-line Lessons*

If you select either Getting Started or Learning Word from the Help menu, Word displays a series of on-line lessons. To start either set of lessons, either press or click on M to learn about both the mouse and the keyboard, or press or click on K to learn about the keyboard.

**21**

*Getting Started* provides lessons about the screen, basic skills, and a quick lesson on creating a document from the first keystroke through saving and printing.

*Learning Word* provides lessons in Formatting; Editing; Proofing; Tables, Frames, and Pictures; Organizing Documents; and Viewing and Printing.

To travel through either set of screens, follow the prompts. Either click on a button or press Alt and the underlined letter. To leave the lessons, press Alt,X (Exit). You can display the Controls menu by pressing Alt,C; then select an option to go to another area of the tutorial or press X to exit.

# Reducing Word to an Icon

If you need to reduce Word to an icon so that you can run the program more quickly or get to another program, you can either click on the Minimize button or press Alt-F9. To get back to the screen display, double-click on the icon or highlight the icon and press Enter.

# Quitting Word

There are several ways to quit Word. You can

▶ Choose the File menu and select the Exit command.
▶ Double-click on either the Application or Document Control menu (the two buttons at the top left part of the screen).
▶ Press Alt-F4.

If you change your mind, click on Cancel or press the Esc key.

If you have made any changes to a document, Word displays a dialog box. To save the changes, either press Y, click on the Yes button, or press Enter. For detailed information on saving a file, see the next chapter.

**22**

# What You Have Learned

▶ You can start Word for Windows from within Windows or from DOS, and you can use either the mouse or the keyboard.
▶ The easiest way to issue commands in Word is to use the mouse. As you move the mouse, you will see the mouse pointer move on the screen. The mouse pointer changes shape depending on its location on-screen.
▶ If a command on a menu looks lighter in color than other commands, you cannot use it without taking at least one other action first.
▶ From the Menu bar, you can access Word's menus. With the mouse, simply click on the menu name. When the menu drops down, click again on one of the available commands. From the keyboard, press Alt and the underlined letter in the menu name. When the menu drops down, press the under-lined letter of the command name or use ↑ or ↓ to highlight the command name. Then press Enter.
▶ The Toolbar, Ribbon, and Ruler help you use Word more efficiently. The Toolbar is especially helpful because you

just click on the appropriate command button and Word does the rest.

► The Status bar, located at the bottom of the screen, shows important information about your document.

► You can learn about Word via the help facility or on-line lessons.

► The easiest ways to quit Word are to double-click on the Application or Document Control menu (the two buttons at the top left of the screen) or press Alt-F4.

23

# Creating Your First Document

## In This Chapter

▶ *Entering text*
▶ *Viewing text and symbols*
▶ *Moving through a document*
▶ *Saving, retrieving, and printing a document*

In Chapter 1, you were introduced to the Word Program window and its components, and you learned how to use the mouse and the keyboard to get around Word for Windows. Next you'll learn how to put some of these components to work in creating your first document—from typing the first words to printing the final copy.

## The Document Window

When Word starts, the text area (also called the document window; see Figure 2.1), is empty—except for the insertion point, the endmark, and the I-beam mouse pointer. The document window is the area in which you'll create and edit all your documents. If you have more than one document open, the window in which you are currently working is known as the *active window*.

Notice that the Title bar reads Microsoft Word - Document1. Because you are just starting your first document and haven't named it yet, Word automatically gives the document the *default,* or starting, name, which is Document1. At any time, you can give the document a name of your choice by saving it. (You'll learn about saving documents later in this chapter.) If you haven't named your document by the time you try to exit the program, Word asks if you want to save changes to Document1—even if it contains only one character. If you select Yes, Word displays a dialog box into which you can type a file name for the document. If you select No, Word exits without saving Document1.

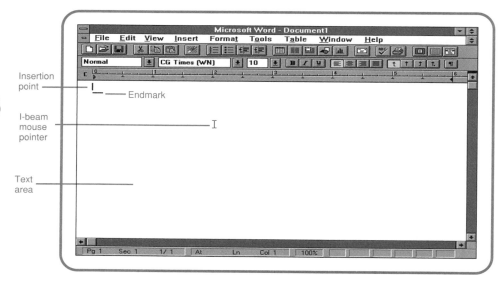

Insertion point
Endmark
I-beam mouse pointer
Text area

*Figure 2.1  A new document window in Word for Windows.*

In Chapter 1, you learned that the Ribbon, the Ruler, and the Toolbar provide shortcuts to using Word efficiently. As a beginner, you'll find the Ribbon, the Ruler, and the Toolbar useful so make sure that all of them are displayed on-screen before you start entering text. Later, as you get more comfortable with Word, you can decide whether to keep the Ribbon, the Ruler, and the Toolbar open or use Word's commands instead. Chances are you will use a combination of both.

To turn on the Ribbon, the Ruler, and the Toolbar, use Word's **V**iew menu (see Figure 2.2). From the **V**iew menu, you can also choose **N**ormal, **O**utline, **P**age Layout, and **D**raft modes (which you'll learn about shortly); create headers and/or footers (see Chapter 5); and add footnotes, annotations, and field codes to your document. You can also use the **Z**oom command as a form of page preview, with one difference—you can edit your document while it is zoomed. See Chapter 9 for a description of the **Z**oom command.

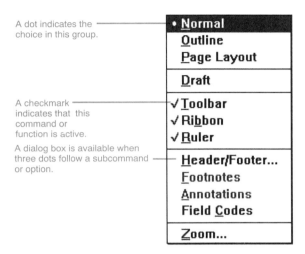

A dot indicates the choice in this group.

A checkmark indicates that this command or function is active.

A dialog box is available when three dots follow a subcommand or option.

*Figure 2.2   The View menu showing the commands that control how your document appears on-screen.*

The following Quick Steps show you how to turn the Ribbon, Ruler, and Toolbar on and off.

 **Turning the Ribbon, the Ruler, and the Toolbar On and Off**

1. Select **V**iew from the Menu bar or press Alt,V.

   Word opens the **V**iew menu. A check mark or bullet preceding any command or function on a list indicates that this command or function is either turned on or is on display.

2. To switch between displaying and hiding the Ribbon, the Ruler, or the Toolbar, move the mouse pointer to the appropriate word on the list and click, or press B, R, or T, respectively.

   Word either places a check mark next to the selected option or removes the check mark.

□

27

> ☐ Another way to open a new document window is to click on the New button on the Toolbar.

## *An Overview of Setting Preferences in Word*

Word provides a mind-boggling array of settings that affect almost every aspect of using Word: the screen display, the document's appearance on-screen, the printing of a document, and the use of Word's commands. When you first start Word, the default settings are activated. However, you can change these settings—including the look of the new document window—to suit your particular needs.

Word provides a straightforward method for displaying and/or changing the default settings. Using the **O**ptions command in the **T**ools menu, you select one of 11 categories. After you select a category, Word displays the settings pertaining to that category. You then select the settings you wish. Because you will be selecting some of these categories in this chapter, an overview of the 11 categories is presented here.

From the **T**ools menu, select the Options command (Alt,O,O). On the left side of the Options dialog box, you will see a list of categories from which you can select. Click on the down arrow to scroll down the list. Each of the categories is explained in the following list:

▶ The *View* dialog box controls how your document looks on-screen. For example, you can turn on and off the vertical and horizontal scroll bars and the Status bar. See Chapter 1 and later in this chapter for more information about the parts of the Word screen affected by the View category.

▶ The *General* dialog box enables you to display or change some general settings, such as defining the measurement unit with which you want to format or choosing between Insert and Overtype modes. If you are familiar with WordPerfect, use the General dialog box to customize settings so that Word behaves like WordPerfect. You will learn about Insert and Overtype later in this chapter. Other general settings are described throughout the book.

▶ The *Print* dialog box allows you to adjust print settings, such as whether hidden text, footnotes, and annotations are included in your printed output. You can also control how paragraphs are split between pages. Chapter 9 is devoted to printing Word documents, and Chapter 7 includes a section on hidden text.

▶ The *Save* dialog box provides a way to review or change save options. For example, at predetermined intervals, you can have Word automatically save the document on which you are working; you can save a backup copy whenever you save a document; or you can decide whether to provide Summary Info for a document. You'll learn about saving documents later in this chapter.

▶ The *Spelling* dialog box, which enables you to define custom dictionaries for a specific document, is described in Chapter 4.

▶ The *Grammar* dialog box allows you to determine how strictly your grammar will be reviewed. Chapter 4 contains information about Word's grammar checker.

**29**

▶ The *User Info* dialog box shows you personal information, such as your name, initials, and mailing address, and allows you to change it.

▶ The *Toolbar* dialog box enables you to customize the icons and actions on the Toolbar. Chapter 13 shows you how to modify the Toolbar defaults, and the inside back cover of this book illustrates Word's default Toolbar settings.

▶ The *Menus* dialog box displays current commands and macros that are associated with Word menus. Use this dialog box to add or remove commands. Chapter 12 shows you how to use macros.

▶ The *Keyboard* dialog box allows you to display or modify keys assigned to commands and macros.

▶ The *WIN.INI* dialog box shows you the current startup settings for both Windows and Word for Windows. The Windows WIN.INI file contains these settings.

You will work with the View, Save, and Print categories in this chapter. Later in the book you will work with many other categories.

# Entering and Viewing Text

Once the document window appears on-screen, you can start entering text. As you type, text appears to the left of the insertion point, the vertical blinking line. You don't have to press the Enter key when the text reaches the right margin because Word automatically controls the amount of text that appears on a line. If you are near the right margin and the word you are typing won't fit on the line, Word moves the word to the beginning of the next line. This is known as *word wrap*.

By default, Word aligns text with the left margin of the page and keeps the text at the right side of the page *ragged* (not aligned with the right margin). This is *left alignment* or *left justification*. Word also provides *right alignment* (the text is aligned with the right margin and ragged on the left), *centered alignment* (the text is balanced on either side of a center point), and *full justification* (the text is aligned with both left and right margins). Chapter 6 contains detailed information about alignment.

30

## *Paragraphs and New Lines*

Whenever you want to signify the end of one paragraph and start a new paragraph, press the Enter key. Word places a paragraph mark (¶), a special nonprinting symbol, at the end of the first paragraph. The display of paragraph marks and other nonprinting symbols can be turned on and off, as you will learn shortly.

Some documents require that you override the word-wrap feature and define your own lines. For example, if you are writing a poem, you might want to specify the number of lines in each paragraph. To create new lines within a paragraph, press Shift-Enter. Word places a newline mark (↵) at the end of the line.

To display the paragraph and newline marks as well as other nonprinting symbols, click on the Show All button, the last button on the Ribbon. You can also control the display of nonprinting symbols from the Options dialog box for the View category. You'll learn how to use this dialog box and find an overview of its features later in this chapter.

## *Insert versus Overtype*

When you enter text in Word, you have a choice of two typing modes—Insert or Overtype. In *Insert* mode, every time you type a character, everything to the right of the insertion point is pushed ahead. No text is deleted as you type. Insert mode is the default typing mode.

In *Overtype* mode, text to the right of the insertion point is erased as you type new text. To get to Overtype mode from Insert mode, press the Ins key. To switch back to Insert mode, press Ins again. When you press the same key to switch between two modes or settings, it is called a *toggle* key. Word's Status bar indicates whether you are in Insert or Overtype mode. When the Status bar displays OVR, you are in Overtype mode. If OVR is not displayed, you are in Insert mode. Table 2.1 lists all the Status bar indicators and gives a description of each.

*Table 2.1    Status bar indicators.*

**31**

| Indicator | Description |
| --- | --- |
| CAPS | The Caps Lock key is on. All text you type is uppercase. |
| COL | The Column Selection key combination (Shift-Ctrl-F8) is on. |
| EXT | The Extend Selection key (F8) is on. |
| MRK | Mark Revisions is on. |
| NUM | The Num Lock key is on. You can use the numeric keypad to enter numbers. |
| OVR | Overtype mode is on. |
| REC | The Word macro recorder is turned on. |

## *Viewing Text in Different Modes*

If you are writing an informal memo, it doesn't matter whether you see headers, footers, footnotes, and graphics because there are probably none to see. However, if you are creating an instruction book using advanced desktop publishing tools, you'll want to view each page in WYSIWYG (what-you-see-is-what-you-get, pronounced "wizzy-wig") format, which shows exactly how the printed page will look.

In this chapter, you've already used the **V**iew menu to turn on and off the Ribbon, the Ruler, and the Toolbar. Next you'll use the **V**iew menu to choose to view your text in one of three different modes: Normal, Page, and Outline.

► **N**ormal, the default, shows text as you have formatted it but does not display all page layout formats, such as headers, footers, page and line numbers, and footnotes. An example of Normal mode is shown in Figure 2.3.

► **P**age Layout shows how the body text, headers, footers, and footnotes appear on the printed page (Figure 2.4). Page Layout mode also shows the edges of the page, allowing you to see text relative to the page dimensions. Because all the formatting is displayed, this is the slowest mode.

► **O**utline shows the heading levels of your document.

**32**

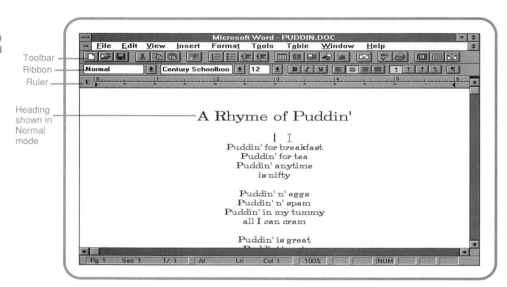

*Figure 2.3    Normal view mode showing most formats.*

In addition, under either Normal or Outline, you can select **D**raft mode to view your document in one text style, with very limited formatting and no graphics, as shown in Figure 2.5.

Edge of
page

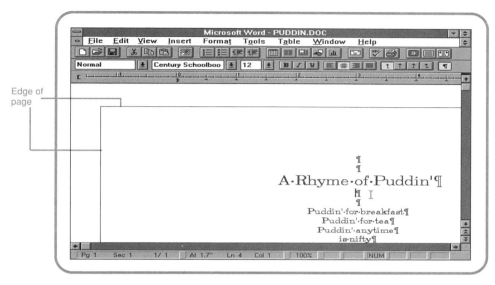

*Figure 2.4    Page Layout view mode showing the place-
ment of the text on the page and showing formatting
symbols.*

**33**

Toolbar
Ribbon
Ruler

Heading
shown in
Draft
mode

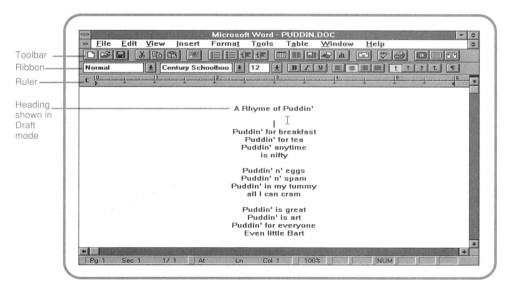

*Figure 2.5    Draft mode shows one text style and limited
formatting.*

> **Tip:** Use Draft mode if you want Word for Windows to run faster. Word runs faster in Draft mode because it doesn't have to load text and graphic formatting. When Word has to load formatting, it needs additional time to "draw" on-screen.

## *Viewing Text As It Will Print*

In Normal mode, you can't see all the page formats. With Page Layout mode, although the formats are there, you can't see the entire page on-screen. However, with the Print Preview command, Word gives you the chance to see one or two pages of your document on-screen as it will print. In this mode, text is illegible and cannot be edited, but you can print or adjust the margins of your document. Select the File menu and the Print Preview command (Alt,F,V), and Word displays the first page of your document (see Figure 2.6). You can scroll through your entire document by pressing PgDn (to move down a page at a time) or PgUp (to move up a page at a time). You can also display your document two pages at a time by selecting Two Pages on the Print Preview screen.

Layout of page is evident, but much of the text may be illegible.

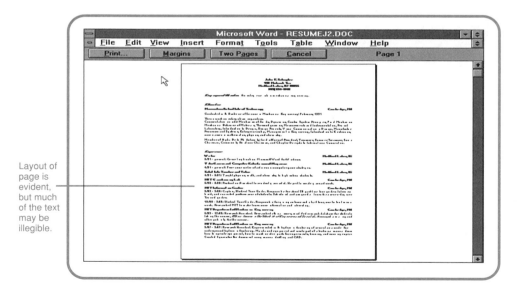

**Figure 2.6** *The first page of a Word document in Print Preview.*

Before you print a document, use Print Preview to check the layout and look of the document. If you don't like what you see, it's easier to change things now. You'll learn all about printing and Print Preview in Chapter 9.

## The Basic Text Elements

Every document is unique—in size, in audience, and in purpose. The pattern of one document is small and plain, that of a second document is large and ornate, and so on. In order to change the appearance of each document, it is important for you to know which text elements are available to you and how you can work with them.

The smallest element used in Word is the character. A *character* is a letter, punctuation mark, number, blank space, or special symbol. Other text units are words, sentences, paragraphs, sections, and documents. Table 2.2 gives the definitions for the text elements discussed in this book.

35

*Table 2.2   Elements of text.*

| Element | Description |
|---------|-------------|
| Character | One alphabetic, numeric, or punctuation symbol |
| Word | One or more characters ending with a space or period |
| Sentence | One or more words ending with a period, a question mark, or an exclamation point |
| Paragraph | One or more characters ending with a paragraph mark |
| Section | One or more characters ending with a section mark |
| Document | A file containing any combination of text and graphics |

As you start to manipulate the text elements of your document, you'll frequently use two Word formatting commands—Format Character (Alt,T,C), which formats one or more characters up to and including your entire document, and Format Paragraph (Alt,T,P), which formats one or more paragraphs up to and including your entire document. In Chapter 3, you'll learn how to manipulate text elements, Chapter 5 details documentwide and section formatting, Chapter 6 describes details of paragraph formatting, Chapter 7 covers character formatting, and Chapter 8 finishes the discussion with advanced formatting.

Unless you are an experienced graphics or document designer, plan to use the default formats for your first Word for Windows documents. You can gradually develop your own styles over time.

## Viewing Formatting Symbols

Every time you press Enter, the space bar, or Tab, and every time you create a new line or introduce an optional or nonbreaking hyphen, Word places a special mark in that location in the text. When you first start Word, you can't see these marks, but there are times when it is important to see them. For example, if you want to see how many tab symbols start each item on a list or if you want to check that a single space follows each sentence, you'll want to see these special nonprinting marks. Table 2.3 shows the most common nonprinting symbols.

**36**

*Table 2.3    Nonprinting symbols.*

| Mark | Represents |
| --- | --- |
| ↵ | New line mark |
| ¶ | Paragraph mark |
| → | Tab mark |
| • | Space mark |
| ¬ | Optional hyphen |
| – | Nonbreaking hyphen |
| ° | Nonbreaking space |

The Options dialog box for the View category controls how a document looks on-screen, including whether nonprinting formatting marks are displayed. You not only can toggle the display of the scroll bars on-screen, but you can also turn the Status bar on and off. In the Nonprinting Characters box, you can control whether you will view formatting symbols. Note that All, the last entry in this box, is a counterpart to the Show All button, which was covered earlier in this chapter. The Show Text With box allows you to control the display of other view options:

▶ The *Table Gridlines* check box controls whether you see lines between the cells of a table and around the tables as a whole. Chapter 10 describes working with tables.

▶ The *Text Boundaries* check box controls whether you see lines indicating the four margins surrounding the text, and whether you see the lines surrounding pictures, graphics, and frames.

▶ The *Picture Placeholders* check box controls whether you see a box or a graphic on the screen. If you choose to see a box instead of a graphic, you'll have faster processing time because no time is devoted to drawing each graphic on the screen.

▶ The *Field Codes* check box determines whether field codes or field results are displayed on the screen.

▶ The *Line Breaks and Fonts as Printed* check box tells Word whether to try to change the current screen font to a font that more closely resembles the printer font.

The following Quick Steps show you how to display nonprinting formatting symbols by using the Options dialog box for the View category.

**37**

 **Displaying Formatting Symbols**

| | |
|---|---|
| 1. From the Tools menu, select the Options command (Alt,O,O). | Word displays the Options dialog box. |
| 2. Select the View category. | Word displays the dialog box for view settings, which is shown in Figure 2.7. An X within a box indicates that an option is turned on. |
| 3. Under Nonprinting Characters, select All. | Word places an X in the box next to All. |
| 4. Select OK or press Enter. | Word closes the dialog box and returns to the document. □ |

---

**Tip:** To quickly turn on or off the display of formatting symbols within your document, click on the paragraph mark (the last button on the right) on the Ribbon.

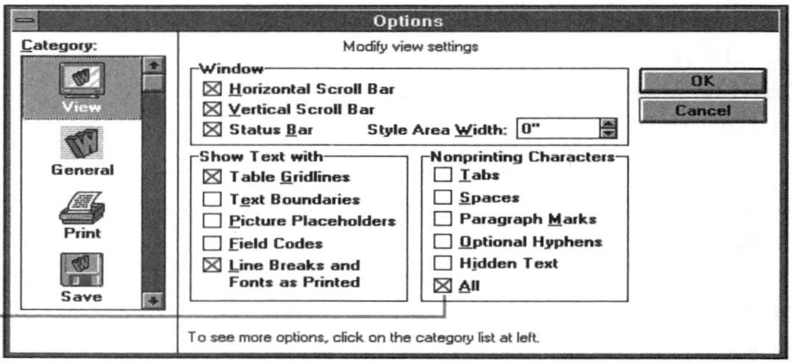

If you select this option, you don't have to check any of the other options in the box.

*Figure 2.7   The Options dialog box for the View category, which allows you to decide whether to display nonprinting options.*

## 38   Moving Around a Document

Word offers three ways to move around a document: the mouse, the keyboard, and the Go To command. With the mouse or the keyboard, you can quickly scroll or jump around a document—from the top to the bottom or from the left margin to the right margin, or anywhere in between. If you know the specific page or section that you want to display, you can use the Go To command. The following sections will explain how to use each of these methods.

### *Using the Mouse to Navigate a Document*

Using the mouse is an easy way to navigate your document. You can either move the mouse pointer around the text area, or you can use the mouse with parts of the scroll bar.

#### Using the Mouse in the Text Area

To use the mouse in the text area, click the left mouse button, hold, and drag the mouse pointer in the direction you want to move. For example, to see the next page of a document, drag the mouse downward. As you drag the mouse, new parts of the document are displayed. The text that you drag over is *highlighted*, as in Figure 2.8 (that is, if text is normally displayed in black on a white background, it will now be displayed in reverse video, or white on a black background). Before making any changes to your document, make sure that you remove the highlight. If you release the left mouse button and then click the mouse outside the highlighted area, the highlight disappears. When you use the mouse in this way, the insertion point remains in its original position unless you specifically click within the text area to move it to a new location.

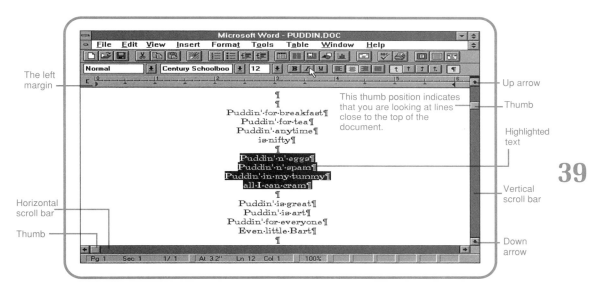

**Figure 2.8** *A screen showing highlighted or reverse video text. The thumbs indicate the specific location of the text on the screen within the document.*

## Using the Mouse with the Vertical Scroll Bar

There are three ways to move through a document by using the mouse and the vertical scroll bar (see Figure 2.8): the scroll bar arrows, the *thumb* (the small box within the scroll bar), and the area within the scroll bar. Since you'll be learning about both the vertical and horizontal scroll bars in this section and the next, make sure that both are displayed as shown in the following Quick Steps.

 **Turning On the Horizontal and Vertical Scroll Bars**

1. Select the Tools Menu and the Options command (Alt,O,O).

Word displays an Options dialog box.

2. Under Category, select View.

Word displays the Options dialog box for the View category (Figure 2.7).

3. In the Window box, make sure that there are check marks on both the Vertical Scroll Bar and the Horizontal Scroll Bar.

Word places Xs next to Horizontal Scroll Bar and the Vertical Scroll Bar, indicating that these options are both active.

4. Select OK or press Enter.

Word closes the dialog box and returns to the document.                    □

You can use any combination of the three parts of a scroll bar to navigate your document:

*Scroll bar arrows*—Move through a document by clicking and holding the left mouse button on the arrows at either end of the scroll bar. As your document scrolls up and down the screen, notice that the thumb moves up and down the dark part of the bar to show you the part of the document currently displayed. If you click once on a scroll bar arrow, the document scrolls up or down one line.

*Within the scroll bar*—Click on the dark part of the scroll bar above and below the thumb. This entire area represents the length of your document. Every time you click, Word moves a screen minus two lines (you can use those lines to be aware of exactly where you are in the document). You won't see a change in the page number displayed in the Status bar until you click in the text area.

*Thumb*—Click and hold on the thumb to drag it to a position on the scroll bar. When you release the left mouse button, you will move to a position in the document relative to the position of the thumb in the scroll bar. For example, if you move the thumb to the middle of the scroll bar, Word displays the middle of the document.

### Using the Mouse with the Horizontal Scroll Bar

When your document is too wide to be completely displayed within the left and right margin of the screen, use horizontal scrolling to view the hidden portions. If you followed the preceding Quick Steps, the horizontal scroll bar is displayed.

The horizontal scroll bar is similar to the vertical scroll bar except that the dark area represents the width of the page (up to 22 inches) if you are in Page Layout mode, or 0–22 inches if you are in Normal mode. To display the edge of the document, drag the thumb to either end of the scroll bar. To alternately display the left and right edges of the document, click on the dark part of the scroll bar.

## Using the Keyboard to Navigate a Document

When your fingers are on the keyboard, sometimes it's easier to use keys to move around a document than to move your hand over to the mouse. Also, if you have to move the mouse and then press and hold a mouse button (when pressing one key can accomplish the same purpose), it might be better to use the keyboard. As we pointed out in Chapter 1, you'll probably end up using both the mouse and the keyboard.

Table 2.4 lists the navigation keys and describes the effect on the insertion point of pressing each key.

**41**

*Table 2.4    Keyboard navigation commands.*

| Press This Key | To Move the Insertion Point |
| --- | --- |
| ↓ | One item down a list or down one line of text |
| ← | One character to the left |
| → | One character to the right |
| ↑ | One item up a list or up one line of text |
| Ctrl-↓ | One paragraph down |
| Ctrl-← | One word to the left |
| Ctrl-→ | One word to the right |
| Ctrl-↑ | One paragraph up |
| Ctrl-End | To the end of the document |
| Ctrl-Home | To the beginning of the document |
| Ctrl-PgDn | To the bottom of a window |
| Ctrl-PgUp | To the top of a window |
| End | To the end of the current line |
| F5 | To a specified location in the current document |

*continues*

*Table 2.4    continued*

| Press This Key | To Move the Insertion Point |
| --- | --- |
| Home | To the beginning of the current line |
| PgDn | Down one screen |
| PgUp | Up one screen |

## The Go To Command

In prior sections of this chapter, you learned two ways to navigate your document—with the mouse and with the keyboard. Word offers yet a third way to navigate your document: with the **G**o To command. When you know the number of the page that you want to jump to in your document (especially if the document is very long), the **G**o To command on the **E**dit menu is a quick way of doing so.

42

 **Using the Go To Command**

1. From the **E**dit menu, select the **G**o To command (Alt,E,G).

   Word opens the Go To dialog box, shown in Figure 2.9.

2. At the insertion point, enter a page number and select OK or press Enter.

   Word closes the dialog box and displays the top of the page that you requested. □

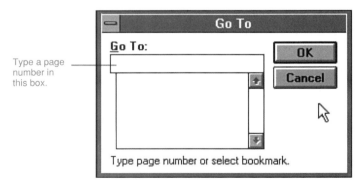

Type a page number in this box.

*Figure 2.9    The Go To dialog box. Type the page number that you want to jump to.*

A shortcut for using the **G**o To command is to double-click anywhere in the Status bar or press F5. Word displays the prompt Go To in the Status bar. Type the appropriate page number and press Enter.

Go To is a very powerful command, which you can also use to jump to sections, lines, bookmarks, and annotations.

---

**Tip:** Word remembers four insertion-point locations. You can press Shift-F5 to cycle through all four locations. If you press Shift-F5 after you open a document, Word displays the document at the page at which you last saved it, with the insertion point at its last location.

---

# About the File Menu                                     43

The commands on the **F**ile menu manage documents and related files. Use this menu to save, create, retrieve, and print documents. Most of the commands in the following list are described in this chapter.

The **N**ew command creates a new document and enables you to enter summary information or attach a *template,* a predefined format, to this document. (Chapter 12 describes templates.)

The **O**pen command opens an existing document or template. Word allows you to have as many as nine documents open at one time.

The **C**lose command closes the current document in the current window.

The **S**ave command saves the current document; if it is unnamed, this command enables you to name it.

The Save **A**s command saves the current document and enables you to name it. You can also lock a file or assign a password.

The Sav**e** All command saves all open documents and other open files.

The **F**ind File command searches for a file that meets certain criteria. See Chapter 13 for detailed information about finding files.

The Summary **I**nfo command allows you to display or edit summary information for the current document.

The **T**emplate command displays the Template dialog box so that you can attach a template to the current document.

The Print Pre**v**iew command displays the document in Print Preview mode. You can also edit margins, headers, footers, and page breaks in Print Preview.

The **P**rint command prints the current document and/or changes print settings for Word.

The Print **M**erge command merges data into the current document (to create form letters, for example).

The P**r**int Setup command selects an active printer and its associated port.

The E**x**it command exits from Word.

The items numbered 1–4 represent the last four documents you closed. Selecting a number causes Word to open and display that document.

44

# Saving Your Work

In this chapter, you've learned the elements of a document and the basic steps to create it—entering and viewing text, and navigating a document. When you have completed your first document, it is time to save it. Word offers several ways to save your work.

▶ Use the **S**ave command from the **F**ile menu whenever you want to save a complete copy of a document.

▶ Use the Autosave feature to automatically save a document every few minutes as you are working on it. Simply tell Word that you want this feature turned on and then indicate the number of minutes between each save.

▶ Use the Fast Save feature to save only the changes that you have made since the last save, rather than saving the entire document.

▶ Use the **File** Save **As** command to create a backup document as you save the original document or to save a copy of a document under a different name. In both cases, you will have two copies of the document.

You'll learn how to use each of these save commands in the next sections of this chapter.

## *Saving Your Document*

Whether you have created a new document or changed an existing document, the only way to store a permanent copy on your hard drive is to use one of the save commands. Otherwise, when you turn off your computer or exit Word, the document will be lost forever.

> Click on the Save button to save the current document or template (see Chapter 12) or to open the Save As dialog box in order to save and name a new document.

**45**

To save a document, select the Save command from the File menu. Depending on whether you are saving a new document or an existing (previously saved) document, Word opens either the Save As or the Save dialog box. If the document is a new document, Word opens the Save As dialog box, shown in Figure 2.10. This dialog box looks complex but is easy to use. The parts of the Save As dialog box are:

*File Name*—This section of the Save As dialog box lists all the documents in the current directory so that when you type the name of the document to be saved, you have had an opportunity to make sure that the new name does not match any of the names on the list. However, if you do type a duplicate name, Word asks you if you want to replace the current file with this file, and you can answer Yes or No. For more information on naming documents, see the discussion following this list.

*Save File as Type*—This box allows you to save a document and, at the same time, convert it to a different file type. Use this feature when you have to edit a document using another word processor or you need to transfer a document to another location—either to a mainframe computer at your office or to a remote site, using a communications service (such as CompuServe). You'll learn about file conversion in Chapter 13.

*Directories*—This section provides information about directories. The current directory is displayed at the top of this box, and other directories, including the current directory and the root directory, are listed in the box. A computer's directory system resembles a family tree. The *root* directory is the ancestor from which all the parents and children come. A directory like winword is a parent; it is one level below the root directory. winword has its own subdirectories, which are created during installation. As you create families of documents, you'll probably want to create other subdirectories under winword. Directories listed in the Directories box are aligned according to their relationship with the root directory and other directories. If a directory name is aligned farther from the left margin of the box than the prior name on the list, it is a subdirectory of the prior name. This is an illustration of the directory organization of your computer system.

*Drives*—This box displays the name of the current drive. If you click on the underlined down arrow at the right of the box, Word displays all the drives it sensed during installation. For many computer systems, c: represents the hard drive, and a: and b: indicate floppy disk drives. However, your computer might be set up with other disk-drive identifiers.

In addition to the standard OK and Cancel buttons, there are File Sharing and Options buttons. Use **F**ile Sharing to lock or unlock a document and **O**ptions to go to the Options dialog box for the Save category.

---

**Tip:** Use the Save **A**s command to create a format for a new document. For example, if you have created a standard cover letter, with margins and tabs carefully placed, save the original letter under a file name appropriate for a new cover letter. Then edit the new document.

### Naming Your Document

When you save a document for the first time, Word asks you to provide a file name for the document. Recall that until you name your document, it has the default name of Document1. When naming a document, follow these guidelines. File names are from one to eight characters in length, and valid file-name characters are alphanumeric (that is, letters or numbers) and the symbols ! @ # $ % & - ( ) _ { } ~ ^ . Try to give your documents file names that easily identify them. For example, name a letter LTR11281 (meaning that this is a letter created on November 28, 1991), or name a document about your company's inventory changes INVNCHGS. Start the names of a group of related files with the same combination of characters (W-CH01, W-CH02, W-CH03, and so on). When Word saves a document, it automatically adds a period (.) and the extension DOC to the file name (for example, W-CH01.DOC).

### Saving a New Document

47

When you save a document for the first time, Word asks you to supply summary information in the Summary Info dialog box, shown in Figure 2.11. It's a good idea to fill in as much information as you can so that you can find this document at a later time. You'll have the opportunity to give your document a title and a subject. The name in the Author box is the name that you typed during installation, but you can edit it, if needed. In the Keywords box, you'll enter words to be used at a later time to search for this document. Chapter 13 provides information about finding files using any information in the Summary Info dialog box. You can type any information in the Comments box. You can select Statistics to see additional information about this document, or you can choose OK to save the information in the dialog box or Cancel to leave the dialog box without making any changes.

Now you are ready to use the following Quick Steps to save a new document.

 **Saving a New Document**

1. With a new document that you want to save for the first time displayed on the screen, select the **F**ile menu and the **S**ave command, or press Shift-F12.

   If this is a new unnamed document, Word opens the Save As dialog box, shown in Figure 2.10.

2. In the File Name box, type a file name from one to eight characters long.

   If you want the file saved into another directory, click anywhere in the **D**irectories box (or press Alt-D), which names the current directory.

   If you want the file saved to another drive, click anywhere in the Dri**v**es box (or press Alt-V), which names the current drive. Select OK or press Enter.

3. Whether you have entered summary information or not, select OK or press Enter. You can also select Cancel to leave the Summary Info dialog box.

Word opens the Summary Info dialog box (see Figure 2.11).

Word returns to the document and displays its new name in the Title bar.

□

**48**

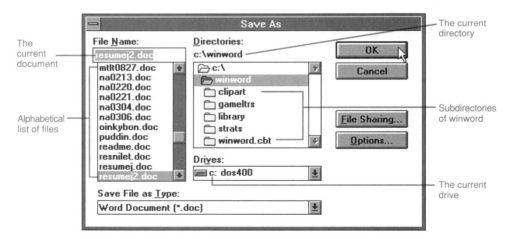

*Figure 2.10    Save a new document using the Save As dialog box.*

From now on, when you save this document, either select the File menu and the Save command (Alt,F,S) or press Shift-F12 or click on the Save button on the Toolbar, and Word automatically saves the document without displaying any dialog boxes.

| Summary Info | | |
|---|---|---|
| File Name: RESUMEJ2.DOC | | **OK** |
| Directory: C:\WINWORD | | **Cancel** |
| <u>T</u>itle: `Letter to Alfred D. Peters` | | **Stati<u>s</u>tics...** |
| <u>S</u>ubject: `Thanks` | | |
| <u>A</u>uthor: `John E. Schnyder` | | |
| <u>K</u>eywords: | | |
| <u>C</u>omments: | | |

*Figure 2.11    The Summary Information dialog box allows you to provide identification information for a new document.*

You can add summary information to this document at any time by selecting the File menu and the Summary Info command (Alt,F,I).

**49**

---

> ✏ **Tip:** If you do not want Word to display the Summary Info dialog box every time you save a new document or save using the Save As command, select the Tools menu and the Options command (Alt,O,O). Under Category, select Save. In the Options dialog box, make sure that the Prompt for Summary Info check box is not checked.

---

### Saving an Existing Document

When you saved the document the first time, you gave it a name and entered appropriate summary information. Because you have to provide this information only once, saving an existing document involves just one step, which follows.

 **Saving an Existing Document**

1. With the document that you want to save displayed on the screen, select the File menu and the **S**ave command (Alt,F,S).

As Word saves the document, it displays status information in the Status bar. Then it returns to the current document.    □

## Using the Autosave Feature

How much of your time are you willing to waste? Let's say that you've spent an hour working on a new document and suddenly there is an electrical blackout. When the lights come back on, you'll have to spend another hour re-creating the document unless you have saved it. Don't wait until you complete your work before you save it. Periodically use the File Save command to save your document, or let Word automatically save your document at a regular time interval that you determine.

When you have Autosave turned on, Word counts the minutes (up to 120) since the last save. While this count goes on, you can continue working without interruption. When the count equals the number of minutes that you have chosen, Word automatically saves your document. Then the cycle starts all over again.

Turn the Autosave feature on by displaying the Options dialog box for the Save category. You can open the dialog box by using Tools Option (Alt,O,O) or File Save As (Alt,F,A). The Options dialog box for the Save category provides four choices, all of which you will learn about in this section. You can choose:

*Always Create Backup Copy*—When you select this option, Word saves the new version of a document as well as the prior version.

*Allow Fast Saves*—This option, which is already selected when you open the dialog box for the first time, allows Word to save only the most recent changes rather than the entire document.

*Prompt for Summary Info*—This option, which is also a default, automatically displays the Summary Info dialog box when you first save a document.

*Automatic Save*—When you select this option and set a time interval, Word automatically saves the current document every few minutes as you work on it. This means that you'll have a current copy no older than the interval that you defined.

To start the Autosave feature, use the following Quick Steps.

50

**Using the Autosave Feature**

1. From the **F**ile menu, select the Save **A**s command (Alt,F,A).

   Word opens the Save As dialog box (see Figure 2.10).

2. Select the **O**ptions button.

   Word opens an Options dialog box.

3. Select the Save category.

   Word displays the Options dialog box for the Save category (Figure 2.12).

4. Click on the Automatic **S**ave Every box.

   Word displays 10 in the Minutes box.

5. Choose the frequency with which you want Word to save (from 1 to 120 minutes). Select OK or press Enter.

   Word returns to the Save As dialog box.

6. Select Close.

   Word returns to the document. From now on, Word calculates the time and saves the document automatically at the interval that you set if you have changed the document since the last time it was saved. As an automatic save occurs, you'll see a message in the Status bar. □

**51**

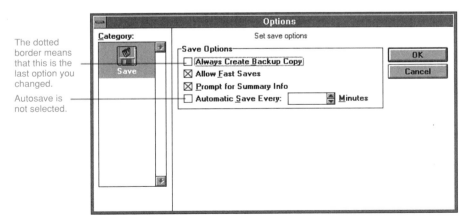

*Figure 2.12   The Options dialog box, which results from selecting the Save category and allows you to define or change save options.*

## *The Fast Save Feature*

Fast Save, which is a Word default setting, saves only the changes made since the last save. This means that processing time is lessened because the computer does not have to save the entire document. However, Fast Save actually increases the size of a document because it doesn't change the document file; rather, it adds the changes to the end of the file. If this feature is turned off, Word saves the entire document.

Note that Word occasionally consolidates all the changes you have made to your document since the last regular save by automatically performing a regular save. If you automatically create a backup copy of a document whenever you save, Word will not use the Fast Save feature, even if has been turned on. Before using a feature that consumes a great deal of memory (for example, sorting or building an index), it's a good idea to do a regular save; otherwise, you may run out of memory during processing. This wastes time because you then have to start your task all over again.

Follow these Quick Steps to activate the Fast Save feature.

 **Setting the Fast Save Feature**

1. Select the **File** menu and the **Save As** command (Alt,F,A).

   Word opens the Save As dialog box (Figure 2.10).

2. Click on the **O**ptions button.

   Word opens an Options dialog box (Figure 2.12).

3. Optionally, click on the Fast Save box.

   If Word displays an X in the Allow Fast Saves box, the Fast Save feature is turned on. If there is no X, this feature is turned off.

4. Select OK or press Enter.

   Word returns to the Save As dialog box.

5. Select OK or press Enter.

   Word returns to the document.  □

## *Backing Up Your Files*

What if you make many changes to a document and find that the original version is better? What if you discover that the most recent

52

copy of a document has been saved to an unreadable part of your hard drive? In either case, if you are using Word's Always Create Backup Copy feature, you can recover the previous version of a document.

As you learned at the beginning of this section, when Word saves a document, it automatically adds the extension .DOC after the file name. If you activate the Always Create Backup Copy feature, Word renames the prior saved version from .DOC to .BAK when you save the current version of a document. Each time you save this document, Word renames the previous .DOC file to .BAK, thus erasing the previous backup file. You can select either the Fast Save feature or the Always Create Backup Copy feature. You cannot select both.

 **Creating Backup Copies**

1. Select the **F**ile menu and the Save **A**s command (Alt,F,A). — Word opens the Save As dialog box (Figure 2.10).
2. Click on the **O**ptions button. — Word opens an Options dialog box (Figure 2.12).
3. Click on the Always Create **B**ackup Copy box. — If Word displays an X in this box, the last document saved becomes the backup document when a save occurs. The result is two documents with the same file name but different extensions.
4. Select OK or press Enter. — Word returns to the Save As dialog box.
5. Select OK or press Enter. — Word returns to the document. ☐

**53**

Besides creating a backup, another way you can protect the original document is to use the Save **A**s command to give a different name to another copy of the document. For example, if the original document is named MEMO0822.DOC, save a "test" document as MEMOTEST.DOC.

Although regularly saving documents to the hard drive and using the Always Create Backup Copy feature is important, it's equally important to *back up,* or copy, all your files to floppy disk periodically. Backing up your documents and then storing the backup floppy disks away from your office may save you a great deal of work if there is a catastrophe at your workplace.

An additional security measure is to invest in a UL-approved electrical power strip containing a surge protector. Plug your computer system into the power strip rather than directly into a wall socket. Although this is not foolproof, the power strip helps to protect your computer system from power surges and brownouts.

# Retrieving a Document

Now you have created your first document, and you have also learned how easy it is to save a document. When you save a document to your hard drive or to floppy disk, you have a copy that you can use at a later time. But how do you move a copy of a document back to your computer screen? You won't always create a document from scratch. Many times, you will use Word to edit existing documents.

 Click on the Open button to display the Open dialog box from which you can retrieve an existing document.

To retrieve your document, select the Open command from the File menu. Word displays the Open dialog box, as shown in Figure 2.13. When you see this Open dialog box for the first time, it will look quite familiar. In fact, it's almost identical to the Save As dialog box. The left side of this dialog box lists file names, directories, drives, and file types. On the right side, instead of File Sharing and Options, you'll see Find File and a Read Only check box. Find File allows you to view a document in a special window in the Find File dialog box. To see the contents of a document, click on the document name in the File Name list and the contents will appear (slightly shrunken but legible) in the window on the right. Check the Read Only box so that this document can be reviewed on-screen but not edited or saved. You can, however, save the file under a different name. The new document will not have the Read Only restriction. See Chapter 13 for more information about the File Find command.

54

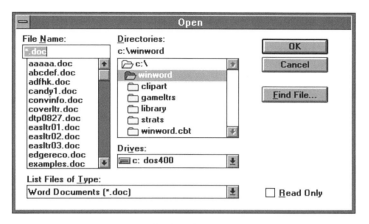

*Figure 2.13   The Open dialog box with a list of the documents in the current directory and a list of other directories on your hard drive.*

The following Quick Steps show you the simple procedures for retrieving a document from the hard drive.

55

 **Retrieving a Document**

| | |
|---|---|
| 1. From the File menu, select the **O**pen command (Alt,F,O), or press Ctrl-F12. | Word displays the Open dialog box. The File Name box lists the .DOC files in the current directory, and the Directories box allows you to display a list of .DOC files in other directories and drives. |
| 2. Select the name of the file that you want to retrieve, and choose OK or press Enter. | Word displays the retrieved document on the screen. □ |

## *Shortcuts for Retrieving a Document*

If you don't know either the name of the file that you want to retrieve, the extension of the file, or its location, Word provides alternative ways to retrieve a document from the Open dialog box:

▶ To retrieve a file whose name you don't know and with any extension, in the List Files of Type box, select the arrow button (the underlined down arrow). When the list of types opens, select a type. Word displays all documents of that type in the File Name box.

▶ To retrieve a file whose name you don't know but with an extension other than .DOC, move the mouse pointer to the File Name box and type *, then a period (.) and the desired extension.

▶ To retrieve a file when you are not sure of its exact name, move the mouse pointer to the File Name box and type as many characters as you remember followed by *, a period, and the extension. Word displays a list of all the files starting with the characters that you typed and with that specific extension.

▶ To display a complete list of files in the current directory, type *.* in the File Name box.

**56**

An asterisk (*) entered in place of a file name and/or extension is a *wildcard*, which can represent any group of characters. If you enter * in place of a file name, but enter the .DOC extension, Word lists any files having the .DOC extension. If you enter a specific file name and then enter * instead of an extension, Word lists any files having that file name and any extension.

Another Word wildcard character is the question mark (?), which represents a single character. For example, if you enter LTR?????.DOC, you'll find every file starting with LTR, followed by any five characters, and with a .DOC extension. So you will find LTR11110.DOC, LTRABCDE.DOC, but not LTRABCD.DOC, LTRGHIJK.BAK, or LTR0928.TXT.

---

**Tip:** To retrieve one of the last four documents that you edited, you can save yourself some time and look for it at the bottom of the **F**ile menu. To open the appropriate file, either click on it or, on the keyboard, press the number to the left of the file name.

# Printing a Document

Now that you have created your first document, you are ready to print it. Word for Windows' printing options are so extensive that they warrant their own chapter, but, for now, just accept Word's default settings. Remember that earlier in this chapter, you were introduced to the Print Preview print option, which will be described more thoroughly in Chapter 9.

 Click on the Print button to print this document using the default print options.

When you start the print process, Word displays the Print dialog box, as shown in Figure 2.14. Here is an overview of the items in the Print dialog box. Chapter 9 will cover them in detail.

57

*Printer*—At the top of the dialog box, Word displays the name of the active printer and the port to which it is attached (for example, LPT1:, COM1:, etc.).

*Print*—You can print the document, *or* you can print summary information, annotations, styles, glossary entries, or macro keys for the document.

*Copies*—To print more than one copy of this document, enter a value (from 1 to 32767) in this box.

*Range*—You can print the entire document, the current page, or a range of pages.

*Print to File*—Check this box to print this document to file rather than to the printer. This means that you have saved the document with its print format, and you can print it at a later time.

*Collate Copies*—If you are printing more than one copy of a document, check this box to print multiple copies from the first page to the last, or clear the box to print all the copies of the first page, then all the copies of the second page, and so on.

Select the Setup button to make another printer the active printer or to change any number of printer setup options. Select the Options button to display the Options dialog box for the Print category, which you'll learn about in Chapter 9. Either select OK to apply the changes and start printing or Cancel to return to your document without applying any changes.

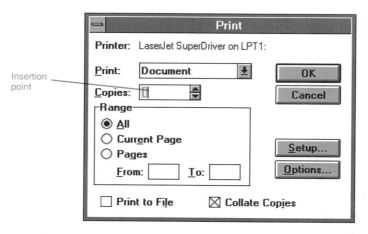

*Figure 2.14   The Print dialog box with its default settings.*

58

Before you print a document, it's a good idea to preview it on-screen, so from the File command, select Print Preview (Alt,F,V); then select Cancel to return to your document so that you can issue the **P**rint command from the **F**ile menu. Assuming that your document looks great, follow these Quick Steps to print it.

### *Q* Printing a Document

1. Select the File menu and the Print command (Alt,F,P), or press Ctrl-Shift-F12.

   Word opens the Print dialog box. Notice that the insertion point is in the Copies box.

2. Select OK or press Enter.

   As Word prints the document, it advises you of its status. After printing, Word returns to the current document on-screen.   □

# What You Have Learned

▶ Once the new document window appears on your screen, you can start entering text. Don't press the Enter key when the text reaches the right margin; press Enter only to end a paragraph.

▶ You can view your text in three different modes—Normal, Page Layout, and Outline. Under Normal and Outline, you can view text in Draft mode. Select any of these modes from the **View** menu.

▶ Word offers three ways to move around a document: the mouse, the keyboard, and the **G**o To command (F5). Use the **G**o To command if you know the exact location to which you want to jump.

▶ Scroll bars provide three ways of navigating a document: the arrows at either end, the thumb, and the area within the scroll bar. The location of the thumb within the scroll bar shows you the approximate location within the document.

**59**

▶ Word has several save options, including Automatic Save, Allow Fast Save, and Always Create Backup Copy. When you save a document for the first time or intend to save under its current name, select the **S**ave command. Use the Save **A**s command to save a copy of a document under a new name.

▶ You can retrieve one of the last documents on which you worked from the bottom of the **F**ile menu. If you do not know the complete name of a file to be retrieved, you can use wildcards to help in your search.

▶ Although Word for Windows printing options are extensive, you can successfully print a document using the default settings. However, before you print a document, use the **F**ile Print Preview (Alt,F,V) command to view your document on-screen.

# Manipulating Text

## In This Chapter

- ▶ *Selecting blocks and columns of text*
- ▶ *Moving, copying, and deleting text*
- ▶ *Undoing and repeating actions*
- ▶ *Finding and replacing text*

Creating a document is only the first step in its evolution. Chances are you'll have to edit your document many times during its lifetime. For example, you might have to write a proposal that must be reviewed in order to get to its final form, or you might have to create a monthly report that must reflect the latest sales figures. In Chapter 2, you learned how to move around a document using both the mouse and the keyboard. In this chapter, you'll build on that knowledge by navigating a document in order to select text on one page and move or copy it to another. You'll also learn how to find text and replace it with other text.

# Selecting Text

*Selection* is a key technique in Word for Windows. When you select text in your document, you identify for Word the particular unit of text, called a *block,* that you want a Word command to act on. The selected text appears highlighted on your screen. You can use either the mouse or the keyboard to select text; the upcoming sections will explain both techniques.

As you work on a document, you select blocks of text—words, sentences, lines, paragraphs, blocks, columns, even the entire document—so that you can perform an operation such as copying, moving, or deleting. For example, suppose your manager likes the contents of a document but doesn't like the order in which the information is presented. If you have to shuffle several sections around, simply select one section and move it to its new location, and then continue the process until your document is completely reorganized. On a smaller scale, you might be working on a letter with four paragraphs. To move the second paragraph after the third is an easy process using Word.

Word provides a special selection feature—column selection. You can use either the mouse or the keyboard to select a column. Regular text selection extends from the left margin to the right margin if you select one line or more of text. Although you can also use column selection from margin to margin, you'll probably use it to select a segment of a line (the width of the column) and then extend that selection up or down (the length of the column). For example, if you have to edit a document with lines that have been indented by repeated pressing of the space bar, you'll start out with many spaces in front of the first character in every line. Rather than deleting the spaces line by line, you can delete a column of excess spaces. You then can indent using tabs. You also could remove the bullets preceding a list while keeping the list format. Just select the column of bullets and delete it.

## *Using the Mouse to Select Text*

For a beginner, the mouse is easier to use than the keyboard for selecting large sections of text. When you use the mouse, you can easily define and, at the same time, view the boundaries of your selection, and you don't have to learn special keys to do so.

To select a block of text, move the mouse pointer to either the beginning or the end of the block of text to be selected. Then click the left mouse button and drag the mouse pointer toward the other end of the block of text. As you move the mouse, Word highlights the selected block of text. When you reach the end of the selection, release the left mouse button. The highlight remains until you click the left mouse button or press a key.

---

 **Caution:** When text is highlighted, be careful that you do not accidentally press a wrong key. Pressing any of the alphanumeric keys or keys such as the space bar, Tab, and Enter causes the highlighted text to disappear and be replaced by the character or symbol that you typed. If this happens, press Ctrl-Z to reverse your action and make the highlighted text reappear.

---

Use these Quick Steps to select any block of text—from one character to your entire document.

**63**

### Selecting a Block of Text with the Mouse

1. Move the mouse pointer to the first character to be selected. Then press and hold the left mouse button. (To select a column of text, press and hold the right mouse button.)

   The insertion point remains at the first character that you select.

2. Drag the mouse to the other end of the selection and release the mouse button.

   Word highlights the selected text.

   □

Word also provides these mouse shortcuts for selecting specific text units:

*Selecting a word*—To select a word, move the mouse pointer to any character in the word and double-click the left mouse button. Word highlights both the word and the space immediately to the right of the word.

*Selecting a line*—Select a line of text by moving the mouse pointer to the selection bar (see Figure 3.1), the invisible blank column located at the left edge of the text area. When the mouse pointer is in the selection bar, it changes shape from an I-beam to an arrow pointing up and to the right. Move the arrow to the left of the line you want to select and click the left mouse button. To select more than one line at a time, you can continue to hold the left mouse button down and drag the mouse up or down from the point at which you first clicked.

*Selecting a sentence*—Select a sentence by moving the mouse pointer anywhere within the sentence, holding down the Ctrl key, and clicking the left mouse button.

*Selecting a paragraph*—Select a paragraph by moving the mouse pointer to the selection bar; move the mouse pointer in front of any line in the paragraph, and then double-click the left button.

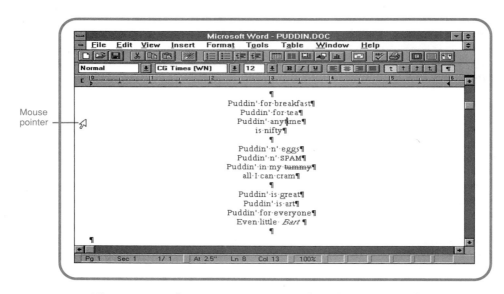

Mouse
pointer

*Figure 3.1    The mouse pointer within the selection bar.*

*Selecting multiple paragraphs*—Select multiple paragraphs by moving the mouse pointer to the selection bar in front of any one line in the first or last paragraph to be selected, double-click the left mouse button, and then drag the mouse pointer within the selection bar.

*Selecting text without dragging the mouse pointer*—Move the mouse pointer to the beginning of the text that you want to select and click the left mouse button. Then move the pointer down to the other end of the text to be selected, hold the Shift key down, and click the left mouse button. This command is useful when the text you want to select extends beyond the boundaries of the computer screen.

*Selecting the document*—Move the mouse pointer to the left of the screen into the selection bar. Hold down the Ctrl key and click the left mouse button.

*Selecting a column*—Move the mouse pointer to the beginning of the column that you want to select. Press and hold the right mouse button and drag the pointer diagonally down to the opposite corner of the column. If any character is at least halfway in the selection area, Word considers it to be selected. When you've highlighted the area that you want to select, release the mouse button.

If you change your mind about the current text selection, just move the mouse pointer off the selected text and click. Word turns off the highlight. If you accidentally select too much text, you can "back up" by continuing to hold down the left mouse button and moving the mouse pointer to the left.

**65**

## *Using the Keyboard to Select Text*

As you learned in Chapters 1 and 2, although the mouse is easier to use, utilizing the keyboard can be more efficient. For example, press F8 to begin a text selection at the insertion point. This action turns on the EXT indicator in the Status bar, as shown in Figure 3.2. EXT is an abbreviation for Extend Selection mode, which is the keyboard equivalent of pressing and holding the left mouse button. When Extend Selection mode is active, text selection is cumulative; each time you select text, the new selection is added to the text that you've already selected. Every time you press F8, the next larger text unit is selected, from word, sentence, paragraph, section, to finally your entire document.

Extend Selection mode indicator

*Figure 3.2   The* EXT *on the Status bar, which indicates that Word is in Extend Selection mode.*

No matter how large a block you have selected, you can press a combination of arrow keys to adjust the characters selected. For example, pressing ← causes the highlight to back up one character for every key pressed. You can also deselect text in reverse order of selection. Press Shift-F8 and the highlight will back up in the reverse order that the text was selected.

You have to specifically turn off Extend Selection mode to stop accumulating selected text. To turn off Extend Selection mode, either press the Esc key or perform an editing command.

When Extend Selection mode is active, you can extend your selection to a specific character to the right of your current selection by pressing that character (letter, number, or symbol) on the keyboard. For example, in the text The quick brown fox jumped over the lazy dog, move the insertion point in front of quick and press F8. If you type x, the selection will be extended to the end of the word fox.

To select text in Extend Selection mode with the keyboard, use the following Quick Steps.

### *Q* Selecting a Block of Text in Extend Selection Mode with the Keyboard

1. Use any combination of arrow keys to move the insertion point to either the beginning or the end of the area you want to select. Then press F8 to turn on Extend Selection mode.

   Word displays the text EXT in the Status bar, as shown in Figure 3.2. This means that Word has entered Extend Selection mode.

2. Keep pressing F8 until all the desired text is highlighted. Press Shift-F8 to deselect text in reverse order.

   Word highlights the selected text.

   □

Remember that Word remains in Extend Selection mode until you press Esc or perform an editing command.

You don't always have to enter Extend Selection mode to highlight text. For example, to start a selection at the insertion point, hold down the Shift key and use the arrow keys to define the block of text to be selected. Table 3.1 lists text selections and the keys used to make those selections.

*Table 3.1    Text selection keys.*

| To Select | Press |
|---|---|
| A document | Ctrl-5 (on the numeric keypad) |
| To the end of a paragraph | Ctrl-Shift-↓ |
| To the beginning of a word | Ctrl-Shift-← |
| To the end of a word | Ctrl-Shift-→ |
| To the beginning of a paragraph | Ctrl-Shift-↑ |
| To the end of a document | Ctrl-Shift-End |
| A column of text | Ctrl-Shift-F8 |
| To the beginning of a document | Ctrl-Shift-Home |
| One line down | Shift-↓ |
| One character to the left | Shift-← |
| One character or graphic to the right | Shift-→ |
| One line up | Shift-↑ |
| To the end of a line | Shift-End |
| To the beginning of a line | Shift-Home |
| One screen down | Shift-PgDn |
| One screen up | Shift-PgUp |

**67**

**Tip:** A shortcut for selecting a large block of text is to move the insertion point to one end of the text you want to select, press F8 (to start Extend Selection mode), press F5 (the **G**o To command), enter a page number, and press Enter. Then Word extends the selection to the top of the page that you just jumped to. If you change your mind about the selection, press Shift-F5; then Word places the insertion point back at the previous location.

You can also select a column of text using the keyboard. For example, you can use column selection to switch the positions of columns in a table. To select the first position in a column of text, usually starting at the top left of your selection, press Ctrl-Shift-F8. Press any combination of arrow keys to define the last position in the column, usually using a downward diagonal movement to the lower right corner. Word always lets you know the selected area by highlighting the column. To exit column selection, press Ctrl-Shift-F8 again or press Esc.

# About the Edit Menu

When you select text, you usually want to manipulate that text in some way. The Word menu devoted to text manipulation is the **E**dit menu (see Figure 3.3). You will be working with most of these commands in this chapter.

► The **U**ndo command cancels the last action, if it can. If the last action cannot be changed, you'll see the words Can't Undo instead. You'll learn more about this command later in the chapter.

► The **R**epeat command repeats the last action, if it can. If the last action cannot be repeated, you'll see the words Can't Repeat instead. This command is covered later in the chapter.

► The Cut command moves selected text or graphics from your document and stores it in the Clipboard.

► The **C**opy command copies selected text or graphics from your document and stores it in the Clipboard.

► The **P**aste command places the contents of the Clipboard into your document at the location of the insertion point.

Cut, Copy, and Paste are all described in the next section.

► The Paste **S**pecial command places the contents of the Clipboard into your document in a format that you define. You can also use this command to create a link to an application that is able to link to Word. After creating the link, when you update selected information in a document that you define as the source document, the document to which the source document is linked is also updated.

► The Select **A**ll command selects your entire document. Ctrl-5 (on the numeric keypad) is the shortcut key for selecting the entire document.

► The **F**ind command searches for specific text.

► The Re**p**lace command replaces the text found using the **F**ind command.

Find and Replace are discussed later in this chapter.

► The **G**o To command jumps to a page, line, section, bookmark, footnote, or annotation. You learned about Go To in Chapter 2.

► The Glossary command is used to place text or graphics in a permanent storage facility called the Glossary. Chapter 12 describes glossaries.

► Links and Object are used in the linking process.

These commands are not available without a prior action taking place.

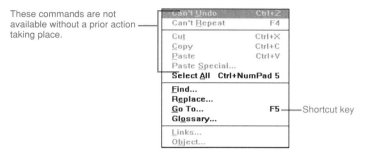

Shortcut key

*Figure 3.3    The Edit menu. When commands are dimmed, they are not accessible until another action takes place.*

**69**

# Moving, Copying, and Deleting Text

After you have selected text, use the Cut, Copy, and Paste commands on the Edit menu to copy or move the text to another location within your document. For example, to transpose two paragraphs, first select the paragraph to be moved and then use Cut and Paste to remove the paragraph from its original position in the document and place it in its new location. Note that if you try to use Cut or Copy without selecting text first, Word displays the Edit menu with these commands dimmed. This is a reminder that you must select text before using these commands.

Although Cut and Copy behave similarly, there is one important difference between the two commands: Cut actually deletes the selected text from its original location, while Copy makes a copy of the selected text but the selected text remains in its original location.

You can paste the same selected text as many times as you like by repeatedly executing the Paste command. For each copy to be pasted, execute the Paste command one time. Note that you can reposition the insertion point for each subsequent paste. Word remembers the pasted copy until you make another text selection.

## *Copying and Pasting Text*

To copy one section of a document to another section, select the text to be copied, and from the Edit menu, choose the Copy command (Ctrl-C, Ctrl-Ins, or Alt,E,C). Move the insertion point to the place the copied text should go. Then paste the text in its new location using the Paste command (Ctrl-V, Shift-Ins, or Alt,E,P). The original text remains in its original location in the document.

 Click on the Copy button to copy the specified text or graphics from the document and to place it in the Clipboard.

 Click on the Paste button to insert the contents of the Clipboard at the location of the insertion point in the document.

## *Cutting and Pasting Text*

To cut a section of a document and place it in another section, select the text to be cut, and from the Edit menu, choose the Cut command (Ctrl-X, Shift-Del, or Alt,E,T). The selected text is deleted from its original location in the document. Then move the insertion point to the place where the copied text should go, and paste the text in its new location using the Paste command (Ctrl-V, Shift-Ins, or Alt,E,P).

 Click on the Cut button to delete the specified text or graphics from the document and to place it in the Clipboard.

 Click on the Paste button to insert the contents of the Clipboard at the location of the insertion point in the document.

>  **FYIdea:** To quickly create multiple copies of a short form, open a document and enter the text. Place blank lines after the text by pressing Enter four or five times; then select the text and all the paragraph marks. Press Ctrl-C to copy the text, and move the insertion point to the bottom of the document. Repeatedly press Ctrl-V to paste the copied text until you have reached the end of the page or until you have created as many forms as you need. Then print and cut the forms apart. For example, teachers could use this technique to create permission slips for a school trip.

## Moving Text with Drag and Drop

Word also provides a shortcut method, *drag and drop,* for moving text. The Quick Steps that follow show you how to move selected text from one location to another.

### Moving Text with Drag and Drop

1. Select the text to be moved either with the mouse or with the keyboard.

   Word highlights your selection.

2. Place the mouse pointer anywhere within your selection.

   Notice that the mouse pointer outside the selection is an I-beam, but inside the selection is an arrow that points up and to the left.

3. Press and hold the left mouse button.

   The mouse pointer changes shape (by adding a dimmed box to its tail) to indicate that it is holding the selected text.

4. Drag the selected text to its new location.

   As you drag the selected text to its new location, a dim insertion point also moves along with the selected text.

5. When you reach the new location, release the left mouse button.

   Word changes the mouse pointer back to its starting shape and drops the dragged text.

6. Click the left mouse button anywhere on the screen.

Word turns off the high-light. □

## Deleting Text

To delete selected text, choose the Cut command. To delete characters, you can press the Backspace key to delete the character to the left of the insertion point or press the Del key to delete the character to the right of the insertion point. If you hold down either of these keys, Word continues to delete characters until you release the key. To delete a block of text, select the text to be deleted and then press the Del key. If you use Backspace or Del to delete characters, the only way you can recover those deleted characters is to choose the Undo command (Ctrl-Z). You'll learn more about the Undo command shortly.

**72**

# The Clipboard versus the Spike

What happens to the selected text between the cutting and/or copying and the pasting? The text is stored in the *Clipboard*, which is a temporary storage facility that holds one piece of text (or graphics) at a time. Another storage facility is the *Spike*, a special Glossary entry that you use by pressing certain keys. The Spike accumulates text and graphics, rather than holding just the last cut or copied text or graphics, as the Clipboard does. In Chapter 12, you'll learn about the Glossary.

There are some important differences between the Clipboard and the Spike:

▶ The Spike doesn't keep just the last cut or copied text or graphics; it accumulates all text and graphics until you choose to clear it.

▶ When you exit Windows, the contents of the Spike remain, but the contents of the Clipboard are lost.

▶ You can use both the mouse and the keyboard to cut, copy, and paste with the Clipboard, but the Spike uses only the keyboard (namely, Ctrl-F3, Ctrl-Shift-F3, and F3).

► While the contents of the Clipboard can be saved to a file, the contents of the Spike cannot be saved to a file.

► You can display the content of the Clipboard on its own small window, but you cannot see the content of the Spike until you insert it into your document.

See Table 3.2 for a summary of the Clipboard and the Spike keys.

*Table 3.2   Clipboard and Spike keys.*

| Press | To Perform This Task |
|-------|----------------------|
| Ctrl-Ins | Copies a selection from a Windows application and puts it into the Clipboard |
| Print Screen (PrtSc) | Copies the current screen into the Clipboard |
| Alt-PrtSc | Copies the active window into the Clipboard |
| Shift-Del | Cuts a selection from a Windows application and puts it into the Clipboard |
| Shift-Ins | Pastes the contents of the Clipboard into a Windows application |
| Del | Clears the contents of the Clipboard completely |
| Ctrl-F3 | Cuts a selection from Word and puts it in the Spike |
| Ctrl-Shift-F3 | Inserts the contents of the Spike into the Word document and empties the Spike |
| F3 | Inserts the contents of the Spike into the Word document but does not empty the Spike. Be sure to type `spike` before you press F3. |

**73**

## Using the Clipboard

The Clipboard is actually a Windows program. Since Word for Windows runs under Windows, the Clipboard is available for Word and other Windows applications or programs. You can thus cut or copy text or graphics between Word and other Windows applications. (See the discussion in Chapter 13 titled "Switching to Other Windows Applications from Word.")

The Clipboard stores only one item at a time. Every time you store text or graphics, the last contents of the Clipboard are overwritten and are lost forever. If you exit Word but stay in Windows, the contents of the Clipboard remain. However, once you exit Windows, the Clipboard is emptied.

You can see the contents of the Clipboard from within Word. Once you have opened the Clipboard, you can use its menus—**File**, **E**dit, **D**isplay, and **H**elp. Use the **F**ile menu to save the contents of the Clipboard to a file, which has a .CLP extension, or open that file to bring the contents back into the Clipboard. For example, if you are in the middle of an editing session and you have to leave the office quickly because of an emergency, just store the contents of the Clipboard. The next day, you can open the stored file and start where you left off. Use the Edit menu in the Clipboard window to delete the contents of the Clipboard, and use the Display menu to change the way you view the contents of the Clipboard. The Help menu provides Clipboard-related help. To learn more about the Clipboard, refer to your Windows manuals.

To get to the Clipboard, you must open the Application Control menu (see Figure 3.4), located at the left end of the Title bar, and select the Run command. (See Chapter 1 to briefly review the Application Control menu.)

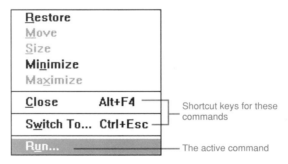

*Figure 3.4    The Application Control pull-down menu showing the active Run command.*

Once you have selected the **R**un command, you will see the Run dialog box (Figure 3.5), which enables you to choose either the Clipboard or the Control Panel. (The Control Panel, another Windows program, allows you to change Windows settings. You'll learn more about the Control Panel in Chapters 7 and 9.) Since the Clipboard option is the default, select OK or press Enter. Word will display the Clipboard window, shown in Figure 3.6.

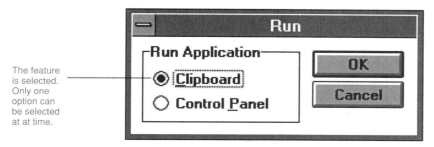

The feature is selected. Only one option can be selected at at time.

*Figure 3.5  The Run dialog box, which allows you to access either the Clipboard or the Control Panel.*

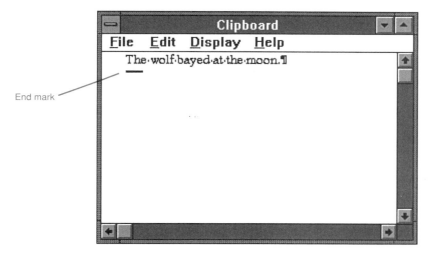

End mark

*Figure 3.6  The Clipboard and its contents—the latest text that has been copied or cut.*

One advantage of using the Clipboard is that you can easily see its contents. Use the following Quick Steps to view or delete the contents of the Clipboard.

 **Viewing and Deleting the Contents of the Clipboard**

1. Click on the Application Control-menu on the left side of the Title bar.

   Word opens a pull-down menu.

2. Select Run.

   Word opens the Run dialog box.

3. Make sure that the Clipboard option is selected (the circle is filled in) and then select OK or press Enter.

Word displays the Clipboard.

4. To delete the contents of the Clipboard, select the **E**dit menu and the **D**elete command (Alt,E,D).

Word prompts you before clearing the Clipboard.

5. Select either the **F**ile menu and the E**x**it command or the Clipboard Application Control menu and select Close.

Word closes the Clipboard window and returns to the current document.

□

## Using the Spike

The Spike is very similar to the Clipboard. However, while the Clipboard replaces its previous contents with the most recent text or graphics that you cut or copy, the Spike appends the cut text or graphics to the end of its current contents. You determine whether and/or when to clear the Spike. If you don't clear it, text and graphics continue to accumulate as you cut them.

Because you have to cut text or graphics in order to insert them into the Spike, it's a good idea to finish your document, save it, and then make a copy from which you can cut. One example of using the Spike to do your job more efficiently is to accumulate text from throughout a document and then insert it at the beginning of the document. This is a quick way to create a summary of your document. If you create a large number of documents with graphics, you can build a portfolio or picture file. Accumulate the graphics in the Spike, insert them into a new document, save, and then print.

These Quick Steps demonstrate how to use the Spike.

 **Using the Spike**

1. Select some text and press Ctrl-F3.

The Spike cuts the text from the document.

2. Repeat step 1 until you have accumulated all the text you want in the Spike.

The Spike accumulates the text in order of deletion and separates each accumulated piece with a paragraph mark.

3. To insert the contents of the Spike and empty the Spike at the same time, move the insertion point where you want to insert the contents and press Ctrl-Shift-F3.

The Spike empties its contents into the document.

4. To insert the contents of the Spike without emptying it, move the insertion point where you want to insert the contents, type **spike**, and press F3.

The Spike copies its contents into the document over the word `spike`.

5. To reinsert the contents of the Spike, repeat step 4.

The Spike copies its contents into the document as many times as you repeat step 4.                □

# Undoing and Repeating Actions

As you go through all the steps in editing your document, you'll inevitably make some mistakes along the way. Fortunately, Word provides the **Undo** command.

 Click on the Undo button to cancel the last action, if Word allows.

Undo is a *context-sensitive* command, which means that it adjusts itself to your last action. Examples of **Undo** commands are Undo Typing, Undo Paste, and Undo Cut. Select the Edit menu and the Undo command (Ctrl-Z or Alt,E,U) to perform this action. If Word can't undo the last action, the entry on the **E**dit menu is `Can't Undo`.

The **R**epeat command (F4 or Alt,E,R) is also context-sensitive. Like the **Undo** command, the action to be repeated is displayed next to Repeat in the menu (for example, Repeat Typing or Repeat Paste). Press F4 to repeat an action. Editing and formatting actions are stored in a buffer, which is cleared when you move the insertion point and start typing or if you perform an editing command. At that point, the current action replaces the previous action in the buffer.

# Finding and Replacing Text

Up to this point, you have edited your document one part at a time. You selected text and moved it to another location, or you've duplicated text in another part of your document. However, when you are editing a document, you sometimes have to make the same change throughout a document. For example, if your company renames a product line from Mountain Lakes to Forest Pines, use Word's **F**ind and R**e**place commands to search for every instance of the old name and then replace it with the new name.

You can use Find and Replace to search for and optionally change groups of characters, words, phrases, punctuation, and formatting. You'll learn about finding and replacing punctuation and formatting in Chapter 8.

## *Finding Text*

Use the **F**ind command to move to a place in a document in which a certain word or phrase occurs. For example, you can look for the word printer, or you can look for the sentence I hate my printer; it doesn't work most of the time. The characters, words, or phrase that you are looking for is the *search string*.

You can enter any of the following information in the Find dialog box (see Figure 3.7) to help your search.

Use the Match **W**hole Word Only box to refine your search by telling Word to find complete words rather than parts of words that match. Suppose that you are looking for all the occurrences of the word *cap*. If you simply click on OK or press Enter, Word will find cap and also caption, capitulate, cape, escape, etc. This is fine if you want to find all those words. However, if you want to find only the word *cap,* click on Match Whole Word Only.

The Match **C**ase box allows you to base a search on upper- or lowercase text. For example, to look for *White House* and avoid all occurrences of *white house,* click on this box.

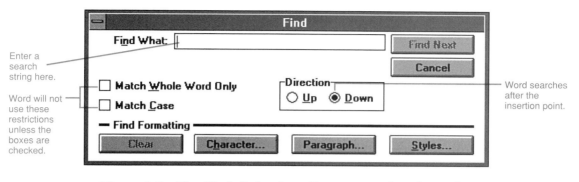

Enter a search string here.

Word will not use these restrictions unless the boxes are checked.

Word searches after the insertion point.

*Figure 3.7   The Find dialog box. Type a search string—the word or phrase that you want Word to find.*

Direction indicates whether you want to search from the insertion point toward the top (Up) or the bottom (Down) of the document. Don't worry too much about choosing the direction, because once the search is at the beginning or end of the document, a small box (Figure 3.8) pops up to ask if you want to continue the search from the other end of the document.

**79**

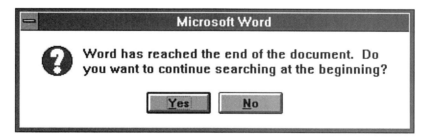

*Figure 3.8   When the search reaches the end of the document, Word displays this box.*

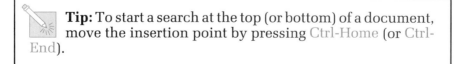

**Tip:** To start a search at the top (or bottom) of a document, move the insertion point by pressing Ctrl-Home (or Ctrl-End).

At the bottom of the Find dialog box, there is a row of buttons, which are used for finding certain formatting in a document. Use the Character, Paragraph, and Styles box to find character, paragraph, and styles formatting, respectively. Chapter 8 tells you how to search for character and paragraph formats, and Chapter 11 covers Styles. Select the Clear button so that you can search for a search string without searching for the formats you have selected.

Normally, the Find command looks throughout your document. To find text in a specific area of your document, select that area before starting. Use the following Quick Steps to find text.

### Finding Text

1. From the Edit menu, select the Find command (Alt,E,F).

    Word displays the Find dialog box.

2. In the Find What box, type the search string—the word or phrase that you would like to find. Select Find Next. Don't worry about the size of the search string—you can type up to 255 characters before you run out of space.

    The Find What text box is filled with the search string.

3. Select the two check boxes— Match Whole Word Only and Match Case—to narrow your search, if you wish. Select Find Next.

    Word searches your document for the search string If Word finds the search string, it displays the page on which the search string is located and highlights the search string. If Word does not find the search string before it reaches the end of the document, it displays a message (Figure 3.8).

4. To search for the next occurrence of the string, repeat step 3.

    Word continues the search. If you started searching below the top of the document, when Word reaches the end of the document, it asks if you want to continue the search at the top.

5. If you want to end the search, select Cancel.

    Word closes the Find dialog box and returns to the current document. □

**80**

## Searching with Wildcards

If you are not sure of the spelling of the word for which you are searching, fill in the questionable area of the word with question marks (?), inserting one question mark for each character that you are unsure of. For example, if you type `p?t`, Word looks for all three-letter words or parts of words starting with the letter *p* and ending with the letter *t*. If you are looking for a word or phrase that actually has a question mark in it, put a caret (`^`) in front of the question mark (for example, `Do bears roam the woods^?`).

## Replacing Text

Finding text is easy, but most times you search for a search string to replace it with some other text. If you wanted to replace every instance of the word *duck* with the word *goose,* it would be a chore to find each *duck,* cancel out of the dialog box, replace it with *goose,* and then repeat the process all over again. Word's **R**eplace command searches for a string of characters and replaces that string of characters with another string.

**81**

The options in the Replace dialog box, shown in Figure 3.9, are very similar to those in the Find dialog box.

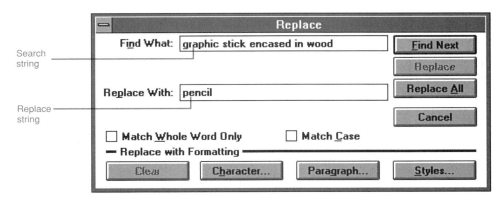

*Figure 3.9    The Replace dialog box. Type a search string and a replace string.*

The Match Whole Word Only and Match Case boxes have the same function as the boxes in the Find dialog box.

At the bottom of the Replace dialog box, there is the same row of Clear, Character, Paragraph, and Styles buttons. However, in this case, you are replacing one format for another. Chapter 8 describes finding and replacing formats, and Chapter 11 talks about Styles.

Use the following Quick Steps to replace text. If you want to replace text in a specific area of your document, select that area before starting.

 **Replacing Text**

1. From the Edit menu, select the Replace command (Alt,E,E).

   Word displays the Replace dialog box. If you have used the Find command earlier in this Word session, your last search string will appear in the Find What box; otherwise, the Replace dialog box is empty.

2. In the Find What box, type the search string that you would like to replace. Select one of the two check boxes— Match Whole Word Only and Match Case—to narrow your search if you wish.

   As you fill in the search string, notice that Word makes the Find Next and Replace All buttons available.

3. In the Replace With box, type the replace string. You can type approximately 500 characters—don't worry about the size of a replace string.

   As you fill the box, Word moves the first characters in the replace string beyond the left margin of the box to make room for additional characters.

4. To find the first occurrence of the search string after the insertion point, select Find Next.

   Word highlights the search string but does not replace it. Word now makes the Replace command available.

5. To replace the highlighted search string, select Replace.

   Word replaces the search string with the replace string and highlights the next occurrence of the search string.

| | |
|---|---|
| 6. Repeat step 5 to replace the next highlighted search string. | When there are no more occurrences of the search string, Word dims the **Re**place command and moves the dialog box insertion point to the Find What box. |
| 7. To replace all occurrences of a search string, select Replace All. | Word replaces all occurrences of the search string, dims the **R**eplace command, and moves the dialog box insertion point to the Find What box. |
| 8. At any time, you can select Close to stop the find-and-replace process. | Word closes the Replace dialog box and returns to the current document.    □ |

 **Tip:** You can replace text with the contents of the Clipboard by typing ^c in the Replace With box.

# What You Have Learned

▶ You can select blocks of every text element—from one word to the entire document. Word for Windows also allows you to select a column of text. Select blocks of text in order to manipulate them with other Word commands.

▶ Word provides the Clipboard and the Spike, which store deleted, cut, and copied text or graphics. The Clipboard stores the last deleted, cut, or copied text or graphics. The Spike accumulates all the deleted, cut, or copied text.

▶ The **U**ndo command (Ctrl-Z or Alt,E,U) can reverse most actions. The **R**epeat command (F4 or Alt,E,R) can repeat most actions.

▶ Use the **F**ind (Alt,E,F) and **R**eplace (Alt,E,E) commands to search for and replace both text and paragraph, character, and style formats.

# Proofing Your Document

## In This Chapter

- ▶ *Checking your spelling, word usage, and grammar*
- ▶ *Creating and choosing a custom or an exclude dictionary*
- ▶ *Customizing grammar rules*
- ▶ *Viewing document statistics*

After you have created a document, it's important to review it. Unless the document is a note to yourself, others will see it and will evaluate its content. After you have edited one or two drafts of a document, consider using Word for Windows' proofing tools—the spell checker, the thesaurus, and the grammar checker.

Use the spell checker to correct misspelled words. Word uses the main dictionary as well as user-defined dictionaries that are unique to your occupation or business. It's a good idea to run the spell checker on every document you create.

While you're writing your document, use the thesaurus to find the best substitute for a selected word.

You can set the grammar checker to one of three levels and then customize the settings within the selected level. This means that you can use the grammar checker to polish a document or you can use it as a tool to improve your grammar and style. By using the readability statistics, you'll know whether the document is aimed at the appropriate audience.

# Checking Your Spelling

Another step in editing your document is checking for spelling mistakes. No matter how beautifully your document is formatted and edited, a spelling error damages its image.

Word's spell checker is an invaluable writing tool. During a full installation of Word for Windows, three dictionaries are provided—the main dictionary, which cannot be modified or even viewed, and two custom dictionaries, CUSTOM.DIC (a startup custom dictionary that you can rename) and STDUSER.DIC (standard user dictionary). You can add words not found in the main dictionary to either of these custom dictionaries by using the **To**ols menu and the **S**pelling command or by editing it with Word. If the dictionaries are not installed on your computer system, you can use the SETUP program at any time to install them. Select Custom Installation and follow the prompts. See Appendix A for installation instructions.

> ABC. Click on the Spelling button to run the spell checker for this document. If the spell checker finds any errors, it displays the Spelling dialog box.

You can use STDUSER.DIC with any document. If you work on a variety of documents, you might want to create a new custom dictionary for a certain type of document that you feel needs one. Suppose you are a pediatrician whose hobby is raising horses, and you write articles on children's medicine and horse raising. You'll probably have two custom dictionaries that contain the appropriate terminology. You don't need to enter every word in your lexicon into the custom dictionary because many words will already be in the main dictionary. When you use the spell checker, Word looks through the main dictionary and as many as four custom dictionaries. Since the main dictionary contains hundreds of thousands of words, it also includes many abbreviations and acronyms. As you work with the spell checker and find gaps, simply add the words to a custom dictionary.

You can use the spell checker to review the entire document, part of a document, or a single word—depending on how much of the document you select. For example, in the process of creating your document, you can check the spelling of a single word by selecting that word, and using the Tools menu and the Spelling command (Alt,O,S).

The Spelling dialog box, shown in Figure 4.1, contains four options and nine buttons:

The *Not in Dictionary* box displays a word that is not in the main dictionary or any active custom dictionary.

The *Change To* box contains the first word in the Suggestions box. You can either accept one of the suggested words or type in a replacement word. If there are no suggestions, the word in the Not in Dictionary box is displayed here. You can also delete a word from your document by deleting the word in the Change To box. When you press Del to delete the word in the Change To box, Word alters the Change and Change All buttons to read Delete and Delete All, respectively. Then click on the Delete or Delete All button.

The *Suggestions* box lists potential replacement words that Word finds in the active dictionaries.

The *Add Words To* box displays the name of the custom dictionary to which you can add a word. Press the list arrow to reveal the names of all active custom dictionaries.

**87**

To choose a replacement word, highlight it and select Change.

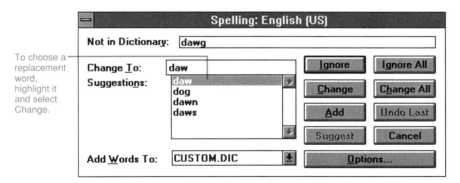

*Figure 4.1    The Spelling dialog box.*

The Spelling dialog box has several buttons, which provide a wide variety of functions. You can act either on a single word or on every occurrence of that word throughout your document.

*Ignore/Ignore All* skips the selected word or all occurrences of the selected word and then moves to the next word not found in the active dictionaries.

*Change/Change All* changes the selected word or all occurrences of the selected word and then moves to the next word
not found in the active dictionaries.

*Delete/Delete All* deletes the word or all occurrences of the
selected word from your custom dictionary once you have
deleted the word from the Change To box. The Delete/Delete
All buttons are only available if you have deleted all the text
from the Change To box. The spell checker then moves to
the next word not found in the active dictionaries.

*Add* places the selected word in the custom dictionary
named in the Add Words To box.

> **Tip:** To view and edit the words in your custom dictio-
> nary, open the dictionary just as you would another file.
> The extension is .DIC. It's a text-only (ASCII) file, which Word
> converts if you answer Yes to a prompt. Then edit the dictionary
> as you would any document. When you have finished, save it.

**88**

*Suggest*, which is dimmed if you have checked the Always
Suggest box in the Options dialog box for the Spelling category, allows you to type a word in the Change To box so
that you can see suggestions based on that word. If the
Always Suggest box is cleared, you can select Suggest whenever the spell checker finds a word that is not in one of the
active dictionaries, but you can also type a word in the
Change To box.

*Undo Last* changes the last word replaced back to the original word.

*Cancel/Close* cancels the dialog box without making any
changes or closes it after making a change that cannot be
undone anymore.

*Options* displays the Options dialog box for the Spelling
category, which is explained right after the following Quick
Steps.

Now that you have some grounding in the Spelling dialog box,
use these Quick Steps to check the spelling in a document.

**Checking the Spelling in a Document**

1. Select the part of the current document that you want Word to check. (You can select the whole document, a single word, or anything in between.) If you want Word to check the entire document, you don't have to select anything. Then select the Tools menu and the Spelling command (Alt,O,S or press F7).

   Word displays the Spelling dialog box and highlights the first word not found in either the main dictionary or an active custom dictionary. The spell checker also suggests a replacement word and lists other replacement words.

2. To ignore or change the word using Word's suggestions, you can press one of the applicable buttons.

   Word looks for the next word not found in a dictionary. If it finds another word, it highlights it and names replacement words.

3. To suggest a word to replace the highlighted word, type it in the Change To box and select Suggest. This is a way to replace a word with a synonym and check its spelling in one step.

   Word looks for the next word not found in a dictionary. If it finds another word, it highlights the word and names replacement words.

4. To add a word to the active custom dictionary, select the Add button.

   Word reviews the remainder of the selected text. If it finds another word, it highlights the word and names replacement words.

5. Repeat step 2, 3, or 4 until Word has reviewed every word in the selected text.

   If you have not started the spell check at the top of the document and Word does not find another word before it reaches the end of your selection, it displays a dialog box asking if you want the spell check to continue at the top of the document. When the spell check is complete, Word displays an informational message.

89

6. Select OK or press Enter.　　　Word returns to the current
　　　　　　　　　　　　　　　　　　document.　　　　　　　□

If you check an entire document for spelling errors, Word asks you if you want to continue checking at the beginning of the document unless you started the check there.

If the spell checker finds a word that is an odd combination of uppercase and lowercase letters, Not in Dictionary changes to Capitalization. You can fix the word, select Ignore, or add the word to your dictionary.

If the spell checker finds duplicate words (for example, *the the*), it informs you so that you can correct the error by pressing Delete.

---

 **Note:** While the Spelling dialog box is displayed, Word allows you to return to your document to manually apply any changes.

---

## *Using the Spelling/Options Dialog Box*

In Chapter 2, you were introduced to the Options dialog box for the View, Print, and Save categories. The spell checker has its own options dialog box, which allows you to define as many as four active custom dictionaries, to ignore certain words, and to determine whether the spell checker suggests replacement words. For example, if you are checking a document with a number of words that are all uppercase characters but you know that they are spelled correctly, check the Words in UPPERCASE check box. Then the spell checker will ignore the all-uppercase words. Suppose you are working with a report that contains a number of inventory codes that are combinations of letters and numbers. If you don't check the Words with Numbers check box, you'll spend a great deal of time ignoring the inventory codes that the spell checker identifies.

If you check the Always Suggest check box, a list of suggested words for each "misspelled" word appears in the Spelling dialog box. If Always Suggest is clear, Word does not suggest replacement words. If you're working with a technical document containing words that are not likely to be in the dictionary, you're probably using the spell checker to "flag" the common words that are misspelled. In this case, clear the Always Suggest check box. You'll find that you save time, and if you want suggestions during a spell check, you can press Suggest in the Spelling dialog box.

You can display the Options dialog box for the Spelling category (see Figure 4.2) from within the Spelling dialog box or by choosing the Tools menu and the Options command (Alt,O,O).

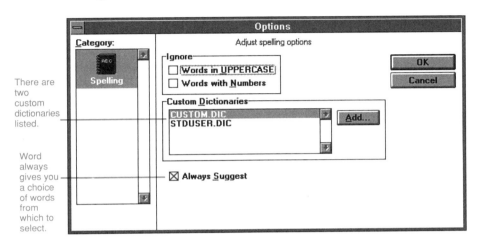

There are two custom dictionaries listed.

Word always gives you a choice of words from which to select.

*Figure 4.2    The Options dialog box for the Spelling category.*

91

## Creating a Custom Dictionary

If you are the pediatrician in the earlier example and, in addition to your horses, you dabble in the stock market and develop electronic equipment, you may need to create four different custom dictionaries. (Actually, you can create as many different custom dictionaries as you want, but you can use only four at a time.)

To create your first custom dictionary, use the following Quick Steps.

 **Creating a Custom Dictionary**

1. From the Tools menu, select the Spelling command (Alt,O,S).

   Word opens the Spelling dialog box.

2. Select Options.

   Word opens the Options dialog box (Figure 4.2).

3. Select Add.

Word displays the Add Dictionary dialog box (see Figure 4.3).

4. Enter the name you would like to give the dictionary.

Word reminds you to add a .DIC extension. However, if you ignore the reminder, you can give your dictionary any extension you want (or no extension at all) and Word will not protest or remind you to add an extension.

5. Select OK or press Enter.

Word returns to the Options dialog box for the Spelling category and adds the new dictionary to the list in the Custom Dictionaries box.

**92**

6. Select OK or press Enter.

Word returns to the Spelling dialog box, from which you can use the spell checker.

7. If you don't want to continue to use the spell checker, select Cancel.

Word returns to the current document.

□

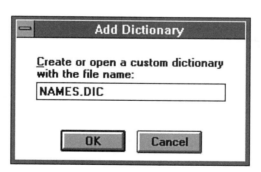

*Figure 4.3  You can create a new custom dictionary or open as many as four custom dictionaries at a time from the Add Dictionary dialog box.*

## *Opening and Closing a Custom Dictionary*

Before Word can use a custom dictionary to check spelling in the current document, the dictionary must be on the list of selected custom dictionaries in the Spelling Options dialog box. The dictionary must be opened before you run the spell check. The next set of Quick Steps explains how to open and close a custom dictionary.

**Q** **Opening and Closing a Custom Dictionary**

1. Select the Tools menu and the Options command (Alt,O,O).

   Word opens the last Options dialog box used during this session.

2. Under Category, select Spelling.

   Word opens the Options dialog box for the Spelling category.

3. If you use the mouse, move the mouse pointer to the the name of a custom dictionary in the Custom Dictionaries box. Then click to open or close that dictionary.

   Word indicates that a custom dictionary is open by highlighting it; otherwise, there is no highlight.

4. If you use the keyboard, press the Tab key to move to the Custom Dictionaries box. Then press any combination of ↑ or ↓ to highlight a custom dictionary.

   Word surrounds your choice with a dotted border.

5. Press the space bar to open or close that dictionary.

   Word indicates that a custom dictionary is open by highlighting it; otherwise, there is no highlight.

6. Select OK or press Enter.

   Word returns to the current document. □

**93**

## *Adding Words to a Custom Dictionary*

The simplest way to add words to a custom dictionary is during a spell checker session. Make sure that you have chosen the custom dictionary to which you want to add words. Then check one or more documents and add words where needed.

If you want to add many words to the custom dictionary at one time, you can create a special document containing the words, each separated by a space. Then run the spell checker against this document. When Word finds a word that is not in either the standard or the custom dictionary, you can add it.

### Creating an Exclude Dictionary

You can create a dictionary that excludes words that the main dictionary may consider to be misspelled. For example, in your workplace, you may use a word such as *correx,* which does not appear in the main dictionary. Instead of adding *correx* to all custom dictionaries, you can create a document containing *correx* and any other unique words. If you use the main dictionary SP_AM.LEX, you must name the exclude dictionary SP_AM.EXC. Make sure that you save the exclude dictionary using the File Save As command (Alt,F,A), and in the Save Text as Type box, select Text Only. Otherwise, Word adds formats that the spell checker will read incorrectly.

# Using the Thesaurus

The next step in refining your document is to use the thesaurus. A thesaurus adds spice to your documents by letting you choose words with similar meanings instead of using the same word repeatedly. You can also use the thesaurus to choose a word that is slightly closer to what you mean in a sentence. For example, does the word *improve* mean *advance* or *repair?* Does *loud* mean *deafening* or *powerful?* In both examples, the groups of words are synonyms but the meanings are not identical.

Word's **Thesaurus** command allows you to replace a word with a synonym from a list. The Thesaurus dialog box includes four boxes and three buttons, as shown in Figure 4.4. These are the options:

*Synonyms For* displays the word or phrase that you selected before you displayed this dialog box. If there is no synonym for a selected word, the box is labeled Word Not Found.

*Replace With* displays the suggested replacement word or phrase. If you're starting a new document and use the Thesaurus command, this box is labeled Insert.

*Meanings* displays definitions of recently displayed words or phrases so that you can make an informed decision. If there is no meaning, this box is labeled Alphabetical List and the thesaurus displays words or phrases that are in alphabetical order but not synonyms of the selected word or phrase.

*Synonyms* displays synonyms for the word or phrase in the Synonyms For box.

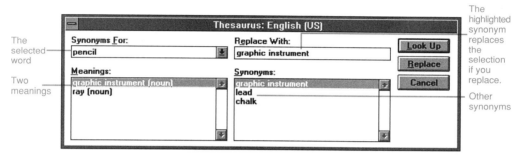

The selected word

Two meanings

The highlighted synonym replaces the selection if you replace.

Other synonyms

*Figure 4.4    The Thesaurus window displays words from which you can choose.*

You can either select the Look Up button to display synonyms for the suggested replacement word or phrase or select Replace/Insert to replace the selected word or phrase with the word or phrase in the Replace With box.

 **Using the Thesaurus**

1. Position the insertion point anywhere in a word or to its immediate right, and select the **T**ools menu and the Thesaurus command (Alt,O,T). You can also press Shift-F7.

   Word displays the Thesaurus window with the selected word in the Synonyms For box.

2. Highlight an appropriate word in the Meanings box.

   For the highlighted word in the Meanings box, Word displays synonyms (and sometimes antonyms) in the Synonyms box.

3. Highlight an appropriate word in the Synonyms box.

Word places the selected word in the Replace With box.

4. To further investigate the word in the Replace With box, click on the **L**ook Up button.

Word displays meanings and synonyms from which you can select.

5. To replace the original word with the selected word, click on the **R**eplace button.

Word replaces the original word with the replacement word and returns to the current document.     □

# Checking Your Grammar

The final step in perfecting the content of your document is to check the grammar and readability of your document with the grammar checker.

Select the Tools menu and the Grammar command (Alt,O,G) to display the Grammar dialog box, shown in Figure 4.5, with these options:

*Sentence box*—In this box, the grammar checker displays a sentence that you should evaluate and perhaps correct.

*Suggestions box*—In this box, the grammar checker either describes the problem or offers one or more corrections.

*Ignore*—Press this button to skip to the next error in a sentence or to the next incorrect sentence without changing the sentence.

*Change*—Press this button to have the grammar checker correct a sentence. If the button is not available, move the insertion point to the document and make the change.

*Next Sentence*—Press this button to ignore the errors in a sentence and find the next incorrect sentence.

*Ignore Rule*—Press this button to ignore the errors in a sentence and similar errors in other sentences. The grammar checker then finds the next incorrect sentence.

*Cancel*—Press this button, if it is available, to close the dialog box but keep all the changes that have been made up to this point.

*Close*—Press this button, if it is available, to close the dialog box but keep all the changes that have been made up to this point.

*Explain*—Press this button to display a small window expanding the explanation in the Suggestions box.

*Options*—Press this button to open the Grammar/Options dialog box (see Figure 4.6), which allows you to select specific grammar and style rules, show readability statistics, and customize settings.

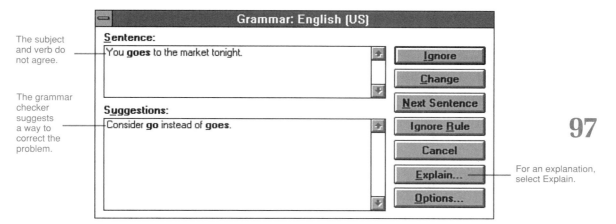

The subject and verb do not agree.

The grammar checker suggests a way to correct the problem.

For an explanation, select Explain.

**97**

*Figure 4.5   When the grammar checker finds problems with your document, Word opens the Grammar dialog box.*

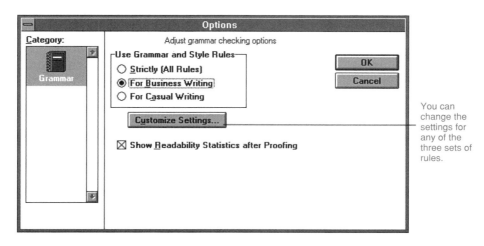

You can change the settings for any of the three sets of rules.

*Figure 4.6   The Grammar/Options dialog box allows you to change grammar and style rules.*

The Options dialog box for the Grammar category enables you to customize the grammar and style rules that the grammar checker uses. You can choose from and customize Strictly (All Rules), For Business Writing, or For Casual Writing. You can also indicate whether you want to Show Readability Statistics after Proofing.

To set your own grammar and style rules, select Customize Settings. The grammar checker then displays the Customize Grammar Settings dialog box. Select Strictly (All Rules), For Business Writing, or For Casual Writing from the top of the screen (you could have also selected one of these from the previous screen). Check or clear the check boxes in the Grammar and Style boxes to adjust the rules to fit your strengths and weaknesses. To learn about individual grammar and style rules, select Explain. In the Catch box, you can set triggering levels for split infinitives, consecutive nouns, and prepositional phrases. To return to the grammar checker's original settings, select Reset All. When you have finished customizing the rules, select another level of severity and repeat the process just described. When you have finally completed customization, select OK or Cancel.

**98**

 **Checking Your Grammar**

1. Select the part of the document that you want Word to check. If you want Word to check the entire document, you don't have to select anything. Then, from the Tools menu, select the Grammar command (Alt,O,G).

   The grammar checker evaluates your document or the selected text. If the grammar checker finds a sentence that is grammatically incorrect, Word opens the Grammar dialog box.

2. Correct your document or ignore the suggestions using the options described previously.

   If the grammar checker finds a misspelled word, Word opens the Spelling dialog box.

3. To switch from the Grammar dialog box to your document, move the insertion point outside the dialog box and click.

   Word dims the dialog box.

4. To switch back to the dialog box, select Start in the dialog box.

   Word activates the dialog box.

5. Correct your document or ignore the suggestions using the options described previously.

When the grammar checker has completed its evaluation of selected text, Word displays a message that it has finished checking (see Figure 4.7). If, however, you have previously chosen to display Readability Statistics, Word now displays those instead of the message.

6. Select OK or press Enter.

Word returns you to the current document. ☐

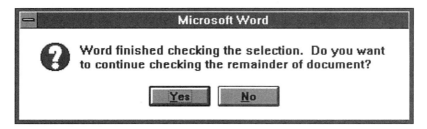

*Figure 4.7   When the grammar checker has finished evaluating the selected text in your document, Word displays this message.*

## Selecting and Customizing Grammar Rules

The grammar checker has three preset levels of severity for grammar and style. This means that you can change grammar rules to fit your environment. For example, suppose you are writing a letter to your grade-school English teacher. If you apply the strictest grammar rules, chances are you'll get that A+ you always wanted. On the other hand, if you're writing an informal note to your best friend, you can loosen the rules somewhat.

Depending on the type of document you are writing, you can select from and/or customize any of three sets of grammar rules using the following Quick Steps.

**Selecting and Customizing Grammar Rules**

1. With a document open, select the Tools menu and the Grammar command (Alt,O,G).

   Word opens the Grammar dialog box.

2. Select Options.

   Word opens the Grammar/Options dialog box.

3. If the selected button is not your choice, select one of the other two buttons.

   Strictly (All Rules) enforces most grammar and style rules in the grammar checker. For Business Writing enforces most grammar rules and some style rules. For Casual Writing enforces most grammar rules and eight style rules.

**100**

4. To display or customize settings for grammar and style rules, select Customize Settings.

   Word opens the Customize Grammar Settings dialog box (see Figure 4.8).

5. Select settings in the Grammar and/or Style boxes to ease or tighten the rules. In the Catch box, you can adjust the settings.

   Word displays the new setting.

6. If you don't understand the selected Grammar or Style entry, select Explain.

   Word opens a Grammar Explanation window (see Figure 4.9), which contains a brief explanation.

7. If you want to reset the rules to Word's default settings, select Reset All.

   Word displays the default settings.

8. When you have completed customizing the rules, Select OK or press Enter.

   Word returns to the Grammar/Options dialog box.

9. Select OK or press Enter.

   Word returns to the Grammar dialog box.

10. Click on Close.

    Word returns to your document.                    □

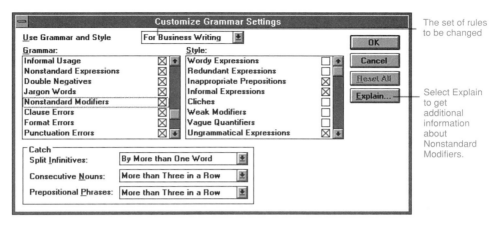

*Figure 4.8   The Customize Grammar Settings dialog box allows you to check or remove the check for a particular grammar or style rule.*

**101**

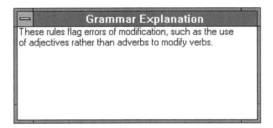

*Figure 4.9   Open the Grammar Explanation window to see a brief explanation about a rule.*

**FYIdea:** To improve your writing skills or to learn more about grammar and style, set the Grammar Settings to **S**trictly (All Rules) and run the grammar checker for most documents.

## *Grammar Statistics*

At the end of a grammar check, Word displays the Readability Statistics window, shown in Figure 4.10. (If you don't want to see Readability Statistics after every grammar check, clear the Show

Readability Statistics After Proofing box in the Options dialog box for the Grammar category.) It is up to you to evaluate the statistics for your document. However, in general, the following information applies:

▶ Don't use passive voice (for example, "the patient was revived by Mike" instead of "Mike revived the patient") if you can avoid it. Keep your passive voice score as low as possible.

▶ The Flesch Reading Ease score decreases as the difficulty of the document increases.

▶ The Flesch Grade Level and Flesch-Kincaid scores both measure the school grade level.

▶ The Gunning Fog Index calculates its score by counting the number of words per sentence and the number of syllables per word. The score increases as the difficulty of the document increases.

**102**

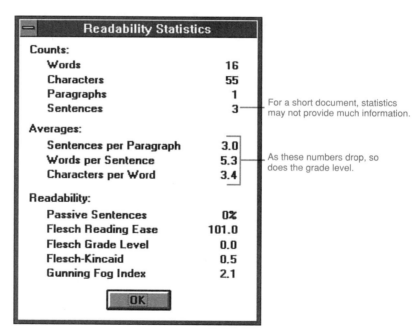

*Figure 4.10   The Readability Statistics window displays statistical information about the document that was just checked.*

# Document Statistics

In Chapter 2, when you saved your first document, you might have filled in the Summary Info box. From that box, you had the opportunity to see document statistics. There is another way to view statistics for your document. After thoroughly checking your document for spelling, word usage, grammar, and style, you can check your document statistics.

Document statistics include the name of this document file, the directory in which it is located, its title, the creation date, the date you last saved it, and the name of the person who last saved the file. Word also tells you the number of times you've saved the document and the time you have spent editing it. Probably the most important statistics are the number of pages, number of words, and number of characters.

To see information about your document, including a count of words, when it was created, and other information, follow these Quick Steps.

**103**

### **Q** Displaying Statistics About a Document

1. From the File menu, select the Summary Info command (Alt,F,I).

Word opens the Summary Info dialog box (see Figure 4.11).

2. Select Statistics.

Word opens the Document Statistics dialog box (see Figure 4.12).

3. Before you look at the statistics, select Update to make sure that they are current.

Word updates the statistics.

4. After you have reviewed the statistics, select OK or press Enter.

Word returns to the Summary Info dialog box.

5. Select OK or press Enter or Cancel.

Word returns to the current document.                    □

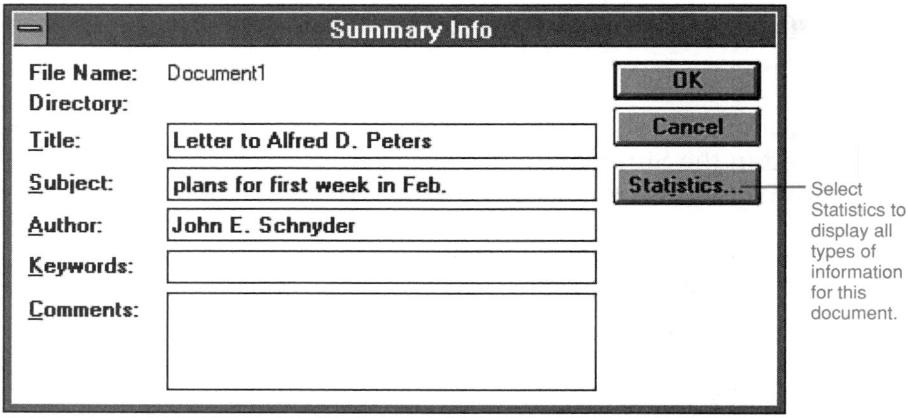

**Summary Info**

| | |
|---|---|
| File Name: | Document1 |
| Directory: | |
| Title: | Letter to Alfred D. Peters |
| Subject: | plans for first week in Feb. |
| Author: | John E. Schnyder |
| Keywords: | |
| Comments: | |

OK
Cancel
Statistics...

Select Statistics to display all types of information for this document.

*Figure 4.11    The Summary Info dialog box displays information about the current document and allows you to add more.*

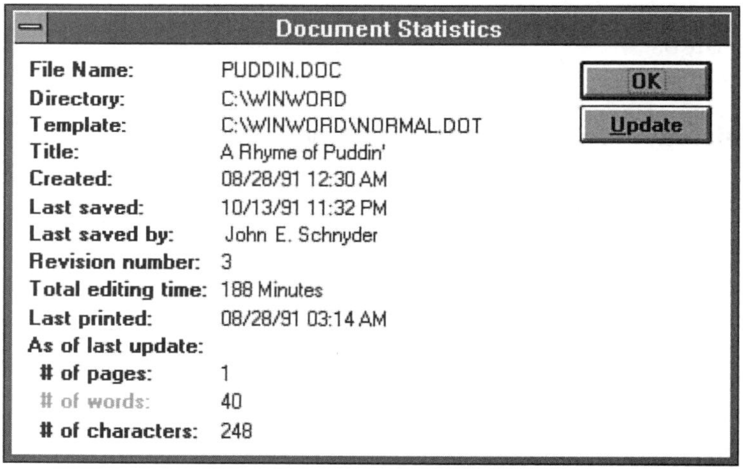

**Document Statistics**

| | |
|---|---|
| File Name: | PUDDIN.DOC |
| Directory: | C:\WINWORD |
| Template: | C:\WINWORD\NORMAL.DOT |
| Title: | A Rhyme of Puddin' |
| Created: | 08/28/91 12:30 AM |
| Last saved: | 10/13/91 11:32 PM |
| Last saved by: | John E. Schnyder |
| Revision number: | 3 |
| Total editing time: | 188 Minutes |
| Last printed: | 08/28/91 03:14 AM |
| As of last update: | |
| # of pages: | 1 |
| # of words: | 40 |
| # of characters: | 248 |

OK
Update

*Figure 4.12    The Document Statistics dialog box provides extensive information about the current document.*

# What You Have Learned

▶ When you use the spell checker, you can have as many as four custom dictionaries open at a time in addition to the main dictionary. From the Tools menu, select the Spelling command (Alt,O,S) to start the spell checker.

▶ Use the Tools Option (Alt,O,O) dialog box for the Spelling category to define the active custom dictionaries. You can create custom dictionaries as well as an exclude dictionary, which excludes words that the main dictionary may flag as being misspelled.

▶ Use the thesaurus to make sure that the words you choose are the closest to the meaning that you intend. Select Tools Thesaurus (Alt,O,T) or press Shift-F7.

▶ Use the grammar checker to evaluate the grammar and readability of a document. You can also use it to improve your grammar and style. To access the grammar checker, select the Grammar command from the Tools menu (Alt,O,G).

▶ Word provides two types of statistics for a document—readability and general document information. Word displays readability statistics after you run the grammar checker. To view or edit document statistics, select File Summary Info (Alt,F,I).

**105**

# Defining Document-wide and Section Formats

## In This Chapter

- ▶ *Defining the unit of measure used throughout Word*
- ▶ *Setting the layout of all pages in the document*
- ▶ *Changing margins, paper size, and text orientation*
- ▶ *Creating headers and footers*
- ▶ *Breaking pages and sections*
- ▶ *Defining and customizing page numbers*

## Formatting in Word for Windows

Once you have finished organizing your document and editing its text, you can enhance the appearance of your document through formatting. Formatting can make the difference between an indifferent and an enthusiastic reception on the part of your reader.

Word for Windows handles formatting through the Format menu. Word has four basic format levels: document, section, paragraph, and character. *Document-wide formatting* encompasses the entire document; *section formatting* defines major changes (such as page orientation, paper dimension, and page numbering) within the document; *paragraph formatting* changes the appearance of one or more selected paragraphs; and *character formatting* determines the appearance of words and characters.

Because these formatting concepts and the associated commands play such a large role in Word, it's important for you to understand them thoroughly.

Document-wide formatting controls the size of margins on a page, the dimensions of the paper on which you will print, and other measures of the printed page. Document-wide formatting applies to every page of your document—from the title page to the index. Although the text on individual pages in the document might look very different (for example, compare body text with the table of contents), you'll print your document on the same size paper, and the page numbers will appear in the same spot on every page.

Section formatting controls major changes within your document. For example, in a sales brochure, most of the text will be oriented across the shorter page dimension, from the left to the right margin. However, there might be one or two pages of tables containing long lines of text that stretch between the top and the bottom margins. You have to create a new section whenever you change the orientation of text in a document. You can also use section formatting to create breaks between chapters, to change the content of headers and footers, or to place endnotes after each chapter. Section formatting sends a strong signal to Word that a major change must take place in order to start the next part of the document.

Paragraph formatting controls strings of text that end with a paragraph mark. You can determine how text is aligned between the margins, whether there are indented or block paragraphs, and how many blank lines are placed between paragraphs. Paragraph formatting also determines where a headline or graphic appears on a page. Paragraph formatting is covered in Chapter 6.

Character formatting changes the appearance of text, changes spacing between characters, and creates special characters. For example, you can use character formatting to create the appropriate text type and size for a headline or footnote. Chapter 7 explains character formatting.

The best way to format a document is to start at the largest level (that is, document-wide) and work your way down to the smallest level (or character). But first, decide whether you want to change the unit of measure used for formatting.

# Changing Units of Measure in Word

Some people are used to measuring with inches, and others are more comfortable with centimeters. A person who is experienced in the printing industry or who requires fine gradations between measurements might want to use picas or points. Word allows you to choose from a list of units of measure so that you can use the one with which you are most comfortable. Table 5.1 shows which measurement units are available and the abbreviation that you type for each.

*Table 5.1    Units of measure in Word for Windows.*

| To Use This Unit | You Type |
| --- | --- |
| Centimeters | cm |
| Inches | in or " |
| Picas | pi |
| Points | pt |
| Lines | li |

All units of measure in Word are set by default to inches. It is an easy matter to change to centimeters, lines, picas, or points. From the Tools menu, select the Options command (Alt,O,O) and select the General category. Display the Measurement Units list box (shown in Figure 5.1) by clicking on the underlined down arrow at the right side of the box or repeatedly pressing the Tab key until you have highlighted the Measurement Units box. Press ↓ to list the contents of the box, shown in Figure 5.2. Select the unit that you want and click on OK or press Enter. The unit of measure on the Ruler will change to reflect your choice (see Figure 5.3). For the rest of this book, you will use the default unit of measure, inches.

Use the following Quick Steps to define a new default unit of measure and to change the unit shown on the Ruler.

 **Changing the Default Unit of Measure**

1. From the Tools menu, select the Options command (Alt,O,O).

   Word displays the last Options dialog box you used in this Word session.

2. In the Category box, select General.

   Word changes the display in the Options dialog box.

3. Select the underlined arrow in the Measurement Units box.

Word displays the available units of measurement. The current default is highlighted on the list of choices and also appears in the arrow box.

4. Select the unit of measurement. Choose OK or press Enter.

Word changes the measurement type on the Ruler and in all boxes containing measurements. □

**Note:** The default unit for vertical measurements is always lines (li).

**110**

Now you are in the General category.

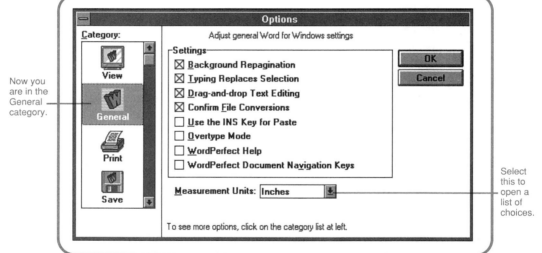

Select this to open a list of choices.

*Figure 5.1   The Options dialog box for the General category.*

This is the current selection.

If you press OK, the highlighted measurement is selected from the list.

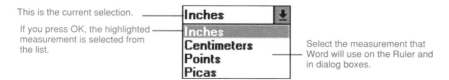

Select the measurement that Word will use on the Ruler and in dialog boxes.

*Figure 5.2   The Measurement Units list box.*

Ruler with points as the unit of measure.

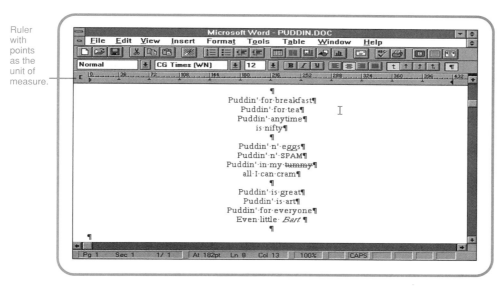

*Figure 5.3    The Ruler as it looks with points as the default unit of measure.*

Whenever you open a dialog box that requires a measurement, you don't have to add an abbreviation if you enter a value that is measured in the same units as the current unit of measure. (For example, if the default value is inches, you can enter 5 and Word knows that you mean "5 inches.") However, if you want to temporarily use another unit of measure, type the number and then the abbreviation of the unit type (for example, 64 pt or 75 cm).

**Note:** You have to use decimal equivalents for fractions (for example, .75 instead of 3/4 or .5 rather than 1/2) because you cannot enter fractions.

# Document-wide Formatting

Once you have chosen your default unit of measure, you can put it to work in determining document-wide formats. You can accept

Word's defaults, which are a good starting point for a beginner, or you can define your own. For example, if you are creating a business letter, using Word's top, bottom, left, and right margins certainly makes sense. However, if you are preparing a one-page advertisement with plenty of white space, you'll want to make those margins larger. For a legal document, you may change the margins as well as the paper size.

Document-wide formats control the overall appearance of your document on a page-by-page basis. These formats include:

▶ The size of margins—left, right, top, bottom, *gutter,* and *mirror.* A gutter margin allows for binding or hole-punching on the left side of a page printed on a single side. A mirror margin allows for binding or hole-punching of a page printed on both sides; the inside margins "mirror" each other.

▶ The size of the paper on which your document prints, for example, 8 1/2 by 11 inches.

▶ The orientation of text on a page, either the way memos and books (such as this one) are oriented, with the page longer than it is wide; or the way some spreadsheets are oriented, with the page wider than it is long.

To set or change document-wide formats, use the Page Setup command on the Format menu (Alt,T,U). Word displays the Page Setup dialog box shown in Figure 5.4. At the top of this box, you will see three attributes that you can modify: Margins, Size and Orientation, and Paper Source. You can choose only one at a time. Word will display a different dialog box for each attribute.

The Page Setup dialog box for Margins includes boxes into which you can type settings for the top, bottom, left, and right margins. You can also determine the size of the gutter and mirror margins. When you select Facing Pages, the left and right margin boxes become the inside and outside margin boxes, respectively. In the Apply To box, you have several choices. You can change the page setup for the entire document or from the location of the insertion point forward (whether or not there is text after the insertion point). To change the margins for a piece of text, select the text and then choose the Selected Text option. When you select text, the This Point Forward option is not available. In the Use as Default box, you can also select the new margins as your default measurements for all new documents that you create until you select a new set of default measurements.

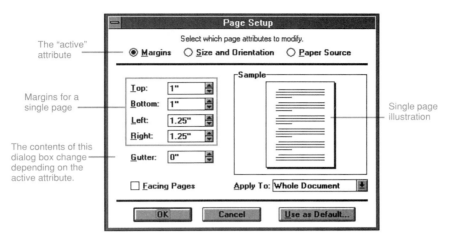

The "active" attribute

Margins for a single page

The contents of this dialog box change depending on the active attribute.

Single page illustration

**Figure 5.4**   *The Page Setup dialog box for Margins with its default settings. The Facing Pages check box is clear.*

113

## Facing Pages versus Single Pages

Now that you've had your introduction to document-wide formatting, consider whether to format one page or two pages at a time.

Documents are either printed on one side of the page (single-sided) or both sides of the page (double-sided). Single-sided documents include business letters, resumes, program listings, and order sheets. Many single-sided documents are easier to use in that format. For example, if you are a programmer who must find the bugs in a program, it's easier to review a listing that's printed on one side of several pages or continuous form paper. When clerks at catalog companies process orders with several items, they are less likely to forget items if the order is on a single side of paper.

Economy is a major reason for double-sided documents. A large report, newspaper, or book can use up a great deal of paper, so why not cut the amount of paper you use in half by printing on both sides? Also, people are used to seeing certain documents in a double-sided format and others on one side of a page.

Designing two pages at a time is a very effective way to create a large document. For example, to design an easy-to-use instruction manual, you might want to present a diagram on the even-numbered, or left-hand, page and the written instructions on the odd-numbered, or right-hand, page. This might require different headers or footers on odd-numbered and even-numbered pages. In a document of this type, the placement of graphics, text, and white space plays a big part in the design of a page.

Use the Format menu and the Page Setup command (Alt,T,U) to display the Page Setup dialog box for Margins shown in Figure 5.4. Then check or clear the Facing Pages check box to determine whether a document is best designed two pages at a time or page by page. The following Quick Steps show how to turn Facing Pages on or off.

 **Turning Facing Pages On and Off**

| | |
|---|---|
| 1. Select the Format menu and the Page Setup command (Alt,T,U). | Word opens the Page Setup dialog box. |
| 2. Select the Margins button. | Word displays the Margins options and shows the Facing Pages check box as clear. |
| 3. To format using facing pages, put a check in the Facing Pages check box. | Word displays two pages in the Sample box. |
| 4. Select OK or press Enter. | Word applies this format to the whole document. □ |

When you are formatting a single page, Word's margins are left, right, top, and bottom. When you use Facing Pages, the left and right margins are called Inside (the margins closest to the binding edge) and Outside (the margins farthest from the binding edge), respectively.

## Changing Margins

After deciding on Facing Pages, the next step in choosing document-wide formats is to set the margins for your document.

Page margin settings control the space between the edge of the page and the text on the page. For example, the top margin is the space from the top of the page to the first line of text. Word's initial top and bottom margins are 1 inch, and the left and right (or inside and outside) margins are 1.25 inches. As the margin measurements increase in size, the amount of text printed on a page decreases.

114

The margins that you set determine the appearance of your document. With narrow margins, your text looks more dense. It's more difficult for some people to read because the number of characters on a line increases. To some readers, a page with a large amount of text and a small amount of white space looks forbidding. Conversely, a page with a great deal of white space and less text area is easier to read and "friendlier" in appearance. Word's default text area is 6 by 9 inches; the default page dimensions are 8 1/2 by 11 inches.

You can change margins whether or not there is a document in the text area. Before you begin the following Quick Steps, clear the Facing Pages check box. If you decide to work with Facing Pages turned on, remember that for two-page formatting, the left margin is called the inside margin and the right margin is the outside margin. Then use these Quick Steps to change all the document-wide margins.

 **Changing Margins**

1. To change the margins of selected text, first select the appropriate text. To set new margins starting at the insertion point through the remainder of your document, move the insertion point to the place at which you want the margins to change. Then select the Format menu and the Page Setup command (Alt,T,U).

   Word opens the Page Setup dialog box.

2. Select the Margins button.

   The Page Setup box appears with the Margins options displayed.

3. Set any combination of Top, Bottom, Left, or Right (or Inside or Outside) margins. With the keyboard, move the insertion point to the number in the desired box and then type a measurement. The measurements for the top and bottom margins must be between –22 and 22. The

   Word changes margins on the page illustrated in the Sample box (Figure 5.5).

measurements for the right and left margins must be between 0 and 22. To use the mouse, move the mouse pointer to the arrow button to the right of that box, and then press and hold the left mouse button, releasing it when the desired number is displayed.

4. To change the Gutter margin, move the insertion point to the number in the Gutter box and then type a replacement number (between 0 and 22 inches). To use the mouse, move the mouse pointer to the arrow button to the right of the Gutter box, and then press and hold the left mouse button, releasing it when the desired number is displayed.

Word shows the gutter margin. Depending on whether you have checked Facing Pages, Word either adds the gutter (in this case, mirror) margin measurement to the inside margin of facing pages (Figure 5.6) or to the left margin of single pages.

**116**

5. To select the part of the document for the margin changes, select the list arrow next to Apply To and select Whole Document or Selected Text (if you have selected text) or This Point Forward (if you have not selected text).

Depending on your choice, Word changes the margins of the entire current document, selected text, or all text beyond the insertion point.

6. To use the new margin settings as the default measurements for every Word document you create from now on, select Use as Default. These new margins apply to documents using the default template, NORMAL.DOT. (*Templates*, which are guidelines to the overall look and content of a document, are described in Chapter 12.) If you use other templates to create a document, their margins are not changed.

Word asks you if you want to use the new settings as the default (Figure 5.7).

7. Select **Yes** (change all new documents based on the NORMAL.DOT template) or **No** (just this document).

If you select Yes, Word returns to the current document or to the screen from which you selected the command. If you select No, Word returns to the Page Setup dialog box.

8. If you have completed filling in the dialog box, select OK or press Enter.

Word returns to the current document or the screen from which you selected the command. □

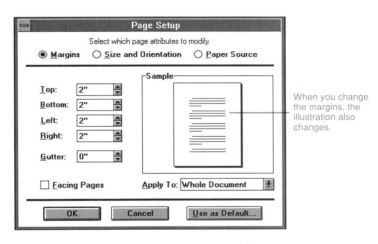

When you change the margins, the illustration also changes.

**117**

*Figure 5.5    The Page Setup dialog box. The Facing Pages check box is cleared, and the Sample document has changed to reflect the new margins.*

If you have a document on-screen, you can see how margins change by using the Ruler, shown in Figure 5.8, to set the left and right margins. For example, if you have just heard that your resume must be on a prospective employer's desk by tomorrow morning, you can adjust formatting "on the fly" by viewing your changes as you make them.

On the Ruler, a single triangle represents the right margin. All text ends at or before the right margin, depending on paragraph alignment. Two smaller triangles indicate the left margin. The top triangle controls the location of the first character in the paragraph's first line; the bottom triangle controls the left margin of the remaining lines in the paragraph.

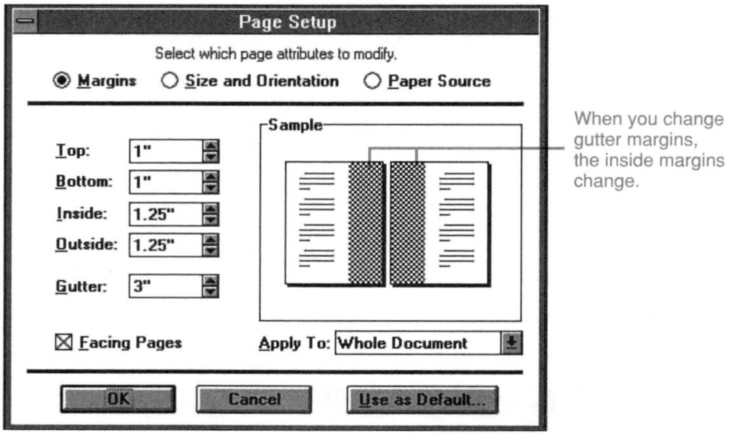

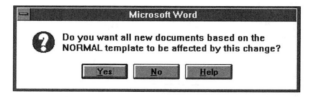

*Figure 5.6    The Page Setup dialog box. The Facing Pages check box is now checked, and the Sample document shows the gutter margin measurement on both pages.*

**118**

*Figure 5.7    Word displays a prompt box when you select the Use as Default option.*

*Figure 5.8    The Ruler showing its default width across the width of the text area.*

The following Quick Steps show how to set margins with the Ruler.

**Using the Ruler to Set Margins**

1. Make sure that the Ruler is turned on (select the **R**uler command from the **V**iew menu, or press Alt,V,R) and click on the brace on the left side of the Ruler.

   Word displays the Ruler across the width of the page instead of the width of the text area from left to right margin. Word also switches the symbols to the left of 0 and below 0. For the differences between these displays, see Figures 5.8 and 5.9.

2. To change the left margin, make sure that there is a brace at the bottom (not to the left) of the Ruler, move the mouse pointer to the brace, and drag it to its new location.

   Word adjusts the left margin of the current document.

**119**

3. To change the right margin, move the mouse pointer to the brace on the right side of the Ruler and drag it to its new location. If you can't see the brace, drag the thumb on the horizontal bar to the right.

   Word adjusts the right margin of the current document.

   □

Brace indicates left margin.

This Ruler measures the width of the page from edge to edge.

Right margin

*Figure 5.9    The Ruler extending across the width of the page.*

Word provides another way to change margins. In Chapter 9, you'll learn how to change margins within Print Preview.

## *Changing Paper Size*

You won't always use 8 1/2-by-11-inch paper for your documents. If you work in a law office, you'll use 8 1/2-by-14-inch paper much of the time. Or you might use Word to print envelopes, create advertising flyers, or even design notepaper and greeting cards.

As you learned earlier, there are three Page Setup dialog boxes. You have just finished learning about the Page Setup dialog box for Margins. Next you'll learn about the Page Setup dialog box for Size and Orientation, shown in Figure 5.10. Use this dialog box to change paper dimensions and orientation. The Paper Size box provides options for changing the height and width of the paper on which the text is printed. The options are dependent on the printer that is active. For example, the Hewlett-Packard LaserJet III provides nine options, including Custom Size and four envelopes, and an Epson FX86E provides one option: Custom Size. You can adjust both the height and width of Custom Size from 0 to 22 inches. The Orientation box allows you to determine the direction in which the text prints, either across the narrower dimension (like a memo) or across the wider dimension of a page (like a spreadsheet). Use the Apply To box to apply these changes to the entire document or to the remaining part of the document either after the insertion point or just to the text selection. In the Use as Default box, you can make the new settings the new Word default measurements for the documents (based on NORMAL.DOT) that you create from now on.

**120**

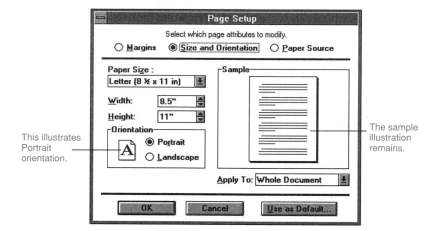

This illustrates Portrait orientation.

The sample illustration remains.

*Figure 5.10    The Page Setup dialog box for Size and Orientation.*

It's a simple process to change the paper dimensions for the active printer. Select the Format menu and the Page Setup command (Alt,T,U). When the Page Setup dialog box opens, select Size and

Orientation. When you select the list button (the underlined down arrow) on the right side of the Paper Size box, Word displays the paper sizes available for the active printer.

The following Quick Steps lead you through the procedures required to change paper size.

 **Changing Paper Size**

1. Either select some text or move the insertion point to the position after which you want the change to take place. Then select the Format menu and the Page Setup command (Alt,T,U).

   Word opens the Page Setup dialog box.

2. Select the **S**ize and Orientation button.

   Word changes the Page Setup dialog box to display page size and orientation options (Figure 5.10).

3. In the Paper Size box, you can select the list key to display a list of choices. You can also enter dimensions in the **W**idth box and/or **H**eight box. Or, move the mouse pointer to the arrows to the right of either box; then press and hold the mouse button to choose from the range of valid dimensions (from 0 to 22 inches).

   Word changes the illustration in the Sample box.

4. You can select the underlined down arrow next to Apply To and select Whole Document, Selected Text (if you have selected text), or This Point Forward (if you have not selected text).

   Depending on your choice, Word changes the margins of the entire current document, selected text, or all text beyond the insertion point.

5. You can select Use as Default.

   Word asks you if you want to use the new settings as the default.

**121**

6. Select **Yes** (change all new documents based on NORMAL.DOT) or **No** (just this document.

If you select Yes, Word returns to the current document or the screen from which you selected the command. If you select No, Word returns to the Page Setup dialog box.

7. If you have finished with the dialog box, select OK or press Enter.

Word returns to the current document or the screen from which you selected the command. □

## *Portrait versus Landscape Orientation*

A typical document is printed with the text oriented to the smaller dimension of the page. For example, with paper that is 8 1/2 by 11 inches, the text is printed across the 8 1/2-inch dimension. This is called *portrait* orientation, which is used for the majority of documents. The main reason that portrait orientation is so popular is that the eye can easily scan across the text that can fit on a line.

If you want to present a great deal of information on a page and that information does not have to be read line by line, use *landscape* orientation, in which the text is printed across the 11-inch dimension of an 8 1/2-by-11-inch page. Probably the most popular use of landscape orientation is for spreadsheets, which contain cells of information rather than lines of text. You don't scan across a spreadsheet; you jump around from cell to cell. Two other examples are time lines and large tables.

To switch between portrait and landscape orientation, use the following Quick Steps.

 **Changing Page Orientation**

1. Either select text or move the insertion point to the position after which you want orientation to change. Then select the Format menu and the Page Setup command (Alt,T,U).

Word opens the Page Setup dialog box.

**122**

2. Select the **S**ize and Orientation button.

Word changes the Page Setup dialog box to display page size and orientation options.

3. In the Orientation box, you can choose either P**o**rtrait or **L**andscape.

Word changes the illustration in the Sample box.

4. You can select the list arrow (the underlined down arrow) next to **A**pply To and select Whole Document, Selected Text (if you have selected text), or This Point Forward (if you have not selected text).

Depending on your choice, Word changes the margins of the current document, selected text, or all text beyond the insertion point.

5. You can select **U**se as Default.

Word asks you if you want to use the new settings as the default.

6. Select **Y**es (change all new documents based on NORMAL.DOT) or **N**o (just this document.

If you select Yes, Word returns to the current document or the screen from which you selected the command. If you select No, Word returns to the Page Setup dialog box.

7. If you have completed filling in the dialog box, select OK or press Enter.

Word returns to the current document or the screen from which you selected the command.  □

**123**

## *Viewing Formatting Changes*

As you apply document-wide formatting to a document, you might want to see the changes before you continue formatting. As you learned in Chapter 2, you can use File Print Preview (Alt,F,V) so that Word displays the first page of your document as shown in Figure 5.11. You can scroll through the document on the screen by using the scroll bar or the PgUp and PgDn keys.

If you are using Facing Pages to format your document, select the Two Pages button at the top of the Print Preview screen. Then you'll see how pages that you formatted as pairs work together. When you use Print Preview this way, the even-numbered page is always the page on the left side of the display, and the odd-numbered page is always on the right side. When you press PgUp or PgDn, Word "flips" two pages at a time. If Facing Pages is not active, the Print Preview display changes one page at a time.

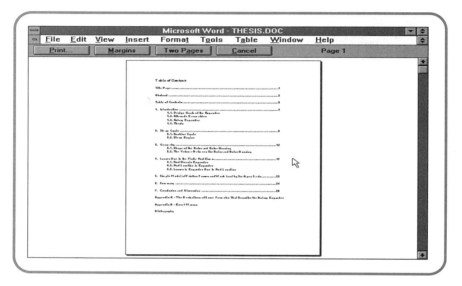

*Figure 5.11    A one-page Print Preview. Facing Pages is not activated.*

Remember that you'll learn a great deal more about all the printing options in Chapter 9.


## Creating Headers and Footers

Up to this point in the chapter, you have learned how to apply document-wide formats to an entire page—margins, paper size, and orientation. You've also learned how to select formatting for single-sided and double-sided pages. Now you'll see how to format parts of each page in your document by using *headers* and *footers,* which are the lines of text within the top and bottom margins, respectively. One key to a professional-looking document is the use of headers and footers.

In this book, the headers on the even-numbered pages identify the chapter number, and the odd-numbered pages display the chapter title. When you flip through the pages of this book, you can quickly find a topic in which you are interested.

Headers and footers are extensively used in technical books, how-to books, dictionaries, and encyclopedias. By using headers and footers in your documents, you can give readers quick information about a document. This information often includes the page number, date of preparation of the document, and the document or section title. However, you can include whatever information is appropriate for your document.

You can't see either headers or footers in Normal or Draft mode, but you can see them using the Print Preview feature or Page Layout mode. You can control where headers and footers appear—on every page, odd-numbered pages, even-numbered pages, every page but the first, and so on.

**125**

> **Note:** The easiest modes in which to start working with headers and footers are Normal, Outline, or Draft because the Header/Footer pane, which is quite easy to work with, is displayed in these modes.

Use the View menu and the Header/Footer command (Alt,V,H) to open the Header/Footer dialog box, which is shown in Figure 5.12. You will see the Header/Footer list box, which displays the types of headers and footers that are available to use. To display different headers and footers on the first page of a document, check the Different First Page check box. To display different headers and footers on odd-numbered and even-numbered pages, check the Different Odd and Even Pages check box. The maximum number of headers and footers that can be displayed if both boxes are checked is six: First Header, First Footer, Even Header, Even Footer, Odd Header, and Odd Footer. You can also determine the distance (ranging between 0" and 22") of a header or footer from the edge of the paper. You can also define page numbering and formats by choosing the Page Numbers button. You'll learn about page numbering later in this chapter.

A *pane* is a portion of a window. When Word displays the header/footer pane, it actually divides the document window into two sections. The top section displays part of the document, and the bottom section is the header/footer pane. One advantage of working with a pane is that you can move between your document and the contents of the pane.

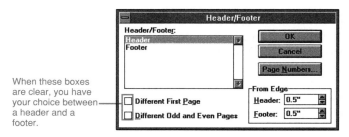

When these boxes are clear, you have your choice between a header and a footer.

*Figure 5.12    The Header/Footer dialog box.*

When you display the header/footer pane, there are three buttons on the left side. These allow you to place a page number, date, and time in the header. Of course, you can place any text as well. You can adjust the size of the header/footer pane by moving the mouse pointer between the two scroll bars on the right side of the screen. When the mouse pointer changes to a horizontal line, press the left mouse button, hold, and drag the pane up and down the screen. Release the left mouse button when the pane is at the location you want.

To define headers and footers, use the following Quick Steps.

 **Defining Headers and Footers**

1. Change to Normal mode (so that you can display the header/footer pane) by selecting the **V**iew menu and the **N**ormal command (Alt,V,N). Then from the **V**iew menu, select the **H**eader/Footer command (Alt,V,H).

   Word displays the Header/Footer dialog box.

2. To place a different header and/or footer on the first page, place a check in the Different First **P**age box.

   Word adds First Header and First Footer to the Header/Footer box.

3. If you want to place a different header and/or footer on odd- and/or even-numbered pages, place a check in the **D**ifferent Odd and Even Pages box.

Word adds Even Header, Even Footer, Odd Header, and Odd Footer to the Header/Footer box.

4. Select one item from the list in the Header/Footer box. Then select OK or press Enter.

Word returns to the current document. If you are in Normal mode, Word displays a header/footer pane, a small document window (see Figure 5.13).

5. Enter the text for your header/footer using the same methods you use for any Word document. You can move the insertion point between your document and the header/footer pane.

Word moves the insertion point and end mark as it does in any document.

**127**

6. You can insert a page number, system date (the date to which your computer is set), and/or system time (the time to which your computer is set) by clicking on any of the three icons at the top of the pane. See Table 5.2.

Word inserts the appropriate information in the header/footer text (see Figure 5.14).

7. Whether or not the header/footer pane is open, you can change the position of the header (or footer) from the default setting of 1/2 inch from the top (or bottom) of the page by selecting the **V**iew menu and the **H**eader/Footer command (Alt,V,H). In the From Edge box (Figure 5.12), adjust the value in the **H**eader or **F**ooter box by moving to one of the arrows to the right of the box, pressing and holding the mouse button down until the value that you want

Word returns to the current document and the header/footer pane.

is displayed. You can also enter a value ranging from 0 to 22 inches. Then select OK or press Enter.

8. After you have completed defining the header/footer, select **C**lose.

Word closes the header/footer pane and displays the current document. □

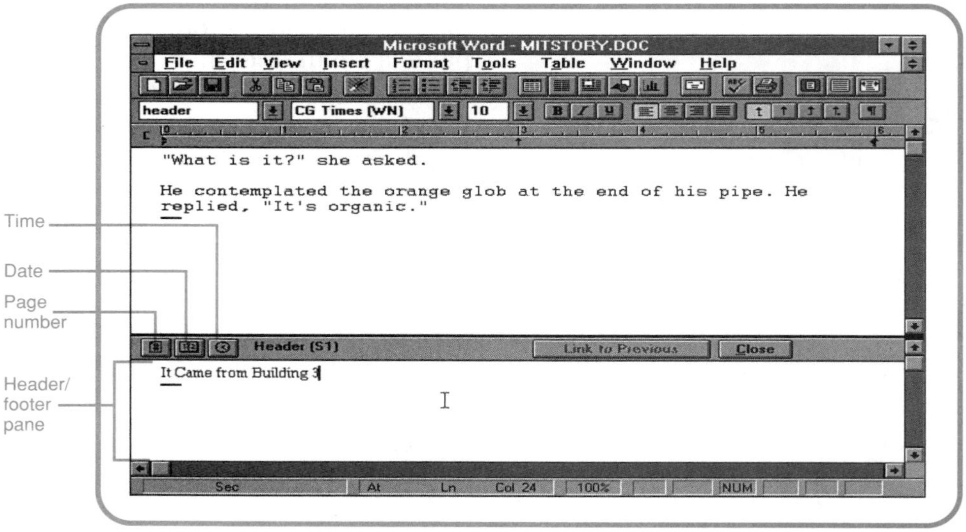

Time

Date

Page number

Header/footer pane

*Figure 5.13    The header/footer pane.*

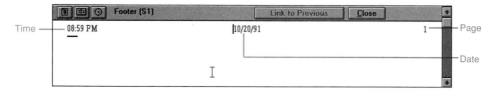

Time —— 08:59 PM        |10/20/91                        1 —— Page

—— Date

*Figure 5.14    A footer with the system time, the system date, and a page number.*

> **Tip:** To customize page numbers (for example, "Page 1"), type the word `Page` in the header or footer and then insert the page number by selecting the page number icon in the header/footer pane.

*Table 5.2   Customizing headers and footers.*

| Feature | Button | Command |
| --- | --- | --- |
| Page Number | # | Shift-F10,P |
| Date | Calendar | Shift-F10,D |
| Time | Clock | Shift-F10,T |

> **Tip:** In longer documents, you can provide a great deal of information in the headers and footers. For example, you can display the chapter number on every even page and the chapter title on every odd page (see the headers in this book). For a document in which date and time are important, "stamp" this information on every page.

**129**

# Creating Page Breaks

Word automatically specifies page breaks by using the measurements for page height and the top and bottom margins. However, there are times when you want to manually determine where to start a new page. For example, you should have a page break between the end of a title page and the beginning of body text or between major sections. Or you may want a list to appear on one page or an entire paragraph (rather than a fragment) to end a page.

To embed a break in your text, select the Insert menu and the Break command (Alt,I,B). The Break dialog box, shown in Figure 5.15, is small and simple. You can select either a Page Break, a Column Break, or a Section Break. (You'll learn about section breaks later in this chapter.) After selecting inserting a page break, select OK or press Enter. Word places a horizontal dotted line across the page at the location of the page break. To learn about placing and removing page breaks in a document, use the Quick Steps that follow.

**Placing and Removing Page Breaks in a Document**

1. Move the insertion point in front of the line that you want to start the new page and select the **I**nsert menu and **B**reak command (Alt,I,B).

    Word displays the Break dialog box.

2. Select **P**age Break and select OK or press Enter.

    Word returns to the current document, places a dotted line at the insertion point, and changes the page number in the Status bar.

3. To remove a page break that you have created, move the insertion point to the beginning of the line below the break and press the Backspace key.

    Word removes the page break line. At the bottom of the screen, the number of the page is displayed (see Figure 5.16).

    □

**130**

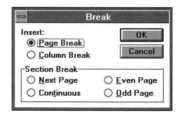

*Figure 5.15    The Break dialog box, which is used to insert page and section breaks.*

---

**Tip:** The only way to remove an automatic page break that Word has inserted is to move the insertion point to a line that is above the page break and then to insert a page break by pressing the shortcut keys Ctrl-Enter.

---

Sometimes you will want to turn off automatic page breaking altogether. For example, long documents with automatic pagination turned on cause Word to process very slowly. Or, if you are creating a document over which you want total control of format, you'll want to make sure that you, and not Word, determines every page break.

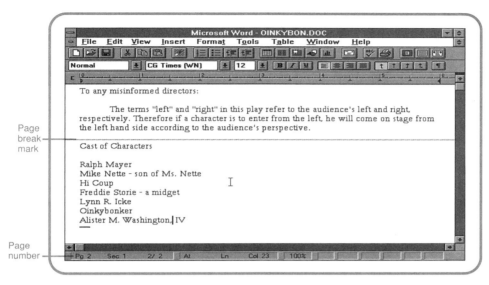

Page break mark

Page number

*Figure 5.16   A page break in a document. Notice that Word has changed the page number at the bottom of the screen.*

**131**

Use the following Quick Steps to turn off automatic pagination.

 **Turning Off Automatic Pagination**

1. Select the Tools menu and the Options command (Alt,O,O).

   Word displays the Options dialog box.

2. Under Category, select General.

   Word changes the dialog box options to general settings (see Figure 5.17).

3. If the Background Repagination box is checked, clear it and select OK or press Enter.

   Word returns to the current document.                                       ☐

---

**Tip:** To paginate a document when automatic pagination is off, select the Tools menu and the Repaginate Now command (Alt,O,A).

Clear this box to turn off automatic pagination.

| | |
|---|---|
| **Options** | |

Adjust general Word for Windows settings

**Category:**

View

**General**

Print

Save

**Settings**

☒ **B**ackground Repagination
☒ **T**yping Replaces Selection
☒ **D**rag-and-drop Text Editing
☒ Confirm **F**ile Conversions
☐ **U**se the INS Key for Paste
☐ **O**vertype Mode
☐ **W**ordPerfect Help
☐ WordPerfect Document Na**v**igation Keys

**M**easurement Units: Inches

**OK**

**Cancel**

To see more options, click on the category list at left.

*Figure 5.17    The Options dialog box for the General category.*

## 132

# Controlling Orphan and Widow Lines

An automatic page break sometimes splits a paragraph between two pages. A single line of a paragraph ending a page is called an *orphan* line; a single line starting a page is a *widow* line. In most cases, you don't want a single line at the beginning or end of a page. The Word default ensures that at least two lines of a paragraph remain at the beginning or end of a page.

To check the status of widow and orphan lines, select the Tools menu and the Options command (Alt,O,O). In the Category list, select Print. When Word displays the Options dialog box, see whether the Widow/Orphan Control box is checked or clear.

In Chapter 6, you'll learn how to ensure that a paragraph starts a new page, how to keep a paragraph on the same page with the following paragraph, and how to keep the paragraph intact on the same page.

**Note:** If a paragraph is only one line long, Word does not consider it either an orphan or widow.

# Customizing Page Numbering

Sometimes, you create a document that is made up of several files. With Word's customized page numbering, you have the ability to define the starting page number for each new file. When you are writing a book in which each file begins a new chapter, this is a handy feature to have. Some books are numbered sequentially from the first page to the last. Other books start numbering at the beginning of each chapter (for example, Page 3 in Chapter 4 is 4-3). Either way, Word can help you set your page numbers quite easily.

When you add a page number to a header or footer, Word starts counting page numbers. You can control where Word starts counting page numbers by selecting the View menu and the Header/Footer command (Alt,V,H). When Word displays the Header/Footer dialog box, select Page Numbers. Word displays the Page Number Format dialog box, shown in Figure 5.18. You can select a number format and determine whether your pages continue from the last page number or start at a specific number that you define.

**133**

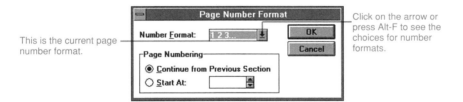

This is the current page number format.

Click on the arrow or press Alt-F to see the choices for number formats.

*Figure 5.18    The Page Number Format dialog box, which is used to customize page numbering.*

To customize the format of page numbers and set the page numbers themselves, use the following Quick Steps.

 **Customizing Page Numbering**

1. From the View menu, select the Header/Footer command (Alt,V,H).

   Word displays the Header/Footer dialog box.

2. Select Page Numbers.

   Word displays the Page Number Format dialog box.

3. Click on the button next to the Start At box.

   Word displays the default starting number.

4. Enter the starting page number in the box, or move to one of the arrows to the right of the box and press and hold the mouse button down until the value that you want is displayed. For example, to start the numbering on page three, type a **3** in the box.

Word keeps the insertion point in the Start At box in case you want to change the number.

5. Move to the Number Format box to show page number formats. Select the underlined down arrow to display all the choices and then select one.

When you make your selection, Word displays the page number format in the Number Format box and closes the display.

6. Select OK or press Enter.

Word returns to the Header/Footer dialog box.

7. Select OK or Close or press Enter.

Word returns to the current document. □

If you want to add page numbers to your document without defining headers or footers, make sure you are in Normal mode. Then select the Insert menu and the Page Numbers command (Alt,I,U), select either the Top or Bottom circle (to tell where on the page the numbers will appear), and then choose Left, Center, or Right (to choose the alignment). Then you can select Format to start or format page numbering. Select OK or press Enter repeatedly until you return to the current document.

## Section Formatting

Use section formatting when there is a major change in your document—starting a two-column layout, placing a headline, or beginning new or reformatted page numbers. Other uses of section breaks are to change the content of headers and footers, or to place endnotes after each chapter.

One example of a section break in some documents is the change between the first part (from the front cover through the table of contents, known as the *front matter*) and the body of the document. In the front matter, page numbers are usually lowercase roman numerals. When the body of the document begins, numbers change to arabic and start at *1*. To make this change, insert a section break at the location of the page numbering change.

Another example is a sales brochure in which most of the text is oriented across the shorter page dimension, from the left to the right margin, with one or two pages of tables containing long lines of text that stretch between the top and the bottom margins. Insert a section break at the location of the change in page orientation.

Although the default is for Word to start a new page at a section break, you can start (and even end) a new section on the same page as the previous (or following) section. A section can be as small as a paragraph or as large as your entire document.

Because sections are so important, you'll read more about them throughout this book.

**135**

## *Creating a Section Break*

Creating a section break is very similar to creating a page break, as shown in the following Quick Steps.

 **Creating a Section Break**

1. Place the insertion point where you would like to place a section break. Then select the **I**nsert menu and the **B**reak command (Alt,I,B).

   Word displays the Break dialog box. The section break controls are located at the bottom of the box.

2. Select a section break option and select OK or press Enter. Table 5.3 describes section break options.

   Word returns to the current document, places a double-dotted line at the insertion point, and changes the page and section numbers in the Status bar (Figure 5.19).  □

In Draft or Normal modes, the section break mark is a double-dotted line that extends across the document window. Like the paragraph mark, the section break mark contains all the formatting information of the section that precedes it.

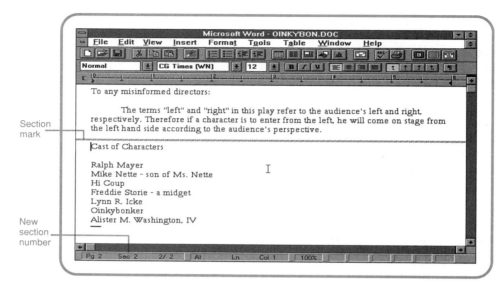

Section mark

New section number

*Figure 5.19 A section break displayed in a document. Notice that Word displays a double-dotted line and changes the page and section numbers in the Status bar.*

*Table 5.3 Section break insertion options.*

| Option | Starts the Next Section |
|---|---|
| Next Page | At the top of the next page |
| Continuous | On the same page as the previous section |
| Even Page | At the top of the next even-numbered page |
| Odd Page | At the top of the next odd-numbered page |

If you are in Page Layout or Print Preview mode, you can look at the section break mark by selecting Tools Options (Alt,O,O). Under Category, select View. When the dialog box opens, place a check mark next to Text Boundaries.

You can edit (selecting, copying, pasting, and deleting) the section break mark like any character. If you delete the section mark, the text preceding the deleted section mark assumes the format of the following section.

The Status bar shows you the section in which the insertion point is located (for example, Sec 1, Sec 2, or Sec 100).

If you want to control page numbering after a section break, move the insertion point anyplace within the section and select the Format menu and the Section Layout command (Alt,T,S). Word displays the Section Layout dialog box shown in Figure 5.20. From the Section Start list box, select one of the options described in Table 5.4. Note that the options are the same as the options in the Insert Break dialog box except for the New Column command.

Word displays the section number.

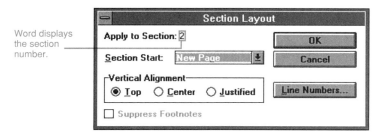

*Figure 5.20    The Section Layout dialog box.*

**137**

*Table 5.4    Section page formatting options.*

| Option | The Current Page Starts at |
| --- | --- |
| New Column | The top of the next column |
| New Page | The top of the next page, whether odd or even |
| Continuous | On the same page as the previous section |
| Even Page | The top of the next even-numbered page |
| Odd Page | The top of the next odd-numbered page |

Another option on the Section Layout dialog box is Vertical Alignment: Top, Center, or Justified. Top allows you to align the top line of text along the top margin (the normal situation for text on a page). Center alignment enables you to center the text on a page. An example of center alignment is the title page of a book report. You can use justified alignment to fill a page from top to bottom. When you use this type of alignment and don't have enough text in the section, there are large spaces between lines of text.

At the bottom of the Section Layout dialog box is the Suppress Footnotes check box. In order to print footnotes at the end of a section, clear this box. If you check this box, footnotes will print at the end of the document.

The Section Layout dialog box also provides a means for numbering lines within your document.

> **Tip:** To quickly display the Format/Section Layout dialog box, place the insertion point on the section mark and then double-click.

## What You Have Learned

▶ Word provides document-wide, section, paragraph, and character formatting. Use the Format menu to apply document-wide formatting first, then section, paragraph, and character formatting, in that order.

▶ The units of measure that Word supports are inches, centimeters, picas, points, and lines. You can change the default unit of measure throughout Word but can override the default whenever you need to. Use the Tools menu and the Options command, and then select General in the Category box.

▶ *Page margin settings* control the space between the edge of the page and the text on the page. *Paper dimensions* control the size of paper on which you print. Use the Format menu and the Page Setup command to change these settings.

▶ Portrait and landscape are Word's page orientations. *Portrait* orientation is used for most text. *Landscape* orientation is used for tabular reports and spreadsheets. Change the page orientation with the Format menu and the Page Setup command.

▶ *Headers* and *footers* are lines of information that appear above and below, respectively, the text on a page. You can embed page numbers, the system time, and the system date in headers and footers. Define headers and footers by using the View menu and the Header/Footer command.

▶ Word automatically specifies page breaks, but you can insert and remove page breaks by selecting the Insert menu and the

Break command. To turn automatic repagination on or off, select the Tools menu and the Options command; under Category, select General.

▶ A *widow* is a single line that begins a page; an *orphan* is a single line that ends a page. Widows and orphans result when paragraphs are split between successive pages.

▶ Use section formatting when there is a major change in your document—a change in page orientation, paper dimensions, or page numbering. Create a section break by selecting the Insert menu and the Break command.

**139**

# Formatting Paragraphs

## In This Chapter

▶ *Aligning and indenting paragraphs*
▶ *Adjusting line and paragraph spacing*
▶ *Controlling pagination for paragraphs*
▶ *Adding borders, lines, and shading to paragraphs*
▶ *Setting and clearing tabs*

## Paragraph Formatting

Chapter 5 explained the first two of Word for Windows' four formatting levels: document-wide and section formatting. *Document-wide* formatting affects the overall appearance of a document—the margins, paper size, page orientation, and headers and footers. *Section* formatting defines the appearance of a particular section within a document.

This chapter will explain the next formatting level: *paragraph* formatting. As you might suspect, paragraph formatting affects the text within a *paragraph*—a string of text that ends with a paragraph mark. Paragraph formatting defines six different aspects of a paragraph. These are the alignment of text between the left and right margins, the space between the lines of text in the paragraph, the space before and after the paragraph, the page breaks involving the paragraph, the indentations in the paragraph, and paragraph enhancements (borders, lines, and shading).

In the discussion of section formatting in Chapter 5, you were introduced to both the section mark and the paragraph mark, which end a section and a paragraph, respectively. Like the section mark, which contains all the formatting information of the section that precedes it, the paragraph mark (¶) contains all the formatting information of the paragraph that precedes it. To display the paragraph mark and other nonprinting formatting symbols, select the Show All button on the Ribbon, shown in Figure 6.1.

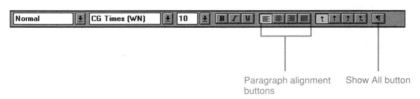

Paragraph alignment buttons    Show All button

*Figure 6.1    The Ribbon contains four paragraph alignment buttons.*

To format a single paragraph, place the insertion point anywhere in the paragraph that you want to change. To format multiple paragraphs, select the paragraphs by using the mouse or the keyboard. Word provides several methods for applying paragraph formats: the Ruler, the Ribbon, the Toolbar, keyboard shortcuts, or the Format menu and the **P**aragraph command. This chapter will explain each method and point out its advantages.

Some paragraph formatting features (such as line spacing, adding white space above and below paragraphs, and applying borders, lines, and shading) are available only via the Format menu. As you learn about Format **P**aragraph, you'll be using all but one of the options in the Paragraph dialog box. The exception is line numbering.

## *Aligning Paragraphs*

Paragraph alignment is the first of Word's paragraph formats featured in this chapter. You can align paragraph text so that it is flush with either the left or the right margin, centered between the margins, or flush with both the left and the right margins. Word's options for these paragraph alignments are left, right, centered, and justified, respectively. Figure 6.2 shows you a sample of each type of paragraph alignment.

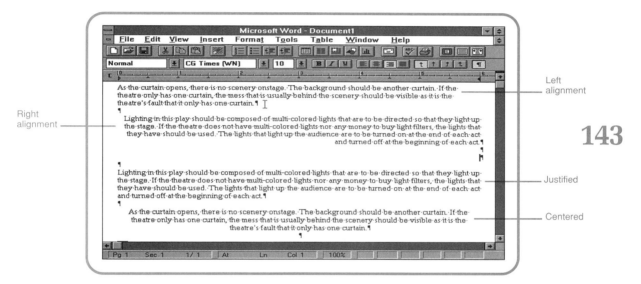

Right alignment

Left alignment

Justified

Centered

**143**

*Figure 6.2    A sample document showing the four types of paragraph alignment.*

Paragraph alignment is one way to emphasize a paragraph or to differentiate it from the rest of the document. For example, if you write a term paper that contains extensive quotations, you can center the quotations within the margins. (You can further enhance the quotation by indenting it, which is covered later in this chapter, or by changing the appearance of its text format, which you'll learn in Chapter 7.) Another example of a change in alignment is a poem which has verses that are left-aligned, centered, and right-aligned successively. Newspapers and magazines use justified alignment to create neat, clean-looking columns. However, the disadvantage of justified text is that the spacing between words can appear uneven and therefore distracting to the eye.

If you want a document with paragraphs aligned with the left margin, you don't have to do a thing, since this setting is the Word default. However, if you want to change paragraph alignment to right, centered, or justified, you can use either the Format **P**aragraph command or the Ribbon.

### Using the Format Paragraph Command to Align Paragraphs

Use the Format **P**aragraph command to change paragraph alignment and then to format your paragraph in other ways. The following Quick Steps show you how to align one or more paragraphs by using the Format **P**aragraph command.

### *Q* Aligning Paragraphs

| | |
|---|---|
| 1. Select one or more paragraphs to align. | Word highlights the selected text. |
| 2. From the Format menu, select the **P**aragraph command (Alt,T,P). | Word opens the Paragraph dialog box (Figure 6.3). |
| 3. In the Alignment box, select the list arrow (the underlined down arrow). | Word displays your choices—Left, Centered, Right, and Justified. See Table 6.1 for a description of the alignment types and keyboard shortcuts for each. |
| 4. Select one of the alignments. | Word changes the alignment in the highlighted paragraph in the Sample box of the Paragraph dialog box. |
| 5. Select OK or press Enter. | Word returns to the current document and aligns the text in the selected paragraphs as you specified and as you saw in the Sample box. □ |

If you wish to change back to the previous paragraph alignment, select Edit Undo (Alt,E,U) or press Ctrl-Z before you perform another action. You can learn more about the **U**ndo command in Chapter 3.

Select this arrow. —

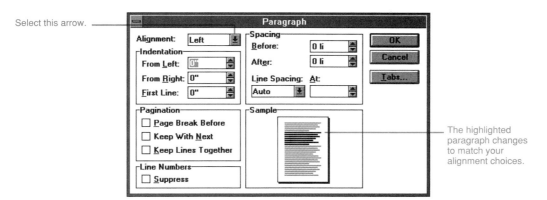

The highlighted
paragraph changes
to match your
alignment choices.

*Figure 6.3    The Paragraph dialog box.*

**Tip:** To quickly open the Paragraph dialog box using the
mouse, place the mouse pointer in the Ruler, just above
the scale, and double-click.

**145**

Table 6.1 sums up the types of paragraph alignment and
provides shortcut keys for each type. Just select one or more
paragraphs in a document and press the shortcut keys. Word
changes the alignment.

*Table 6.1    Types of paragraph alignment.*

| Alignment Type | Keys | Description |
|---|---|---|
| Left | Ctrl-L | Text aligns with the left margin. The right margin is ragged. |
| Right | Ctrl-R | Text aligns with the right margin. The left margin is ragged. |
| Center | Ctrl-E | Text is centered between the margins. |
| Justified | Ctrl-J | Text aligns with both the left and right margins by adding extra spaces between words. |

### Using the Ribbon to Align Paragraphs

Use the Ribbon to change paragraph alignment. When you use the Ribbon, you don't have to spend time in a dialog box. This means that you can make changes more quickly. To change alignment with the Ribbon, either move the insertion point to a paragraph or select one or more paragraphs. Then move the mouse pointer to the Ribbon and select one of the paragraph alignment buttons.

If you are starting out with a new document or have not changed paragraph alignment in the current document, notice that the Left Alignment button appears to be pressed. This indicates that the paragraph is left-aligned. To change from this paragraph alignment to another, you can press another paragraph alignment button on the Ribbon.

## *Adjusting Line Spacing*

In the last section, you learned how to emphasize a paragraph by changing its alignment. Next you'll see how to adjust the *leading*, which is the spacing between the lines within a paragraph. Two common examples of line spacing are business letters, which are normally single-spaced, and term papers, which are usually double-spaced. You can also use different line-spacing settings to emphasize particular paragraphs within a document (for example, to set off quotations). Don't confuse line spacing with paragraph spacing, which adjusts spacing before and after paragraphs.

Word's default line-spacing setting is single spacing, which is the measurement between the bottom of one line of text and the bottom of the next line. This measurement includes the text as well as the white space between the lines of text. As the size of the type in a document increases, Word increases the white-space measurement as well. You'll learn more about selecting text types (fonts) and size (points) in the next chapter.

Use Format Paragraph (Alt, T, P) to choose line spacing. Then open the list in the Line Spacing box to view the available options. You can select either fixed or adjustable spaces between lines (see Figure 6.4). Fixed spacing options are Single, 1.5 (1.5 times Single), Double (twice the measurement of Single), and Exactly, which enables you to choose line spacing ranging from 0 to 132 lines. If you choose Exactly, you can type the measurement in the At box or use the arrow button at the right side of the At box to cycle through the range of measurements. Fixed spaces always remain the same, regardless of the height of letters, although as the size of characters increases, Word automatically adjusts the amount of Single, 1.5, and Double line spacing. Exactly remains at the measurement that you set, even if the text lines run into each other.

**Tip:** You can use keyboard shortcuts to set single, one-and-a-half, and double line spacing. Ctrl-1 sets single spacing, Ctrl-5 sets one-and-a-half spacing, and Ctrl-2 sets double spacing.

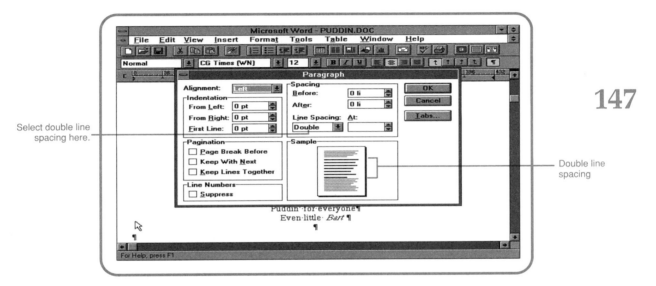

Select double line spacing here.

Double line spacing

*Figure 6.4    The Paragraph dialog box after the Double spacing option has been chosen. Notice that the high-lighted paragraph in the Sample box reflects the chosen settings.*

Word also provides two adjustable spacing options: Auto and At Least. Auto measures the tallest *ascender,* the part of a letter above the body of the letter (for example, *h, b, d, f,* and *h* are letters with ascenders) to determine the line-spacing measurement. At Least requires you to enter a minimum measurement or cycle through the measurements in the At box (from 0 to 132 lines) but adjusts line spacing when it encounters a large character. Table 6.2 summarizes Word's line-spacing options.

*Table 6.2   Line-spacing options.*

| Spacing Option | Key Shortcut | Option Type | Description |
| --- | --- | --- | --- |
| Auto | — | Adjustable | Automatic spacing. Word selects the spacing for you based on the tallest ascender in a line of text. |
| Single | Ctrl-1 | Fixed | Single spacing, based on a single line of text. |
| 1.5 | Ctrl-5 | Fixed | One-and-one-half spacing, based on 1 1/2 lines of text. |
| Double | Ctrl-2 | Fixed | Double spacing, based on two lines of text. |
| At Least | — | Adjustable | A specific minimum measurement that you decide but that Word can increase, if needed. |
| Exactly | — | Fixed | A specific measurement that you decide, and that Word will not change. |

The following Quick Steps show you how to adjust the line spacing in a paragraph.

 **Adjusting Line Spacing**

1. After selecting one or more paragraphs, select the Format menu and the **P**aragraph command (Alt,T,P).

Word Opens the Paragraph dialog box.

2. Next to the Line Spacing box, select the list arrow (the underlined down arrow).

Word displays the line-spacing options (see Table 6.2).

3. To set your own line-spacing measurement, select At Least or Exactly and in the At box, either type the number of lines (from 0 through 132) or move to one of the arrows to the right of the box, pressing and holding the left mouse button down until the value that you want is displayed.

As you select an option, the Sample document in the dialog box changes.

4. To let Word select the line-spacing measurement, select Single, 1.5, Double, or Auto.

As you select an option, the Sample document in the dialog box changes.

5. Select OK or press Enter.

Word returns to the current document and adjusts the line spacing of the selected paragraphs as you just saw in the Sample box.  □

**149**

To return to the previous line-spacing setting if you haven't performed any other actions, select Edit Undo (Alt,E,U) or press Ctrl-Z. Chapter 3 explains the **U**ndo command in greater detail.

## Setting Paragraph Spacing

In the last section, you learned about line spacing, which adjusts spacing within a paragraph. Next you'll see how you use paragraph spacing, which adjusts spacing above and below a paragraph. Word's default paragraph spacing is no lines between paragraphs. If you add a space between each paragraph in a letter, each will stand out and be easier to read.

You can use either Format Paragraph (Alt,T,P) or keyboard shortcuts to adjust spacing between paragraphs. Using the Forma**t P**aragraph command provides more flexibility than using keyboard shortcuts because you can adjust in increments of half a line and you have more spacing options before and after a paragraph. Word's default settings are 0 lines before and after each paragraph. To create an extra line before one or more selected paragraphs, press the keyboard shortcut Ctrl-O. There is no keyboard shortcut for adding line spacing after a paragraph.

The following Quick Steps show you how to use the Format **P**aragraph command to adjust paragraph spacing.

### Adjusting Paragraph Spacing

1. Select one or more paragraphs and then select the Format menu and the **P**aragraph command (Alt,T,P).

   Word displays the Paragraph dialog box.

2. Type a value in the Before box. Alternatively, press and hold down the left mouse button on either the up or the down arrow (located to the right of the box) until the desired value (ranging from 0 to 132 lines) is displayed. Enter a value in the After box in the same way.

   As you change the settings, Word changes the Sample document in the dialog box (Figure 6.5).

3. Select OK or press Enter.

   Word returns to the current document and changes its paragraph formatting. □

**150**

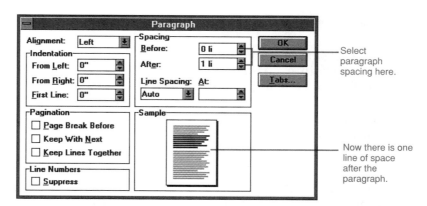

*Figure 6.5    The Paragraph dialog box showing paragraph spacing options.*

Press Ctrl-Z or choose Edit Undo to change back to the previous paragraph spacing format before you perform another action. See Chapter 3 for an explanation of the Undo command.

It's a good idea to apply spacing using either Before or After but not both. The reason is that you'll have better control over your entire document if you choose one type of paragraph spacing. For example, suppose a document consists of four paragraphs. If you use the After option to change spacing for the second paragraph and Before for the third paragraph, you'll have extra space between paragraphs two and three but not enough space between paragraphs one and two as well as paragraphs three and four.

## *Controlling Page Breaks for Paragraphs*

In Chapter 5, you learned about inserting page breaks and preventing widow and orphan lines in your document. The page breaks that you insert are called *hard page breaks*. They remain where you put them regardless of the addition or deletion of text throughout the document. As you create a document, Word inserts *automatic page breaks*, which are calculated based on the amount of text that fits on a page. When you add or delete text, Word recalculates the text on the page and moves the automatic page break to a new location. Then it automatically recalculates the remaining pages in the document and places automatic page breaks where needed. Both types of page breaks are displayed as dotted lines that extend between the left and right margins. However, the hard page break symbol consists of more densely packed dots than the automatic page break symbol.

**151**

Next you'll learn how to insert a hard page break before a paragraph. This is a way of ensuring that the paragraph starts a new page. For example, for a document consisting of a memo and an attachment, you can place a hard page break before the first paragraph of the attachment. You can insert a page break using **I**nsert **B**reak, as you learned in Chapter 5, but if you're formatting the paragraph using the Paragraph dialog box, you can insert the page break as you change formats. It is best to select only one paragraph when you use this option. Otherwise, Word places a page break before every paragraph that you select.

Word allows you to keep a paragraph on the same page with the following paragraph by providing the Keep With Next option. For example, suppose you write a term paper containing quoted material. Each quotation is preceded by a paragraph giving background information about the quotation. You'll probably want to keep the introductory paragraph and the quotation on the same page. You can also use this option if you have a list consisting of separate paragraphs and you want to print the list on one page.

As you learned in Chapter 5, controlling widow and orphan lines prevents single lines of a paragraph from printing separately from the rest of the paragraph. However, a paragraph can still print with two or three lines on one page and two or three lines on the next. To force a paragraph to print on one page, select Keep Lines Together. In our term paper example, you may want to make sure that each line of a quotation prints on the same page. Table 6.3 summarizes Word's pagination options for paragraphs.

*Table 6.3    Pagination options for paragraphs.*

| Pagination Option | Description |
| --- | --- |
| Page Break Before | Inserts a page break before each of the selected paragraphs. |
| Keep With Next | Prevents a page break between the selected paragraphs and the following paragraph. |
| Keep Lines Together | Prevents a page break within the selected paragraphs. |

The following Quick Steps describe how to control page breaks for paragraphs.

 **Controlling Page Breaks for Paragraphs**

1. Select one or more paragraphs. From the Format menu, select the **P**aragraph command (Alt,T,P).

   Word displays the Paragraph dialog box.

2. In the Pagination box, you can check any combination of the three options. For an explanation of each, see Table 6.3.

   Depending on the option selected, Word changes the illustration in the Sample box (see Figures 6.6 through 6.8).

3. Select OK or press Enter.

   Word returns to the current document and changes its paragraph formatting.    □

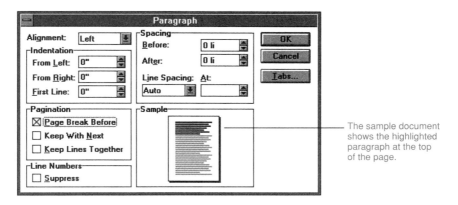

The sample document shows the highlighted paragraph at the top of the page.

*Figure 6.6    When you select the Page Break Before option, Word changes the illustration in the Sample box.*

**153**

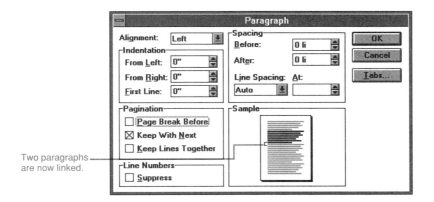

Two paragraphs are now linked.

*Figure 6.7    When you select Keep With Next, Word displays this illustration.*

## Indenting Paragraphs

Early in this chapter, you learned about aligning paragraphs with respect to the left and right margins. Another paragraph formatting option that uses margins as a guide is indentation, which moves either the entire paragraph or the first line away from the left and/or right margin.

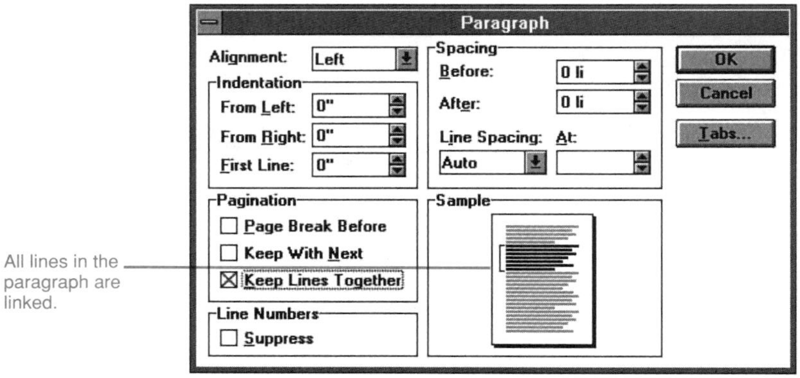

All lines in the paragraph are linked.

*Figure 6.8    The Sample box illustration looks like this when you select Keep Lines Together.*

There are four ways to indent paragraphs—the Toolbar, the Ruler, the Format **P**aragraph command, and shortcut keys. Use the Format **P**aragraph command to indent using precise measurements with any of Word's units of measurements, use the Ruler and the Toolbar as a quick method of indenting using the current unit of measurement, and use shortcut keys to indent using tab positions.

There are five types of indents:

*First-line indent*—Start the first character in the first line of a paragraph several spaces after the left margin but align succeeding lines with the left margin. Use the first-line indent for letters or for documents where there is minimal spacing between paragraphs but you want to show where a new paragraph begins. The right margin can be either justified or ragged, depending on the paragraph alignment you have set for this paragraph.

*Hanging indent*—Start the first line in a paragraph either at the left margin or close to it. Then, following lines are further indented from the left margin. The right margin can be either justified or ragged, depending on the paragraph alignment you have set for this paragraph. Hanging indents are ideal for bulleted and numbered lists.

*Left or right indent*—Indent all the lines of a paragraph from either margin. This is also known as a block indent.

*Centered indent*—Indent all the lines of a paragraph from both margins. This emphasizes the text in the paragraph and makes it stand out from the rest of the text. This is also known as a block indent.

*Tabbed indent*—You can press the Tab key to indent the first line of a paragraph or to indent within a paragraph. The last topic in this chapter explains the use of tabs in Word.

Click on the Unindent button to align the selected paragraph or paragraphs with the previous tab position (to the left). The current indentation format (hanging, first-line indent, etc.) remains.

Click on the Indent button to align the selected paragraph or paragraphs with the next tab position (to the right). The current indentation format (hanging, first-line indent, etc.) remains.

**155**

### Using the Ruler to Indent

The quickest way to indent paragraphs and lines is by using the small triangles on the Ruler, shown in Figure 6.9. The left margin markers on the Ruler are two triangles—the top triangle is the first-line indent marker, and the bottom triangle is the left margin marker. To indent paragraphs from the left, simply move the bottom triangle with the mouse pointer. When you move the bottom triangle, the top triangle moves along with it. To create first-line or hanging indents, move the top triangle, which moves without also causing the bottom triangle to move. The right margin marker on the Ruler is represented by a single triangle. To indent paragraphs from the right, move the right margin marker. When you use the Ruler to indent paragraphs, you see the result instantly.

### Using the Format Paragraph Command to Indent

Another way to indent paragraphs is by using the Forma**t P**aragraph command. When the Paragraph dialog box is displayed, either type values in the From Left, From Right, and First Line boxes, or move the mouse pointer to the arrow keys and press and hold down the left mouse button until the value that you want is displayed. You can indent selected paragraphs by a value ranging from −22 inches through 22 inches. However, Word won't allow a line of text in a document to be narrower than 1 inch or allow the first-line indent to be closer than .1 inch from the right margin.

First-line indent marker

Left margin marker                                      Right margin marker

*Figure 6.9   You can indent paragraphs and immediately see the results by using the Ruler.*

**156**

Use the Forma**t P**aragraph command when you must set an indent based on a unit of measurement that is not your regular one. For example, if you use inches as your normal unit of measurement, and you need to indent a certain number of centimeters, it's easy to display the Format dialog box and enter the measurement in the appropriate box.

To create a first-line indent, enter a value in the First Line box that represents the amount of indentation of the first line in the paragraph. The value in the First Line box can be any positive number. Word uses the value in the From Left box as the left margin, and indents the paragraph by the amount in the First Line box from the left margin. If you type a negative number in the First Line box, you are creating a hanging indent. Word changes the sample in the Paragraph dialog box to match the indent (see Figure 6.10).

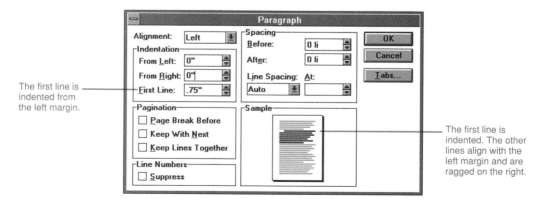

The first line is indented from the left margin.

The first line is indented. The other lines align with the left margin and are ragged on the right.

*Figure 6.10   A first-line indent. Following lines do not indent on the left.*

To create a hanging indent, enter the value of the left indentation of the paragraph in the From Left box. In the First Line box, enter a value that moves the first line back toward the left margin. To align the first line with the left margin, the value in the First Line box (for example, –.5) should be the negative counterpart of the value in the From Left box (for example, .5). Word changes the sample in the Paragraph dialog box to match the indent (see Figure 6.11).

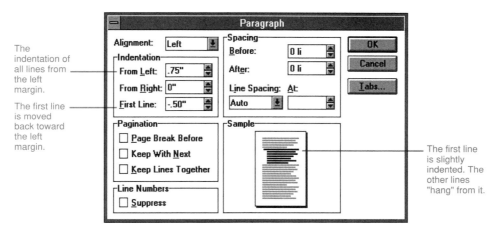

*Figure 6.11    A hanging indent. The entire paragraph is indented and the first line is moved back toward the left margin.*

To indent selected paragraphs from both margins, enter values that represent the indentation from the left and right margins in the From Left and From Right boxes. If you want to indent both margins equally, enter the same value in each box. Word changes the sample in the Paragraph dialog box to match the indent (see Figure 6.12). To indent selected paragraphs from the left margin, enter a value in the From Left box; to indent from the right margin, enter a value in the From Right box.

The following Quick Steps show you how to create a first-line indent.

 **Creating a First-Line Indent**

1. Select one or more paragraphs.    Word highlights the selected paragraphs.

157

2. Select the Format menu and the **P**aragraph command (Alt,T,P).

Word displays the Paragraph dialog box.

3. In the First Line box, type any positive number. In the From Left box, type a value that represents the left margin. Word indents the first line in the paragraph by the value in the First Line box.

Word changes the illustration in the Sample box.

4. Select OK or press Enter.

Word returns to the current document and changes its paragraph formatting.  □

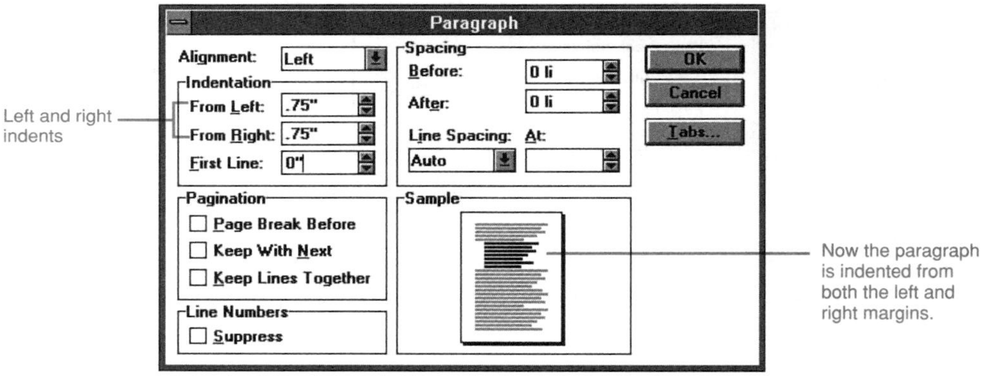

Left and right indents

Now the paragraph is indented from both the left and right margins.

*Figure 6.12    A left and right indent. The text indents from both left and right margins.*

## Indenting Paragraphs with the Keyboard

Word also provides shortcut keys for paragraph indentation. Select one or more paragraphs and the paragraph is indented to the next or preceding tab stop, depending on the shortcut key you press. Table 6.4 presents a synopsis of the keys along with a description of each.

*Table 6.4   Indenting paragraphs with the keyboard.*

| Key | Type of Indent | Description |
| --- | --- | --- |
| Ctrl-T | Hanging Indent | Indents all but the first line of selected paragraphs. Press repeatedly to increase the indent by moving to the next tab stop. |
| Ctrl-N | Indent | Indents all the selected paragraphs from the left margin, one tab stop at a time. |
| Ctrl-M | Unindent | Unindents selected paragraphs, one tab stop at a time. If the paragraphs are already formatted for hanging or other indents, those formats are not changed. |
| Ctrl-G | Decrease | Decreases all but the first line indent by one tab stop. |
| Ctrl-Q | Remove all indents and formats | Removes all indents and paragraph and character formatting from the selected paragraphs. |

**159**

# Enhancing Paragraphs

Up to this point in the chapter, you have formatted paragraphs for emphasis by aligning, indenting, and adding space. However, if there are paragraphs that you want to stand out from the rest in a distinctive way, consider adding borders, lines, and/or shading with the Forma**t B**order command.

For example, you can use borders to call attention to one or two paragraphs in a document. Perhaps they warn the reader or emphasize an important step in a set of instructions. You can also use a combination of text and border to quickly make a poster. If you select several paragraphs, Word places borders or lines around the entire selection. When you choose the Forma**t B**order command, Word displays the Border Paragraphs dialog box, shown in Figure 6.13, which provides these options:

▶ The Border box shows you an illustration of the options that you have selected.

▶ The From Text box allows you to determine the amount of white space (from 0 pt to 31 pt) between the text and the border.

▶ The Preset box presents three types of borders: None, which represents no border; Box, which is a standard border; and Shadow, which is a drop-shadow border.

▶ The Line box provides a variety of single and double lines from which you can select.

▶ The Color box gives you a choice of 17 border colors that you can use if your computer system has a color monitor, plotter, and/or a color printer.

▶ If you select the Shading button, the Shading dialog box is displayed. You'll learn about shading later in this chapter.

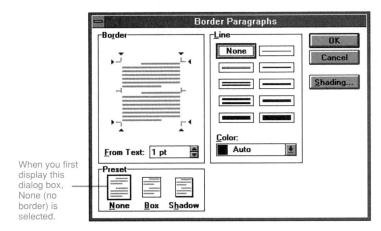

When you first display this dialog box, None (no border) is selected.

*Figure 6.13    The Border Paragraphs dialog box, which allows you to define or change borders around paragraphs.*

## Placing Borders Around Paragraphs

The easiest way to emphasize a paragraph is to surround it with a border. All you need to do is select Format Border (Alt,T,B), select Box, select a Line type, and press OK. Suppose you are writing instructions for installing a light fixture or switch. You'll want to warn your customers to turn off the electricity when they are working with bare wires. These Quick Steps describe how to apply a border.

**Applying a Border to a Paragraph**

1. Select one or more paragraphs, and from the Format
   menu, select the **B**order command (Alt,T,B).

   Word displays the Border
   Paragraphs dialog box.

2. In the Line box, select the
   appropriate border.

   Word displays your selection in the Border box
   (Figure 6.14).

3. Move to the Border box and
   select **F**rom Text to define
   the space between the text
   and the border.

   Word changes the illustration in the Border box
   (Figure 6.15).

4. If you have a color monitor,
   printer, or plotter, select the
   **C**olor list box to display a list
   of colors from which you
   can choose.

   Word displays a list of
   colors and their names.

5. You can select the type of
   border—**N**one, **B**ox, or **S**ha-
   dow—in the Preset box.

   Word changes the illustration in the Border box
   (Figure 6.16).

6. When you have completed
   your selection, select OK or
   press Enter.

   Word returns to the current
   document and applies the
   border to the selected
   paragraph.                      □

**161**

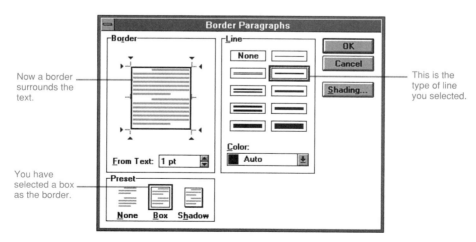

*Figure 6.14   When you select a border, Word changes the
illustration in the Border box.*

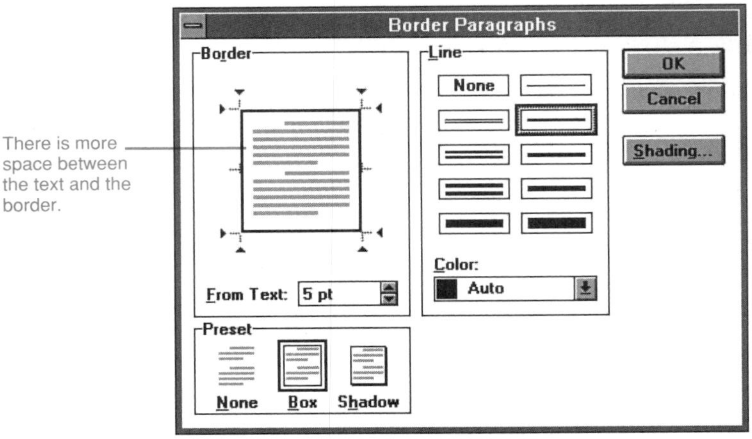

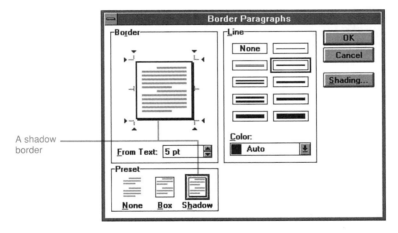

There is more space between the text and the border.

Figure 6.15   *The Border Paragraphs dialog box, with more white space added between text and the border.*

**162**

A shadow border

Figure 6.16   *The Border Paragraphs dialog box. When you select the type of border, Word adds to the illustration in the Border box.*

**Tip:** Simplicity is the rule when designing effective documents. Select one type of border and stick with it throughout. However, there are exceptions: You might consider giving a caution box a slightly thicker border than that for a note.

## *Emphasizing Paragraphs with Lines*

Another way of emphasizing a paragraph is to place lines against one, two, three, or four sides. (Of course, lines around four sides of a paragraph are a border.) Remember that in earlier sections of this chapter, we used a term paper with extensive quotations as an example. Another way to emphasize each quotation is to put lines above and below it. To emphasize a list, you could place a vertical line to the left and a horizontal line below. This emphasizes the paragraph but also demonstrates that this paragraph has different content than the paragraph surrounded by a border.

The next set of Quick Steps describes how to add lines around a selected paragraph.

 **Adding Lines Around a Paragraph**

1. First select one or more paragraphs, and then select the Format menu and the **B**order command (Alt,T,B).

   Word displays the Border Paragraphs dialog box.

2. In the Preset box, select None, which indicates that you want no border.

   Word deletes any borders from the illustration in the Border box (Figure 6.17). The triangles at the corners of the illustration are the points between which any line or border is drawn.

3. In the Border box, click one of the sides of the illustration to which you want to apply a line.

   Word changes the illustration in the Border box (Figure 6.18).

4. In the Line box, select the type of line or None (to remove lines).

   Word changes the illustration once again.

**163**

5. To add a line to more than one side, hold down the Shift key after you select the first line, and then select the additional sides. Alternatively, press Ctrl-R and press any arrow key to cycle through the available combinations of lines until you find what you want.

Word changes the illustration in the Border box (Figure 6.19).

6. When you have completed your selection, press OK.

Word returns to the current document and applies the specified lines to the selected paragraph (Figure 6.20).  □

Note that you can only select one line type at a time to emphasize the selected paragraph.

164

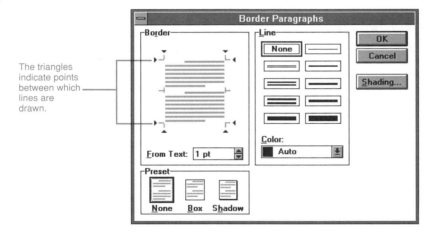

Figure 6.17   *The Border Paragraphs dialog box with no border selected.*

## Shading Paragraphs

Another way to emphasize selected paragraphs, whether or not you have selected borders or lines, is to apply shading. For example, you can make a sign advertising a sale or a school play, surround it with a border, and then shade it. Another example is creating screen illustrations for computer software documentation. First, enter the appropriate text and format it to match the screen image; then add a shadow-box border and light shading. This differentiates the screen images from the rest of the text.

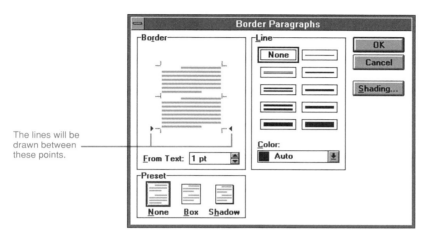

The lines will be drawn between these points.

*Figure 6.18    The Border Paragraphs dialog box. At this point, a line would be drawn between the arrows at the bottom of the sample paragraph.*

**165**

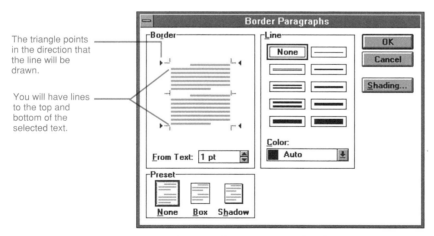

The triangle points in the direction that the line will be drawn.

You will have lines to the top and bottom of the selected text.

*Figure 6.19    The Border Paragraphs dialog box. If you select OK or press Enter, lines will be drawn at the top and bottom of the selected paragraph.*

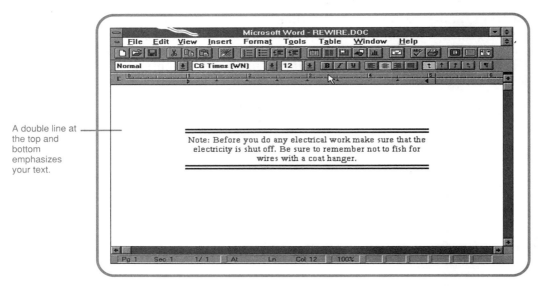

A double line at the top and bottom emphasizes your text.

*Figure 6.20    A paragraph with double lines above and below.*

Select Format Border (Alt,T,B) and, when Word displays the Border Paragraphs dialog box, select Shading. The Shading dialog box, shown in Figure 6.21, allows you to select either no shading or coloring (the default) or Custom, from which you can choose a pattern and foreground or background colors. You don't need to have a color printer, plotter, or monitor to select colors. If you have selected colors, you can use a color printer, plotter, or monitor anytime later.

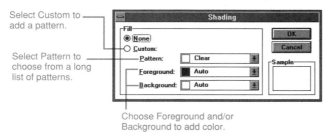

Select Custom to add a pattern.

Select Pattern to choose from a long list of patterns.

Choose Foreground and/or Background to add color.

*Figure 6.21    To add shading or color to a paragraph with a border, choose from the options in the Shading dialog box.*

To shade selected paragraphs, use the following Quick Steps.

**Q Shading Paragraphs**

1. Select one or more paragraphs, and then select the
   Format menu and the Border
   command (Alt,T,B).

   Word displays the Border
   Paragraphs dialog box.

2. If needed, add a border
   or lines.

   Word changes the illustration in the Border box.

3. Select Shading.

   Word opens the Shading
   dialog box.

4. Select Custom.

   If you had selected None
   instead of Custom, Word
   would have cleared the
   previous pattern from the
   Sample box.

**167**

5. Move the mouse pointer to
   the list arrow on the right
   side of the Pattern box. Alternatively, press the Tab key
   repeatedly until you highlight
   Clear in the Pattern box and
   then press ↓.

   Word opens a list of
   patterns.

6. Select a pattern.

   Word closes the list and
   displays your choice.

7. To add colors to the selected
   paragraph, choose Foreground or Background.

   Word opens a list of colors
   from which you can choose
   Auto, the default color,
   uses your monitor's,
   printer's, or plotter's default
   colors.

8. Select a foreground and
   background color.

   Word closes each list and
   displays your choices.

9. Select OK or press Enter.

   Word closes the Shading
   dialog box and returns to
   the Border Paragraphs
   dialog box.

10. After you've made any addi-
    tional changes, select OK or
    press Enter.

    Word returns to the current
    document and applies the
    pattern within the border of
    the paragraph (Figure 6.22). □

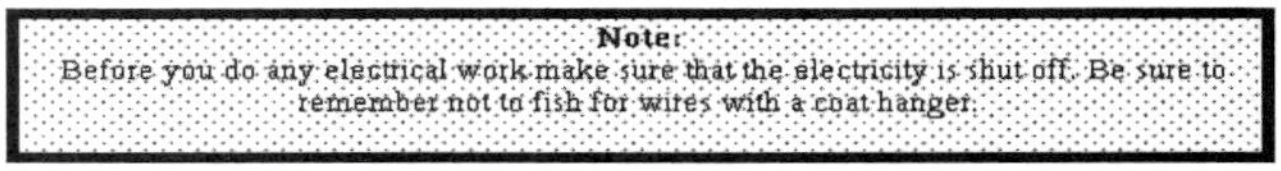

> **Note:**
> Before you do any electrical work make sure that the electricity is shut off. Be sure to remember not to fish for wires with a coat hanger.

*Figure 6.22   Word adds the new border to the selected paragraphs.*

# Using Tabs

Earlier in this chapter, you learned about paragraph indentation and specifically about first-line indents. In this section, you'll be given information about using tabs—how to set tabs at regular intervals or at specific locations, how to clear some or all tabs, and how to use some other tab options.

Tabs indent paragraphs more quickly than when you use Format **P**aragraph. Move the insertion point to the beginning of the paragraph you want to indent and press the Tab key. On-screen, the tab symbol appears as a right-pointing arrow if Word is set to display hidden characters.

Use tabs to indent text within a line or paragraph. For example, to format a computer program, you may need to place parts of each command line at specific tab positions or indent some lines using the same tab positions. Either accept Word's default tab positions (every 1/2 inch) on the Ruler or change the tab settings. Then, in your document, press the Tab key to start text at the next tab position. On the Ruler, the default tab positions appear as inverted *T*s, hanging just below the Ruler scale line.

Another use for tabs is to create tables. Although you should probably use the Table menu to create most tables, occasionally you can use tabs for small tables. See Chapter 10 for a complete description of Word's Table menu.

Use the combination of the Ruler and the Ribbon to set and clear tab positions and to change tab alignment: Left, Right, Decimal, or Center. Use the Forma**t T**abs command to define tab positions at either regular intervals or specific locations, to clear some or all tab positions, to determine the type of *leader* (the dotted lines between a title and a page number in some tables of contents—not to be confused with *leading,* which is related to line spacing) to use, and to set or change tab alignment. Table 6.5 lists each tab alignment setting and provides a description for each.

*Table 6.5    Tab alignment types.*

| Setting | Description |
|---------|-------------|
| Left | The leftmost character aligns with the tab position. The rest of the text flows to the right. |
| Right | The rightmost character aligns with the tab position. The rest of the text flows to the left. |
| Decimal | Any decimal point is aligned with the tab position. The remaining digits flow left and right from the decimal point. If there is no decimal point, this setting behaves like a right tab. |
| Center | The text is centered on the tab position. |

**169**

## *Setting Tabs*

Use the Format **T**abs command to set tabs at regular or varying intervals. To set tabs at regular intervals (for example, every 3/4 inch), type a value in the Default Tab Stops box shown in Figure 6.23. To set tabs at varying intervals (for example, .5", 1.5", 3.3") for tabs, type measurements between –22 and 22, one at a time, in the Tab Stop Position box. (A negative number can be used for tabs within hanging indents.)

All tabs start left-aligned until you change them.

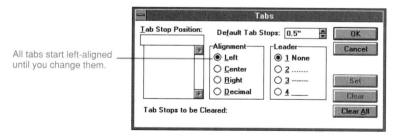

*Figure 6.23    The Tabs dialog box enables you to set tabs and define their alignment.*

Word allows you to set tab alignment in four ways: left, right, center, and decimal. To set left-aligned tab positions (the default) at regular intervals using the Format Tabs command, use the following Quick Steps.

 **Defining Tab Positions at Regular Intervals Using the Format Tabs Command**

1. From the Format menu, select the Tabs command (Alt,T,T).

   Word displays the Tabs dialog box.

2. Move to the Default Tab positions box and enter a new tab setting (from 0.1 to 22 inches). Then select OK or press Enter.

   Word sets new tab positions at the intervals you have defined. So if you enter .25 in the box and select OK or press Enter, the default tabs on your page will start at a quarter of an inch from the left side of the edge of your page and then appear every .25 inch.  □

To find the exact location of a tab setting in a document, select a paragraph with that tab setting, display the Tabs dialog box, and write down the measurement.

---

**Tip:** To quickly display the Format Tabs dialog box, double-click on any tab mark on the ruler.

---

Many times, you will want to set specific tab positions at varying intervals. Use either the combination of the Ruler and the Ribbon (for tab alignment) or the Format Tabs command to set varying tab positions and alignment. There is a set of Quick Steps for each method. Before starting the Quick Steps, make sure that both the Ribbon and the Ruler are displayed by choosing the View menu and then making sure that there is a check mark next to Ribbon (Alt,V,B) and Ruler (Alt,V,R).

**Defining Tab Positions at Varying Intervals Using the Ruler**

1. Select the text for which you want to define tab positions.

   Word highlights your selection.

2. Select one of the tab alignment buttons on the Ribbon, shown in Figure 6.24.

   Word highlights the selected button on the Ribbon and removes the highlight from any other button.

3. On the Ruler, click where you want a tab position. Or, drag an existing tab symbol to a new location and release the mouse button.

   When you insert a tab mark, it causes all of the default tab marks to the left of the one you just inserted to disappear.

4. Repeat step 3 until you have placed all the tab positions you want.

   If the highlighted paragraph includes any tab marks that are affected by the new tab positions, Word changes the format.□

**171**

 **Tip:** To delete a tab symbol, just drag it off the Ruler and release the mouse button.

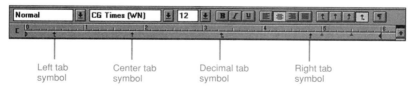

Left tab symbol     Center tab symbol     Decimal tab symbol     Right tab symbol

*Figure 6.24     This Ruler illustrates all types of tab settings.*

A feature that is not available when you use the Ribbon and the Ruler is defining a *leader*, typically a dotted line that extends from the last character or space in the text before the tab and the tab itself (see Figure 6.25). Leaders are used in many tables of contents. The following Quick Steps  show how to define tab positions at specific locations.

**Defining Tab Positions at Varying Intervals Using the Format Tabs Command**

1. Select the text for which you want to define tab positions.

   Word highlights your selection.

2. Select the Format menu and the Tabs command (Alt,T,T).

   Word displays the Tabs dialog box.

3. In the Tab Stop Position box, enter a number representing the tab position. Valid values for tab positions range from –22 inches to 22 inches.

   Word informs you if you enter a number outside the valid range.

4. Select the type of alignment (Left, Center, Right, or Decimal) for the tab position.

   Word fills in the appropriate button.

5. To select a leader, choose one of the four leader types.

   Word places a border around the leader that you have selected.

6. Select Set.

   Word highlights the contents of the Tab Stop Position box.

7. To add more tab positions, repeat steps 3 through 6 until you have finished.

   Word adds each position to the list in the Tab Stop Position box. You can set a maximum of 50 tab positions.

8. Select OK or press Enter.

   Word returns to your document and places the new tab setting on the Ruler.  □

## Clearing Tabs

You can clear one specific tab position or all tab positions. From the Format menu, select the Tab command (Alt,T,T). Word displays the Tabs dialog box. To clear one specific tab position, first select a tab position from the list in the Tab Stop Position box and then select the Clear button. Select OK or press Enter. To clear all tab positions, just select the Clear All button. Select OK or press Enter. To clear a tab position using the Ruler, select a tab position and drag it off the Ruler.

172

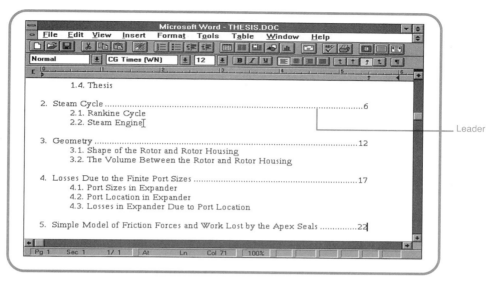

1.4. Thesis

2. Steam Cycle ........................................................................6
   2.1. Rankine Cycle
   2.2. Steam Engine

3. Geometry .............................................................................12
   3.1. Shape of the Rotor and Rotor Housing
   3.2. The Volume Between the Rotor and Rotor Housing

4. Losses Due to the Finite Port Sizes ....................................17
   4.1. Port Sizes in Expander
   4.2. Port Location in Expander
   4.3. Losses in Expander Due to Port Location

5. Simple Model of Friction Forces and Work Lost by the Apex Seals ..............22

Leader

*Figure 6.25   An example of leaders in a document.*

**173**

 **Note:** Once you have cleared a tab position, there is no way to undo this action other than setting the tab again.

# What You Have Learned

▶ A paragraph is a string of text that ends with a paragraph mark. When you delete a paragraph mark, you delete all the paragraph formats for the preceding paragraph.

▶ To display all nonprinting symbols, select the Show All button on the Ribbon.

▶ Choices for paragraph alignment are Left, Right, Centered, and Justified. Left and Right align a paragraph along the left and right margins, respectively. Centered centers text between the margins, and Justified extends the text from the left to the right margins. To set paragraph alignment, either select a button on the Ribbon or from the Format menu, select the Paragraph command. Then select from the Alignment list box.

► You can indent every line in a paragraph or indent the first line and the remaining lines differently. Indentation options are left and/or right, centered, hanging, and first line. There are four ways to indent a paragraph: adjust the arrows on the Ruler, select Format Paragraph and fill in the Indentation box, click on the Toolbar's Indent button, or use shortcut keys.

► Word's default setting for both indentations and tabs is every half inch.

► You can emphasize a paragraph by surrounding it with a border, placing one or more lines around it, and/or shading it. To define borders or lines for a paragraph, select Format Border. To shade a paragraph, select Format Border; then select Shading.

**174**

► There are two ways to set tab positions—the Ribbon and the Ruler combination and the Format Tab command.

# Chapter 7

# Formatting Characters

## In This Chapter

- ▶ *Enhancing characters*
- ▶ *Adjusting spacing between characters*
- ▶ *Hiding and revealing text*
- ▶ *Viewing, adding, deleting, and downloading fonts*
- ▶ *Changing fonts and point size*

## Character Formatting

Up to this point, you have been learning about Word for Windows formats that define large parts of a document. You've created formats for the entire document and for individual paragraphs. There is a smaller text element that you can format—the character.

A character is the smallest unit of text in Word. A *character* is any letter, number, or special symbol. Special symbols are characters like hyphens, punctuation marks, or those symbols that are displayed on the number keys of your keyboard.

Formatting characters lets you emphasize text in a document. For example, a newspaper uses character formatting to emphasize the headlines for its articles. Newspaper headlines are displayed in larger, bolder letters than the text in the articles.

There are two main types of character formatting. The first type of formatting has to do with the design of the characters, or *font*. Characters that have the same font share similarities in their design. For example, if the characters *h*, *k*, *d*, and *l* are in the same font, the straight vertical line that is part of these letters should look the same and have the same *point size* (the vertical size of a character measured from top to bottom). You can differentiate between headlines and normal text by changing the font and point size.

The second type of character formatting concerns the appearance of a character. Keeping the same font and point size, you can change the appearance of a character to give it greater emphasis. You can underline it, slant it, make its lines thicker, move it above or below other characters, or even change its color.

Word for Windows provides three ways of formatting characters. You can use the Ribbon, the Forma**t** **C**haracter command, or keyboard shortcuts.

You can format existing characters or set new formats for characters you are about to type. To format existing characters, select the text to be changed and then use the Ribbon or the Forma**t** **C**haracter command. When you apply a different character format for new text, the new format starts at the insertion point and doesn't change until you change to another character format. Unless you change the character format, text that you type has the same format as the text before it. Word starts out with normal, unemphasized text as the default.

When you use the Forma**t** **C**haracter command, Word displays the Character dialog box. All of its options are explained in this chapter.

## *Emphasizing Characters with the Ribbon*

The easiest way to format characters is to use the Ribbon, shown in Figure 7.1. The Ribbon not only enables you to manipulate characters but also shows you how the characters are formatted. The second box from the left on the Ribbon shows you the current font.

Moving to the right, the next box shows the point size of the current text. The next three buttons allow you to set bold, italic, and underlined text, respectively. You can press any combination of these buttons to enhance text.

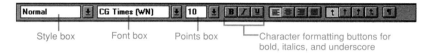

Style box    Font box    Points box    Character formatting buttons for
                                        bold, italics, and underscore

*Figure 7.1    The Ribbon. When a button is selected on the*
*Ribbon, it looks as though it has been pressed.*

Use the following Quick Steps to enhance text using the Ribbon.

 **Emphasizing Characters Using the Ribbon**

1. To use the Ribbon, it must be displayed. If the Ribbon is not displayed on-screen, select the **View** menu.

   Word opens the **View** menu.

2. Select Ri**b**bon if there is no check mark next to it.

   Word returns to the current document and displays the Ribbon.

3. To enhance text already in your document, select it. Then select one or more buttons on the Ribbon.

   When a button is selected, it appears to be pressed. Word also changes the appearance of the selected text (Figure 7.2).

4. To enhance text that you have not yet typed, move the insertion point to the place at which you want to start typing. Then select a button on the Ribbon.

   Word changes the appearance of the Ribbon to reflect the format at the insertion point.

5. To turn off or undo a character enhancement, click on the button or buttons that control that enhancement.

   The buttons that you click on no longer appear to be pressed. If text is selected, it changes to the new format. Any future text assumes the new format.  □

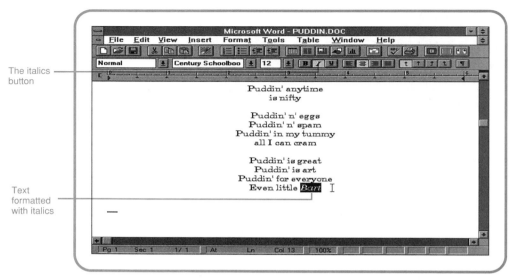

The italics button

Text formatted with italics

*Figure 7.2    A document showing text formatted for italics.*

**178**

## *Emphasizing Characters with the Format Character Command*

Although using the Ribbon is the easiest way to change character formats, it doesn't cover all formatting options. For example, if you have a color monitor, you can display text in different colors, or if you have installed and configured a color printer or plotter, you can print files in color. To use the Format **C**haracter command to apply additional character formatting, follow these Quick Steps.

**Emphasizing Characters Using the Format Character Command**

1. Select existing text to be formatted or move the insertion point to the location at which you want to type formatted text.

   Word highlights the selected text or displays the insertion point in its new location.

2. From the Format menu, select the **C**haracter command (Alt,T,C).

   Word displays the Character dialog box (Figure 7.3).

3. Select one or more choices from the Style box (see Table 7.1 for a list of styles along with their shortcut keys).

In the Sample box, Word displays the format that you selected.

4. If you have a color monitor, printer, or plotter, select Color and select a color from the list of colors.

In the Sample box, Word displays the color that you selected.

5. To change additional character formats, repeat steps 2 and 3.

Word changes the sample text accordingly.

6. When you have completed your selections, select OK or press Enter.

Word returns to your document and either emphasizes the text that you selected or will emphasize the text that you enter at the insertion point. Note that the appearance of the Ribbon also changes, depending on your selections. □

**179**

---

**Tip:** You can quickly open the Character dialog box by moving the mouse pointer anywhere on the Ribbon buttons or boxes. Then double-click.

---

Table 7.1 describes each of the formatting options in the Style box of the Character dialog box, and names shortcut keys for these formats.

***Table 7.1  Character dialog box formats.***

| Style | Shortcut Key | Description |
|-------|--------------|-------------|
| Bold | Ctrl-B | Applies boldface to selected text |
| Italic | Ctrl-I | Applies italics to selected text |
| Strikethrough | None | Strikes through selected text |
| Hidden | Ctrl-H | Hides selected text |
| Small Caps | Ctrl-K | Changes selected text to small capitals |

*continues*

**Table 7.1   continued**

| Style | Shortcut Key | Description |
|-------|--------------|-------------|
| All Caps | Ctrl-A | Changes selected text to full-size capitals |
| Underline | | |
| None | N/A | |
| Single | Ctrl-U | Underlines all selected text, including spaces between words |
| Words Only | Ctrl-W | Underlines all selected text, excluding spaces between words |
| Double | Ctrl-D | Applies double underline |
| Superscript | Ctrl-= | Moves selected text higher relative to other text on the line |
| Subscript | Ctrl-Shift-= | Moves selected text lower relative to other text on the line |

**180**

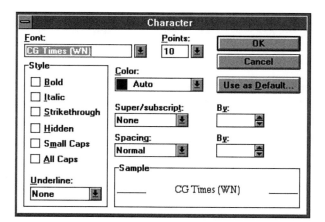

*Figure 7.3   The Character dialog box.*

## Using Superscripts and Subscripts

Up to this point, you have used character formatting to change the way characters look, but you have not changed their size or location. The superscript/subscript format in the Character dialog box is a way to change the location of characters above or below the normal line of text. Use this format primarily for mathematical formulas and other technical material. Suppose you typed the equation $x^2 - y^2$. In order to show that each number is an exponent, you need to raise it above the other characters in the formula. To format the number as a superscript, first select the number; then choose Format Character (Alt,T,C), and use the Super/subscript list box, shown in Figure 7.4. Use the following Quick Steps to apply superscript or subscript formats.

 **Using Superscript and Subscript Styles**

1. Select the text to be formatted.

   Word highlights your selection.

2. Select the Format menu and the Character command (Alt, T,C).

   Word displays the Character dialog box.

3. In the Super/subscript box, select the list arrow (the underlined down arrow).

   Word opens a list from which you can choose.

4. Select None, Superscript, or Subscript.

   In the Sample box, Word shows the alignment of sample text above, on, or below the *baseline,* the invisible line on which characters sit.

5. You can adjust the alignment of your selection by selecting the list arrow to the right of the box. You can select any value from 63.5 points above to 63.5 points below the baseline.

   Word changes the text in the Sample box.

6. Select OK or press Enter.

   Word returns to your document and either realigns the text that you selected (Figure 7.5) or will align the text that you enter. □

181

> **Tip:** Before printing a document with superscript or subscript text adjusted more than three points (the default), check the document in Print Preview or by printing the page in question. The superscript or subscript text may have been moved up or down so much that two text lines are overlaid. You can adjust the superscript and/or subscript until the spacing is correct.

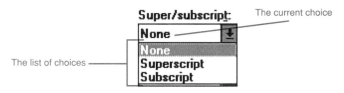

*Figure 7.4    The Super/subscript list box.*

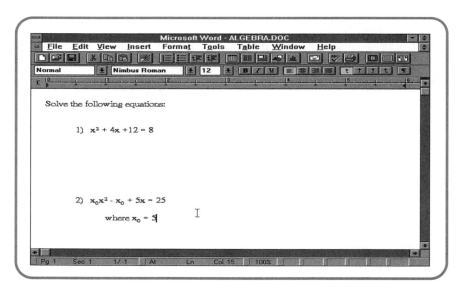

*Figure 7.5    A page showing text formatted with subscript and superscript styles.*

To remove all formatting (including any changes to the font and point size), select the text and press Ctrl-spacebar.

## *Adjusting Spacing Between Characters*

You can adjust the space between characters to subtly change their appearance. Reducing or tightening the space between letters is called *kerning.* Kerning is particularly important for text with a large point size, such as headlines. An unkerned headline can look like a series of letters rather than words. When you tighten the space between letters, the letters become a related group—a word. If you select more than two characters at a time for kerning, it's difficult to fine-tune the separation between letters. You'll find that some letters don't need to be moved at all. For examples of kerned and unkerned text, see Figure 7.6.

Unkerned text

Kerned text

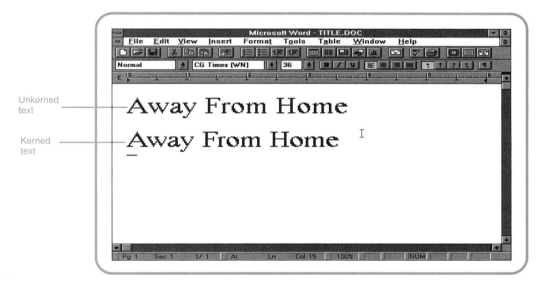

*Figure 7.6    These two headlines are examples of kerned and unkerned text. In each word of the second headline, the space between the first two characters has been tightened. The effect is subtle but effective.*

To adjust the spacing between characters, follow these Quick Steps.

 **Adjusting Character Spacing**

1. Select two adjoining letters.                    Word highlights the
                                                    selected letters.

2. Select the Format menu and the Character command (Alt, T,C).

Word opens the Character dialog box.

3. Choose either the Expanded or the Condensed box. The By box (Figure 7.7) lets you adjust the amount by which you can expand (up to 14 points) or condense (down to 1.75 points) the text.

As you adjust the spacing, Word changes the sample text accordingly, as shown in Figure 7.7.

4. Select OK or press Enter.

Word returns to your document and adjusts the text that you selected.  □

Repeat these Quick Steps to adjust the rest of the headline. Remember to select two adjoining letters at a time.

**184**

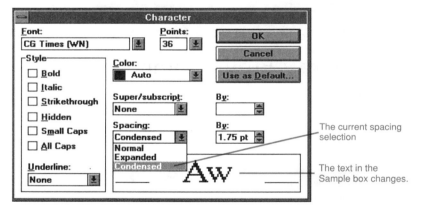

*Figure 7.7   As you adjust the spacing, Word changes the text in the Sample box accordingly.*

---

**Tip:** Use kerning to reformat a paragraph when the last line of the paragraph consists of only one word. Kern the letters and words in the preceding line of the paragraph so that Word moves the single word up from the last line.

---

As you get to be an expert in document creation, you'll start to notice *rivers,* which are spaces between words occurring at approximately the same point on successive lines. These spaces are called rivers because they flow vertically down the page. Often, rivers are caused by justification and the extra spaces placed between words. Use kerning to adjust spaces between words so that rivers are eliminated.

## Hiding Text

Up to this point, all character formatting described in this chapter has changed the appearance or position of characters in a document in order to emphasize the selected characters. Using the Format Character command, you can also *hide* text. Use hidden text to make notes to yourself or to others throughout a document. At a later time, you can print these hidden notes for your records. Before hiding text or typing hidden text, be sure to turn on the Show All button on the Ribbon so that you can see all the characters and symbols in your document, whether they are hidden or not. To hide text, use the following Quick Steps.

185

 **Hiding Text**

1. Select existing text, or move the insertion point to the place at which you want to type hidden text.

   Word highlights the selected text or displays the insertion point in its new location.

2. Select the Format menu and the Character command (Alt, T,C).

   Word displays the Character dialog box.

3. In the Style box, place a check mark next to Hidden. Then select OK or press Enter.

   Word returns to the current document and either hides the selected text or hides the text that you type at the insertion point. As you type hidden text, Word under-lines it (Figure 7.8).

4. To switch back to normal text, repeat step 1, clear the Hidden box, and then select OK or press Enter.

   Word returns to the current document and either reveals the selected text or returns to normal text at the insertion point.       □

 **Tip:** To switch between normal and hidden text format-ting, press the shortcut keys Ctrl-H.

## Displaying or Concealing Hidden Text

When you use the Show All button on the Ribbon, all hidden text and nonprinting symbols are affected. As a way to selectively display or conceal hidden text, tabs, spaces, paragraph marks, and optional hyphens, use the **Tools Options** command. Use the following Quick Steps to display or conceal hidden text using **Tools Options**.

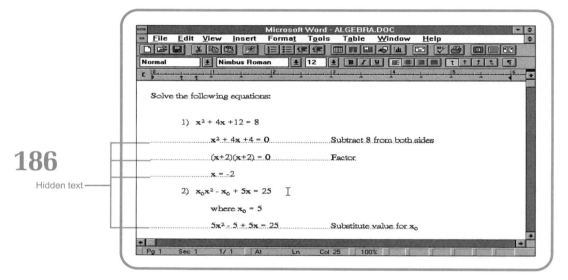

Solve the following equations:

1) $x^2 + 4x + 12 = 8$

   $x^2 + 4x + 4 = 0$ .................... Subtract 8 from both sides

   $(x+2)(x+2) = 0$ .................... Factor

   $x = -2$

2) $x_0x^2 - x_0 + 5x = 25$

   where $x_0 = 5$

   $5x^2 - 5 + 5x = 25$ .................... Substitute value for $x_0$

Hidden text

**Figure 7.8**  *A document with hidden text displayed. Notice that the hidden text is underlined with a dotted line.*

 **Displaying or Concealing Hidden Text**

1. Select the **Tools** menu and the **O**ptions command.

   Word displays the Options dialog box.

2. In the Category area, select View.

   Word displays the Options dialog box for the View category (Figure 7.9).

3. To display hidden text, under Nonprinting Characters, place a check in the Hidden Text box and select OK or press Enter.

   Word returns to the current document and displays all hidden text.

4. To conceal hidden text, remove the check in the Hidden Text box and select OK or press Enter.

   Word returns to the current document and conceals all hidden text.

   □

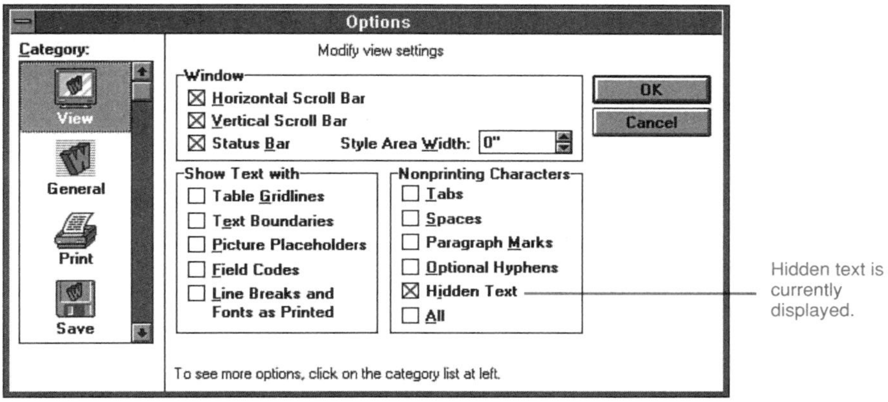

*Figure 7.9    The Options dialog box for the View category.*

### Printing Hidden Text

**187**

Your document can serve two purposes: to inform its ultimate audience and to provide a printed record of the changes it has gone through. Suppose that a document has gone through extensive review by your co-workers, and each reviewer has typed comments that have resulted in a series of changes to the document. The recipients of the document don't need to see the notes, so you have hidden them and printed the final document for distribution. To keep a file copy of the finished document including your co-workers' comments, reveal the hidden text and then print. Note that when you print hidden text, the page breaks and page numbering are affected. The following Quick Steps describe how to print a document with and without its hidden text.

### Printing a Document with and without Hidden Text

| | |
|---|---|
| 1. Select the Tools menu and the Options command (Alt, O,O). | Word displays the last Options dialog box you used in this session of Word. |
| 2. In the Category area, select Print. | Word displays the Options dialog box for the Print category (Figure 7.10). You'll learn all about this dialog box in Chapter 9. |

3. To print hidden text, place a check in the **Hidden** Text box under Include with Document. To exclude hidden text from being printed, remove the check in the **Hidden** Text box.

Word places a dotted line around the Hidden Text box, indicating that this option is your last selection.

4. Select OK or press Enter.

Word returns to the current document.

5. Select the **File** menu and the **Print** command (Alt,F,P).

Word opens the Print dialog box (Figure 7.11).

6. Select OK or press Enter.

Word prints your document with or without hidden text, as you choose. You'll learn more about printing options in Chapter 9. □

**188**

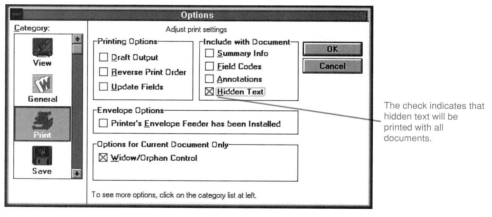

The check indicates that hidden text will be printed with all documents.

*Figure 7.10    The Options dialog box for the Print category.*

**Tip:** You can use Print Preview to check whether you have chosen to print hidden text. Remember that whether you are displaying or concealing hidden text on-screen, Word can print or not print hidden text.

When you want to print your document without hidden text being a factor in page numbering, use the Tools Options dialog boxes to clear the Hidden Text box in the Print category as well as the Hidden Text box in the View category. Also, be sure that you have not accidentally formatted page or section breaks as hidden text.

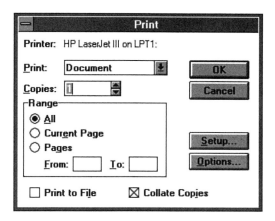

*Figure 7.11    The Print dialog box.*

**FYIdea:** Teachers and those involved in employee training can use hidden text to advantage when constructing tests and quizzes. The test questions can be in regular text and the answers in hidden text. On the student version, the hidden text is not printed.

**189**

# Using Fonts

Earlier in this chapter, you learned about enhancing words in a document. The remainder of this chapter describes setting the overall tone of a document with another type of character formatting.

Fonts add character to a document. With fonts, you can help identify your document as serious or comic, technical or informal.

## *Introducing Fonts and Points*

Fonts are families of typeface designs. For example, two pages of text from different documents (for example, a typewritten letter versus a page from a book) will look different because the sets of characters used for the text probably have different designs. This means each set of characters comes from a different font. For example, the most common typewriter font is Courier. However, typeset technical manuals quite often use a combination of Times Roman for the regular text and Helvetica for headlines, and many textbooks use Century Schoolbook.

Fonts can be either serif or sans serif. *Serif* fonts have decorative lines at the ends of letter strokes, and *sans serif* fonts are simple and undecorated. Font and typeface experts consider serif fonts easier to read, so most body text falls into the serif category.

You can also divide fonts into proportional and monospace fonts. *Proportional* fonts use different widths for each letter. For example, the space for the letter *I* is much narrower than the space used for *W*. Every character in a *monospace* font has the same width, which is very useful when you have to align text vertically or at specific column locations.

**190**

As you become more accustomed to using fonts in your documents, you'll find that the variety of fonts is almost endless. See Table 7.2 for a list of common fonts and descriptions of each.

*Table 7.2   Commonly used fonts.*  ,

| Font | Usage | Description | |
|------|-------|-------------|--|
| Times Roman | Standard body text | Serif | Proportional |
| Optima | Standard body text | Serif | Proportional |
| Courier | Letters | Serif | Monospace |
| Line Printer | Tables | Serif | Monospace |
| Century Schoolbook | Textbooks | Serif | Proportional |
| Bookman | Textbooks | Serif | Proportional |
| Avante Garde | Headlines | Serif | Proportional |
| Helvetica | Headlines | Sans serif | Proportional |
| Zapf Chancery | Invitations | Serif | Proportional |
| Palatino | Invitations | Serif | Proportional |

Not only can fonts differ in style, but they can also differ in size. The size of a character is measured in *points*. The higher the point number is, the larger the character. A point is 1/72 of an inch, so a 72-point character measures one inch from top to bottom. When you are planning a document and deciding upon font, point size, and the length of a line of text, a general rule is that a line should contain no more than 1 1/2 alphabets—about 40 characters. See Table 7.3 for the point sizes and formats of typical text elements.

*Table 7.3    Point size and format of typical text elements.*

| Document Element | Point Size | Format |
| --- | --- | --- |
| Body text | 8–12 | Normal |
| Subheadings | 10–14 | Bold or Bold Italic |
| Headings | 14–28 | Bold |
| Headers/Footers | 8–12 | Italic |
| Captions | 8–12 | Italic |
| Page numbers | 10–14 | Bold or Bold Italic |

191

## Changing Fonts and Point Sizes

When you start Word, a default font and point size is assigned to the new document. For a particular document, you may decide that the default font isn't appropriate for your needs. For example, to subtly encourage people to read a report, select a font with round, easy-to-read characters. However, if you're trying to fool all of the people all of the time, select a font with condensed type and a tiny point size. You can change fonts and point sizes by using either the Format Character command or the Ribbon.

### Changing the Font and Point Size with the Format Character Command

The Format Character command is more versatile than the Ribbon. Both allow you to change the font and point size, but the Format Character command provides formatting options not available with the Ribbon. For example, the strikethrough format can be applied only with the Format Character command. Thus, if you wish to do more than define fonts and point sizes, the Format Character command is probably the better choice.

**Q Selecting a Font and Point Size Using the Format Character Command**

1. Select your entire document by pressing Ctrl-5 (on the numeric keypad).

   Word highlights the document.

2. From the Format menu, select the Character command (Alt, T,C).

   Word displays the Character dialog box.

3. If you don't know the name of the font you want to select, choose the list arrow (the underlined down arrow) next to the Font box.

   Word displays a list of fonts associated with the active printer and displays the highlighted font in the Sample box (Figure 7.12). The symbol next to some fonts represents a printer font (a font that is associated with your printer).

**192**

4. Either select a font name or enter it in the Font box.

   Word displays a sample of the font in the Sample box.

5. If you happen to know the point sizes available for the selected font, enter it in the Points box. Otherwise, select the list arrow next to the Points box.

   Word displays a list of point sizes. If this is a scalable font, you'll see a long list of numbers that increase by one (Figure 7.13). (A *scalable font* is a mathematically defined font that can be expanded or contracted to achieve a wide range of sizes.)

6. Select a point size.

   Word displays a sample of the font in the selected point size.

7. Select OK or press Enter.

   Word returns to the current document and applies the new font to the selected text.             □

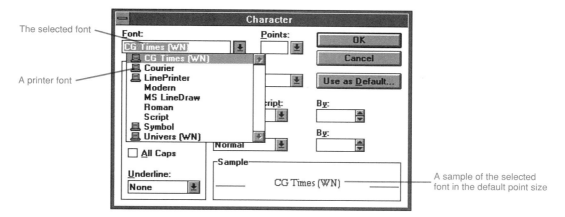

The selected font

A printer font

A sample of the selected font in the default point size

*Figure 7.12    The Character dialog box showing the Font list.*

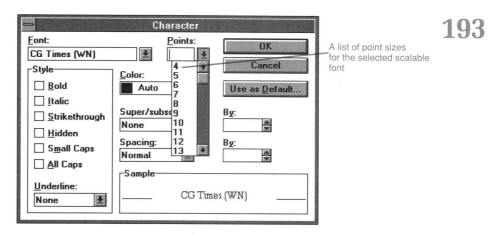

A list of point sizes for the selected scalable font

**193**

*Figure 7.13    The Character dialog box showing a partial list of point sizes for a scalable font.*

### Changing the Font and Point Size with the Ribbon

If all you want to do is change font and/or point size, use the Ribbon (shown earlier in Figure 7.1). In the Font box, either enter the name of a font that has been installed or select the list arrow to open the list of fonts from which you can make a selection. At this point, Word changes the name in the Font box and closes the list. To select a point size, use the same procedures. Enter a number in the Points box or select the list arrow to its right. When the list is displayed, select a point size. Word changes the number in the Points box and closes the list. Then when you start entering new text, Word uses the newly defined font and point size. To specify a font and point size for existing text, select the text and change the values on the Ribbon.

## More About Fonts and Points

Be aware of the fact that Word uses two basic sets of fonts—screen fonts, which come from Windows and Word, and printer fonts, which come from the printers attached to your computer system. If you select a printer font that does not have a screen font counterpart, Word tries to substitute the most closely related screen font. In this way, the printed page will not differ too much from the page on-screen.

194

For a beginner, an easy solution to font selection is to use the same font throughout a document. For example, select the easy-to-read Times Roman 10-point size because it is a good font for body text. Then use 14-point bold Times Roman for headers. Select 12-point bold italic Times Roman for page numbers and 10-point italic for captions.

When you use two fonts in a single document, make sure that they are contrasting and distinct (for example, sans serif vs. serif) and serve two separate purposes (for example, headlines vs. body text). Fonts that come from the same family but are slightly different can be visually distracting.

---

**Caution:** Don't use more than two fonts per page! With more than two fonts, your document will start to look like a ransom note.

---

If you are working with technical documents, make sure that your font clearly shows the difference between the zero (*0*) and the letter *O*; the uppercase letter *Z* and the number *2*; and the lowercase letter *l*, the uppercase letter *I*, and the number *1*.

If you use a copier to duplicate your documents, see how the font that you have chosen copies. Since copied text tends to be lighter than the original, is the text still easy to read? If not, select a font with heavier lines.

Consider your audience. For example, if your readers are older people, think about increasing the point size. Certain fonts look smaller than others, even if they are the same point size. Select fonts for your readers' comfort.

If the text in the body of the document is 10-point type, subtitles should be 10 to 12 points, and the main title 14 points. As a general guideline, increase the point size two to four points as the text element changes. Table 7.3 gives general guidelines.

Most importantly, let your eye and good sense lead the way!

## About Soft Fonts

Word comes with *soft fonts*, which are stored on your hard disk and sent to the printer every time they are in a document for which they are defined. *Cartridge fonts* are "plugged into" your printer and do not need to be sent.

**195**

Regardless of the type of font, there are two production methods for fonts—bit-mapped and scalable. A *bit-mapped* font is made up of patterns formed from dots. These fonts come in certain point sizes and cannot easily be adjusted to a size that is not mapped. Dot-matrix printers use bit-mapped fonts.

Only a few printers can handle *scalable* fonts, which are defined by mathematical formulas. A scalable font can be expanded or contracted in a wide variation of sizes. Before you select a specific point size, the font is represented by a mathematical formula. After you select a point size, the actual font is calculated. Word can handle scalable font sizes from 4 to 127 points, which should be more than adequate for your needs.

For information about soft fonts or cartridge fonts unique to your printer, see your printer's manual.

## Viewing, Adding, and Deleting Fonts

The list of fonts that you can choose to use in your document depends on which active printer you have selected to use with Word. As mentioned earlier, not every printer font has a comparable screen font. When Word tries to display this unmatched font, it chooses the font that is closest in appearance to the printer font.

### Viewing Fonts

You can display a list of printer fonts and screen fonts by using the Windows Control Panel as detailed in the following Quick Steps.

 **Viewing Fonts**

1. Select the Application Control menu (located at the left end of the Title bar).

    Word opens the Application Control menu (Figure 7.14).

2. Select **R**un.

    Word opens the Run dialog box (Figure 7.15).

3. Select the Control **P**anel option button. Select OK or press Enter.

    Word opens the Windows Control Panel (Figure 7.16).

4. Double-click on the Fonts icon.

    Windows displays the Fonts dialog box (Figure 7.17). In the Installed Fonts box, Windows displays a list of the fonts available to your printer. If a printer font doesn't have a comparable screen font, then Windows displays the closest available font. [All res] indicates that the font can be displayed in any size, from 4 to 127 points. □

**196**

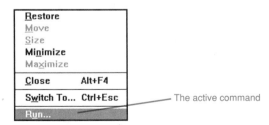

*Figure 7.14    The Application Control menu.*

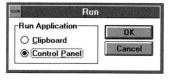

*Figure 7.15    The Run dialog box from which you can select the Clipboard or Control Panel.*

The Fonts icon

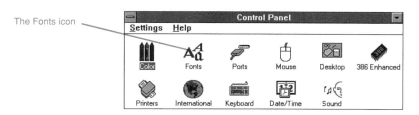

*Figure 7.16    The Windows Control Panel, used for setting up the Fonts dialog box.*

The fonts that
are currently installed

All resolutions, which
indicates a scalable font

Point sizes for
the selected font

Samples in each
point size

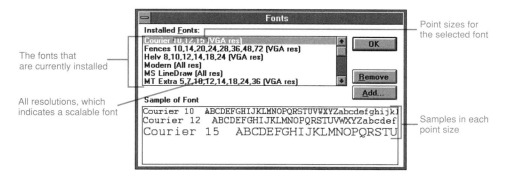

*Figure 7.17    The Fonts dialog box. Notice that the selected font is displayed in each of its point sizes in the Sample box.*

## Adding Fonts

You have already learned how to use the Fonts dialog box to view fonts. You can also use this dialog box to add fonts (for example, soft fonts software). Adding fonts does not cause any Word or Windows software problems, but be aware that font files are large and can take up a great deal of hard disk space and computer memory. Use the following Quick Steps to add fonts.

**Adding Fonts**

1. Select the Application Control menu (located at the left end of the Title bar).

Word opens the Application Control menu.

2. Select Run.

Word opens the Run dialog box.

3. Select the Control Panel option button. Select OK or press Enter.

Word opens the Windows Control Panel.

4. Double-click on the Fonts icon.

Windows displays the Fonts dialog box.

5. Select Add in the Fonts dialog box.

Windows displays the Add Font Files dialog box (Figure 7.18).

6. Type the path in which the fonts that you want to add are located. Type an asterisk (*), which indicates any file name, and the .FON extension; press Enter.

Windows displays a list of the available fonts for the selected directory. If there are none available, the Font Files box is empty.

7. Click on one or more fonts to be added and click on OK.

Windows returns to the Fonts dialog box.

8. Select OK or press Enter.

Windows returns to the Control Panel.

9. Select the Application Control menu.

Windows opens the Application Control menu.

10. Select Close.

Word returns to the current document.  □

**198**

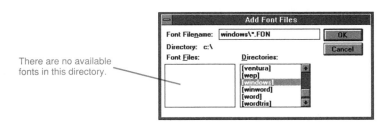

*Figure 7.18    The Add Font Files dialog box.*

Deleting Fonts

You can also use the Fonts dialog box to delete fonts. However, before you delete anything, please think twice. If you delete something that is crucial to your computer system's operations, it may be impossible to reconstruct the missing pieces later on. In particular, do not delete the System or Helv fonts, because these fonts are used to display characters in Word dialog boxes and in Windows.

## *Q* **Deleting Fonts**

| | |
|---|---|
| 1. Select the Application Control menu (located at the left end of the title bar). | Word opens the Application Control menu. |
| 2. Select Run. | Word opens the Run dialog box. |
| 3. Select the Control Panel option button. Select OK or press Enter. | Word opens the Windows Control Panel. |
| 4. Double-click on the Fonts icon. | Windows displays the Fonts dialog box. |
| 5. Click on the Remove button in the Fonts dialog box. | Windows displays a message that asks if you want to remove the selected font. |
| 6. Select Yes or No. | Windows either removes or doesn't remove the selected font and returns to the Fonts dialog box. |
| 7. Select OK or press Enter. | Windows closes the Font dialog box. □ |

**199**

## *Downloading Fonts When You Start Your Computer*

If you have a laser printer, your document will take longer to print if you have soft fonts because the fonts have to be downloaded to the printer. If you often use fonts that have to be downloaded, you might want to automatically install them every time you turn on your computer. These *permanent fonts* stay in your printer until you shut off the printer. Use the following Quick Steps to adjust your

AUTOEXEC.BAT file so that whenever you start your computer, you are asked whether you would like to install fonts to the printer. Before attempting this procedure, be aware that not everyone is able to download soft fonts automatically. Success depends on a variety of factors.

## Q Downloading Fonts to Your Printer

1. Select the Application Control menu (located at the left end of the title bar).

   Word opens the menu.

2. Select Run.

   Word opens the Run dialog box.

3. Select Control Panel and OK.

   Word opens the Windows Control Panel.

4. From the Control Panel, select the Printers icon.

   Windows opens the Printers dialog box (Figure 7.19).

5. Select Configure.

   Windows displays the Printers - Configure dialog box (Figure 7.20).

6. Select Setup.

   Windows displays the Setup dialog box for the active printer (Figure 7.21).

7. Select Fonts.

   Windows displays the Font Installer dialog box for the active printer (Figure 7.22). If Fonts is not an available button, then you cannot download fonts to the printer.

8. In the list of soft fonts, select one font at a time and select Permanent. Repeat this until you have selected all the fonts you want to download. Select Exit.

   Windows displays a Download options box, which prompts you to download now or download at startup (Figure 7.23).

9. Select Download at startup. Then select OK or press Enter.

   Windows installs the selected fonts and appends a line to AUTOEXEC.BAT. Then Windows returns to the Setup dialog box for the active printer.

**200**

10. Select OK or press Enter.

Windows returns to the Printers - Configure dialog box.

11. Select OK or press Enter.

Windows returns to the Printers dialog box.

12. Select OK or press Enter.

Windows returns to the Control Panel.

13. Select the Application Control menu.

Windows displays the Application Control menu.

14. Select Close.

Word returns to the current document. Note that the new font is on the list in the Ribbon. □

*Figure 7.19 The Printers dialog box from the Control Panel. Notice the active and inactive selections.*

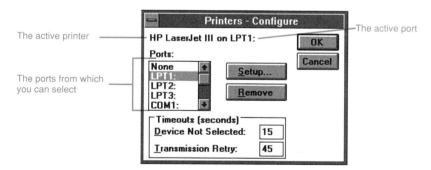

*Figure 7.20 The Printers - Configure dialog box.*

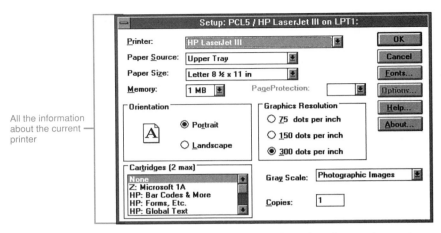

All the information
about the current
printer

*Figure 7.21   The Setup dialog box for the active printer.*

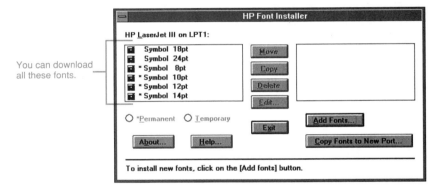

You can download
all these fonts.

*Figure 7.22   The Font Installer dialog box from which you
can select fonts to be downloaded.*

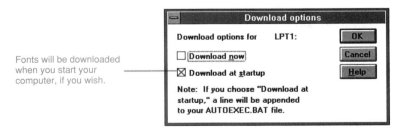

Fonts will be downloaded
when you start your
computer, if you wish.

*Figure 7.23   Download options box from which you down-
load fonts.*

Check your AUTOEXEC.BAT to make sure that a new statement has been added.

## Copying Fonts from One Port to Another

If you have more than one Hewlett-Packard LaserJet printer attached to your computer, you can use fonts from one printer on another printer by copying fonts from one port (for example, LPT1, LPT2, or COM1) to another. Then, whenever you use either printer, you have a greater number of printer fonts at your disposal. Use the "Downloading Fonts to Your Printer" Quick Steps to get to the HP Font Installer dialog box. Select a font from the list at the left side of the dialog box, select the Copy Fonts to New Port button, highlight the port, and select OK or press Enter. Then select the Copy button and the Exit button. Repeat this procedure to copy additional fonts.

---

**Note:** Word provides a special, easy-to-use help facility for the HP Font Installer dialog box. Select the Help button in either the Printer Setup dialog box or the Font Installer dialog box.

**203**

# What You Have Learned

▶ A *character* is the smallest unit of text in Word for Windows. A character is any letter, number, or special symbol.

▶ The easiest way to format characters is with the Ribbon. The Ribbon not only enables you to manipulate characters; it shows you how the characters are formatted. However, the Ribbon doesn't cover all formatting options.

▶ Using the Format **C**haracter command displays the Character dialog box, from which you can select a variety of formatting options: emphasizing characters, adjusting characters vertically or horizontally, hiding text, using superscripts and subscripts, and changing the font and point size of text.

▶ *Fonts* are families of typeface designs. Fonts can be serif or sans serif, or proportional or monospace. To view, add, or delete fonts, select the Run command from the Application Control menu. Then select Control Panel, select OK or press Enter, and double-click on the Fonts icon.

▶ The size of a character is measured in points. A 72-point character measures one inch from top to bottom.

**204**

# Advanced Formatting

## In This Chapter

- ▶ *Finding and replacing paragraph and character formats (including fonts and point sizes)*
- ▶ *Finding and replacing special symbols*
- ▶ *Adding special symbols to a document*
- ▶ *Creating bulleted and numbered lists*
- ▶ *Creating and changing snaking columns*

In the last few chapters, you learned the basics of Word for Windows document-wide, section, paragraph, and character formatting. This chapter completes the job with a variety of advanced formatting concepts.

You'll see that you can use the **E**dit **F**ind and **E**dit **R**eplace commands to find and replace more than text. Word also enables you to search for and replace paragraph and character formatting, nonprinting symbols, special symbols (covered later in this chapter), fonts, and point sizes.

Word enables you to create numbered or bulleted lists automatically. You can use the bullets that Word provides, or you can easily define a custom bullet.

You'll learn the ways to add special symbols (such as copyright and trademark symbols) to a document: via the **I**nsert **S**ymbol command or by inserting a symbol directly.

Finally, you'll see how to create documents with multiple columns and how to manipulate those columns.

# Finding and Replacing Formats and Symbols

As you have learned, a document can go through many changes—in content and in appearance. You saw how to select and manipulate text in order to edit the content of a document. Then, through formatting, you created a specific look for a specific document. In this section, you'll learn how to find an original format and replace it with a new format.

Suppose a company has hired a graphics designer to modernize its logo, stationery, and forms. Formats of all documents will change from indented paragraphs to block format, and all italicized text will be converted to boldface. If you're responsible for converting each document to the new format, you can start at the top of a document and manually change every occurrence, or you can use Word's **E**dit **F**ind and **E**dit **R**eplace commands to quickly make every change.

Most times, you'll search for formats, fonts, or symbols in order to replace them throughout a document, so we'll emphasize the **E**dit **R**eplace command in the next sections. However, there are times when you'll want to search without replacing. For example, what if you've taken a lunch break and upon reopening a document, you can't remember the last page or section in which you worked? You can look for the first occurrence of the old format, and then start replacing after that point.

## *Finding and Replacing Formats*

In Chapter 3, you searched for and replaced text, and in the last two chapters, you learned how to format paragraphs and characters. You can combine these two pieces of knowledge to search for paragraph and character formats and, if you want, to replace them with other formats. As you did in Chapter 3, you'll fill in either the Find dialog box (which is shown in Figure 8.1) or the Replace dialog box (shown in Figure 8.2) to determine the combination of the text and formats to be found or replaced. In this way, you can quickly change the appearance of a document.

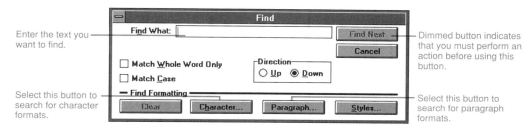

Enter the text you want to find.

Dimmed button indicates that you must perform an action before using this button.

Select this button to search for character formats.

Select this button to search for paragraph formats.

*Figure 8.1    The Find dialog box, which is used for finding text, formats, fonts, and symbols.*

**207**

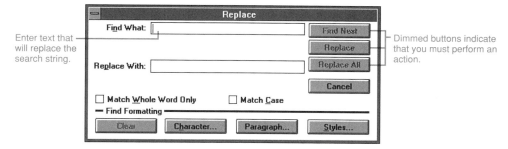

Enter text that will replace the search string.

Dimmed buttons indicate that you must perform an action.

*Figure 8.2    The Replace dialog box, which enables you to find and replace text and formats.*

You can specify a combination of paragraph and character formats to find and/or replace by selecting the Paragraph or Character button at the bottom of the Find dialog box. This reveals the Find Paragraph dialog box (shown in Figure 8.3) or the Find Character dialog box (shown in Figure 8.4), in which you specify search and/ or replacement criteria. When you first see either of these dialog boxes, no values are specified: The boxes next to the options are blank and the check boxes are shaded. Fill in these dialog boxes in the same way you defined the original formats. To put a value in an option box, type the value, display a list, or cycle through the values. When filling in a check box, be aware that it has three states:

checked, clear, or shaded. A checked box indicates that Word includes the presence of this value in its search. A cleared box indicates that Word will search for an absence of this value. A shaded box indicates that Word will not search for the absence or presence of this value. For example, to look for the next occurrence of a paragraph preceded by a page break, the Page Break Before check box must contain a check; to look for the next occurrence of a paragraph not preceded by a page break, the check box must be clear. If you don't want to include this paragraph format option in your search, make sure that the box is shaded. Once you have selected the formats for which to search, select OK or press Enter. Word redisplays the Find dialog box.

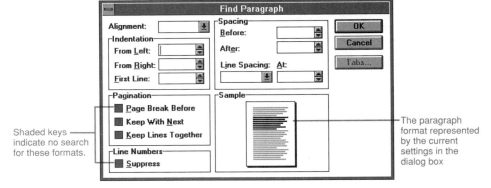

Shaded keys indicate no search for these formats.

The paragraph format represented by the current settings in the dialog box

*Figure 8.3   The Find Paragraph dialog box enables you to fill in specifications for the search.*

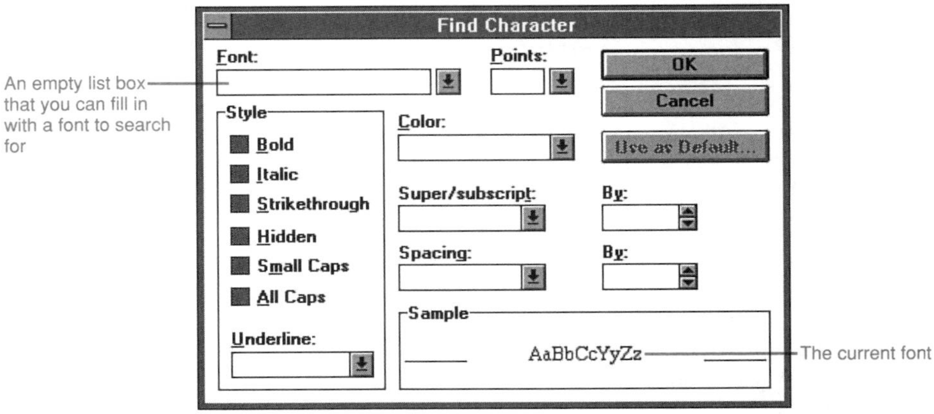

An empty list box that you can fill in with a font to search for

The current font

*Figure 8.4   The Find Character dialog box.*

Finding and Replacing Paragraph Formats

In our example, a company is in the process of changing the appearance of all its documents. Because new letterhead has replaced the old, some paragraph formats will also change. You also can use this opportunity to search for and replace text, as you learned in Chapter 3. To search for text only, fill in the Find What box. To search for formatting only, make sure that the Find What box is empty. Note that if you search for both paragraph formats and text, Word finds only the occurrences of formats *and* text that match the search criteria.

Use the following Quick Steps to search for paragraph formats and, optionally, text.

 **Finding Paragraph Formats**

| | |
|---|---|
| 1. Select part of the document to be searched; otherwise, Word searches the entire document. | If you have selected text, Word highlights it. |
| 2. From the Edit menu, select Find (Alt,E,F). | Word opens the Find dialog box. |
| 3. To search for text, enter it in the Find What box. | In order to make room for text, Word scrolls the text out of the box to the left as you type. |
| 4. To match on a whole-word basis or by case, place a check in the box next to the appropriate option. | Word surrounds your last choice with a dotted-line border. |
| 5. Select the Paragraph button at the bottom of the dialog box. | Word displays the Find Paragraph dialog box. |
| 6. Fill in the combination of formats for which you want to search (Figure 8.5). | Word changes the illustration in the Sample box. |
| 7. Select OK or press Enter. | Word returns to the Find dialog box. Notice that the formats you selected are displayed below the Find What box. |

**209**

8. Select Find Next.

In your document, Word finds the first occurrence after the insertion point of the formats and text for which you are looking. Word highlights the text. If the search is unsuccessful, Word displays a message.

9. To continue the search, repeat step 8. Otherwise, select Cancel.

Word returns to the current document.

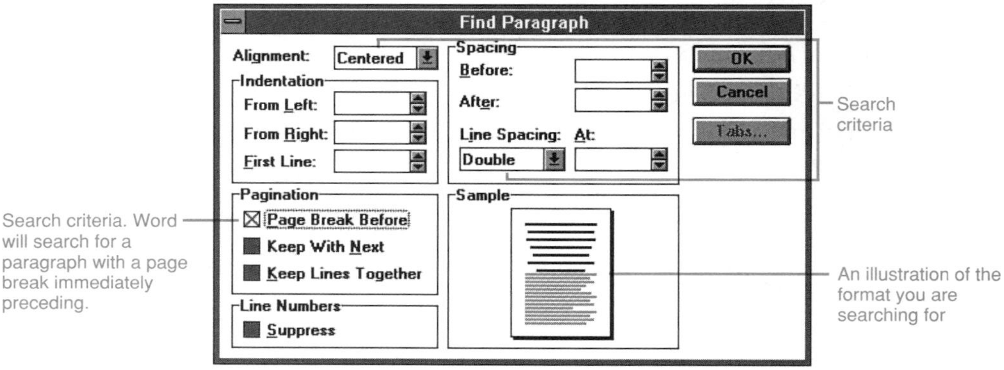

□

**210**

Search criteria. Word will search for a paragraph with a page break immediately preceding.

Search criteria

An illustration of the format you are searching for

*Figure 8.5    The Find Paragraph dialog box with search specifications.*

You'll probably use **E**dit **R**eplace more often than you'll use **E**dit **F**ind. For example, to modernize a document by changing from first-line paragraph indentation to block indentation, you would find all occurrences of first-line indentation and replace each with block indentation.

The main difference between finding formats and both finding and replacing them is that in the latter procedure you'll have to define the formats for which you are looking and the formats that will replace them. For this reason, the location of the insertion point in the Replace dialog box is very important. If the insertion point is in the Find What box (whether or not you type text to be found), Word displays the Find Paragraph dialog box when you select the Paragraph button; if the insertion point is in the Replace With box (whether or not you type text to replace the search string), Word displays the Replace Paragraph dialog box when you select the Paragraph button.

To search for and replace only text, fill in the Find What and Replace With boxes. To search for and replace only formatting, make sure that both the Find What and Replace With boxes are empty. To replace paragraph formats, use the following Quick Steps.

---

**Note:** If you search for and replace both paragraph formats and text, Word finds only the occurrences of formats *and* text that match the search criteria.

---

### *Q* Replacing Paragraph Formats

**211**

| | |
|---|---|
| 1. Select part of the document to be searched; otherwise, Word searches the entire document. | If you have selected text, Word highlights it. |
| 2. From the **Edit** menu, select the **R**eplace command (Alt, E,E). | Word displays the Replace dialog box. |
| 3. To search for text, enter it in the Find What box. | In order to make room for extra text, Word scrolls the text out of the box to the left as you type. |
| 4. To match on a whole-word basis or by case, place a check in the box next to the appropriate option. | Word surrounds your last choice with a border. |
| 5. To search for paragraph formats, select the Paragraph button at the bottom of the dialog box. | Word displays the Find Paragraph dialog box. |
| 6. Fill in the combination of formats for which you want to search. | Word changes the illustration in the Sample box. |
| 7. Select OK or press Enter. | Word returns to the Replace dialog box. The formats you selected are displayed below the Find What box. |
| 8. To replace the text search string with a replace string, enter it in the Replace With box. | In order to make room for text, Word scrolls the text out of the box to the left as you type. |

9. In the Replace with Formatting area at the bottom of the dialog box, select Paragraph.

   Word displays the Replace Paragraph dialog box (Figure 8.6).

10. Fill in the combination of formats for which you want to search.

    Word changes the example in the Sample box as you choose options.

11. Select OK or press Enter.

    Word returns to the Replace dialog box. Notice that the formats you selected are displayed below the Find What box and the Replace With box (Figure 8.7).

12. Select Find Next.

    Word finds the first occurrence for which you are looking and highlights it. If the search is unsuccessful, Word displays a message.

**212**

13. To replace this occurrence of found text and/or format, select Replace.

    Word replaces the text and/or format.

14. To replace all occurrences of found text and/or format, select Replace All.

    Word replaces the text and/or format.

15. To replace another combination of format and/or text, select Clear to clear the Find What box and the formats for which you are searching.

    Word dims the Clear box.

16. To stop searching and replacing, select Cancel.

    Word returns to the current document. □

### Finding and Replacing Character Formats

Word provides the means to search for and optionally replace character formats in conjunction with or separately from paragraph formatting. For example, as long as you are searching for indented paragraphs, you can look for a character format (for example, changing from italics to bold) to be replaced when you convert to block paragraphs. In addition, since you are already using **E**dit **F**ind, you can look for text as well.

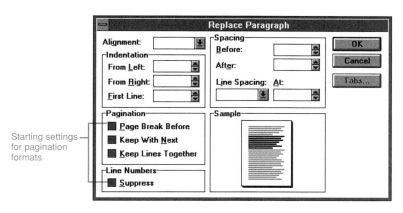

*Figure 8.6    The Replace Paragraph dialog box.*

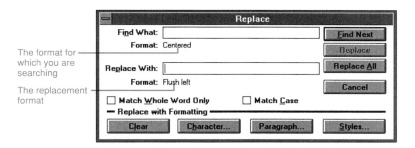

*Figure 8.7    The Replace dialog box with all the formats
that you have selected.*

The procedures for finding character formats are almost the same as those used in finding paragraph formats. Rather than selecting the Paragraph button at the bottom of the Find or Replace dialog boxes, you'll select Character. Just as the Find and Replace Paragraph dialog boxes are almost identical to the Paragraph dialog box, the Find and Replace Character dialog boxes are similar to the Character dialog box.

Use the following Quick Steps to search for character formats and optionally text.

 **Finding Character Formats**

1. Select part of the document to be searched; otherwise, Word searches the entire document.

   If you have selected text, Word highlights it.

**214**

2. From the Edit menu, select Find (Alt,E,F).

Word opens the Find dialog box.

3. To search for text, enter it in the Find What box.

In order to make room for text, Word scrolls the text out of the box to the left as you type.

4. To match on a whole-word basis or by case, place a check in the box next to the appropriate option.

Word surrounds your last choice with a dotted-line border.

5. To search for character formats, select the Character button at the bottom of the dialog box.

Word displays the Find Character dialog box.

6. Fill in the combination of formats for which you want to search.

Word changes the illustration in the Sample box.

7. Select OK or press Enter.

Word returns to the Find dialog box. Notice that the formats you selected are displayed below the Find What box (Figure 8.8).

8. Select Find Next.

In your document, Word finds the first occurrence after the insertion point of the formats and text for which you are looking. Word highlights the text. If the search is unsuccessful, Word displays a message.

9. To continue the search, repeat step 8. Otherwise, select Cancel.

Word returns to the current document.

☐

Just as you learned when replacing paragraph formats, you have to define the character formats for which you are looking and the character formats that will replace them. To replace character formats, use the following Quick Steps.

**Tip:** The position of the insertion point controls whether the Find Character or Replace Character dialog box is displayed.

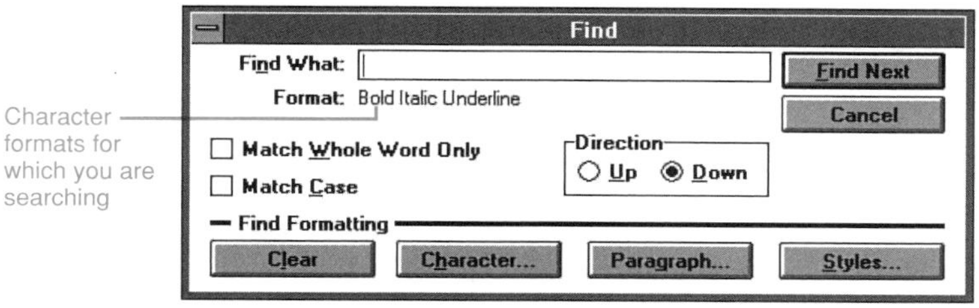

Figure 8.8    *The Find dialog box with the formats you specified.*

##  Replacing Character Formats

1. Select part of the document to be searched; otherwise, Word searches the entire document.

   If you have selected text, Word highlights it.

2. From the **E**dit menu, select the **R**eplace command (Alt, E,E).

   Word displays the Replace dialog box.

3. To search for text, enter it in the Find What box.

   In order to make room for text, Word scrolls the text out of the box to the left as you type.

4. To match on a whole-word basis or by case, place a check in the box next to the appropriate option.

   Word surrounds your last choice with a border.

5. To search for character formats, select the **C**haracter button at the bottom of the dialog box.

   Word displays the Find Character dialog box.

6. Fill in the combination of formats for which you want to search.

   Word changes the illustration in the Sample box.

7. Select OK or press Enter.

   Word returns to the Replace dialog box. The formats you selected are displayed below the Find What box.

**215**

8. To replace the text search string with a replace string, enter it in the Replace With box.

In order to make room for text, Word scrolls the text out of the box to the left as you type.

9. In the Replace with Formatting area at the bottom of the dialog box, select Character.

Word displays the Replace Character dialog box (Figure 8.9).

10. Fill in the combination of formats for which you want to search.

Word changes the example in the Sample box as you choose options.

11. Select OK or press Enter.

Word returns to the Replace dialog box. Notice that the formats you selected are displayed below the Find What box and the Replace With box (Figure 8.10).

12. Select Find Next.

Word finds the first occurrence for which you are looking and highlights it. If the search is unsuccessful, Word displays a message.

13. To replace this occurrence of found text and/or format, select Replace.

Word replaces the text and/or format.

14. To replace all occurrences of found text and/or format, select Replace All.

Word replaces the text and/or format.

15. To replace another combination of format and/or text, select Clear to clear all your choices.

Word dims the Clear box.

16. To stop searching and replacing, select Cancel.

Word returns to the current document. □

## *Using Shortcut Keys to Find and Replace Formats*

When you search for and replace paragraph and character formatting, you can also fill in the Find What and Replace With boxes in the Find and Replace dialog boxes with shortcut keys to represent fonts, point sizes, and other character formats. For example, press Ctrl-B to add bold to your search or replace string. Press Ctrl-F repeatedly to cycle through the list of fonts that are installed on your computer.

However, if this list is long and you pass your choice, you must cycle through the list again. For a complete list of formats and shortcut keys, see Table 8.1.

---

**Tip:** Word will search for and replace spaces, just as it does characters. For example, it is standard practice to insert one space between sentences. If you inadvertently inserted two spaces, you can have Word search for two spaces and replace them with one. In the Replace dialog box, just fill in the Find What text box by pressing the spacebar twice, and fill in the Replace With text box by pressing the spacebar once. Remember, though, that if you select the Replace All button, Word will search for *all* instances of two spaces and replace them with one space, wherever the two spaces occur.

---

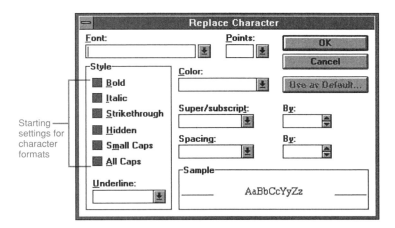

*Figure 8.9    The Replace Character dialog box.*

*Figure 8.10    The Replace dialog box with all the formats that you selected.*

Table 8.1    *Shortcut find-and-replace keys.*

| Keys | Format |
|------|--------|
| Ctrl-A | All Caps |
| Ctrl-B | Bold |
| Ctrl-D | Double Underline |
| Ctrl-F | Font |
| Ctrl-H | Hidden Text |
| Ctrl-I | Italic |
| Ctrl-K | Small Caps |
| Ctrl-P | Point Size |
| Ctrl-U | Single Underline |
| Ctrl-W | Words Only Underline |
| Ctrl-= | Superscript |
| Ctrl-Shift-= | Subscript |

**218**

## Finding and Replacing Symbols

Word also allows you to find and optionally replace symbols in the document. Once again, fill in the Find What and Replace With boxes in the Find and Replace dialog boxes, but this time insert a code for a special symbol. For example, to replace a trademark symbol with a copyright symbol, just search for the trademark symbol and replace it with the copyright symbol. For a complete list of key codes, refer to Table 8.2.

Table 8.2    *Find and search key codes.*

| This Key Code | Represents |
|---------------|------------|
| ? | Any character (e.g., ?*elief* looks for *relief, belief,* etc.) |
| ^- | An optional hyphen |
| ^? | Text ending in a question mark |
| ^^ | A caret (^) mark |
| ^~ | A nonbreaking hyphen |
| ^0*nnn* | A character from the ANSI character set, where *nnn* is the code for the ANSI character |

| This Key Code | Represents |
|---|---|
| ^1 | A graphic |
| ^2 | Automatic footnote reference mark |
| ^3 | Footnote separator |
| ^5 | Annotation reference mark |
| ^9 | A tab symbol |
| ^10 | A linefeed symbol (a character that tells the printer to move to the next line) (¶) |
| ^11 | A newline symbol, which is also known as a line break mark (↵) |
| ^12 | A page or section break symbol |
| ^13 | A carriage return symbol, also called a paragraph mark (¶) |
| ^14 | A column break symbol |
| ^19 | A field symbol |
| ^21 | An end of field symbol |
| ^c | The contents of the Clipboard |
| ^d | Manual page break or section break |
| ^m | Search text to be used as part of the replace text |
| ^n | Line break (see newline symbol) |
| ^p | Paragraph mark (see carriage return symbol) |
| ^s | Nonbreaking space |
| ^t | Tab mark |
| ^w | White space |

**219**

# Adding Special Characters

Sometimes you'll need to add a special character (like a copyright symbol or trademark) to your document. Special characters, which are not on your keyboard, and standard keyboard characters make up a character set. There are more characters in most character sets than there are keys on the keyboard, so Word provides two methods to add special characters: the **S**ymbol command on the **I**nsert menu and the direct insertion of an ANSI (American National Standards Institute) symbol via the numeric keypad.

When you use **Insert Symbol** to display the Symbol dialog box, shown in Figure 8.11, notice that one symbol has a thicker border. If you select OK or press Enter now, this symbol is inserted into your document. If you press and hold down the left mouse button or press an arrow key, that symbol is "magnified" so that you can see it in detail.

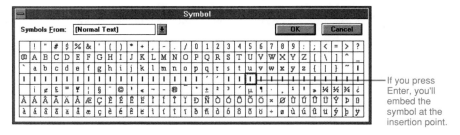

If you press Enter, you'll embed the symbol at the insertion point.

*Figure 8.11   The Symbol dialog box for (Normal Text).*

Most standard text fonts have their own unique set of ANSI symbols—some extensive and some not. When you find a font that has the symbol you need, use the following Quick Steps to embed the symbol. If you wish to insert a symbol from a particular font, make sure that the surrounding text is of the same font. If the symbol and the surrounding text don't match in fonts, and if you later change fonts, the symbol might change in appearance.

A few fonts, which may include some text characters, don't use the ANSI character set. A prime example of this type of font is Zapf Dingbats, which is often used to insert special symbols to emphasize parts of documents. Unfortunately, not all of Word's character formatting capabilities are available for enhancing these non-ANSI symbols. However, you can apply some formats, such as bold and italics. The following Quick Steps show you how to use the **Symbol** command.

 **Adding Special Characters to a Document**

1. Move the insertion point where you want the symbol to be placed. Then select Insert and **Symbol** (Alt,I,S).

   Word displays the Symbol dialog box. The (Normal Text) symbols are those from the font at the insertion point.

2. In the Symbols From box, type the name of the font from which you want this symbol, or select the list arrow (the underlined down arrow) to display a list of fonts from which you can select.

Word changes the symbol display as you select the font.

3. Select the desired character by highlighting your choice. Either move the mouse pointer to your choice and click the left mouse button or press any combination of arrow keys.

As you select a choice, Word automatically displays your choice in a magnified view.

4. Select OK or press Enter.

Word returns to your document and inserts the symbol. □

**221**

You can also use the ANSI symbol set as a source for special characters. To enter a special character at the insertion point, first press the NumLock key so that NUM appears in the Status bar. While holding down the Alt key, enter the four-digit code using the *numeric keypad*. (This procedure will not work if you use the keyboard number keys.) When you release the Alt key, the symbol should appear on-screen at the position of the insertion point. Table 8.3 contains a list of commonly used special characters.

*Table 8.3    Commonly used ANSI special characters.*

| ANSI Code | Character | Description |
|-----------|-----------|-------------|
| Alt-0145 | ' | Starting single quotation mark |
| Alt-0146 | ' | Ending single quotation mark |
| Alt-0147 | " | Starting double quotation mark |
| Alt-0148 | " | Ending double quotation mark |
| Alt 0150 | – | En dash |
| Alt-0151 | — | Em dash |
| Alt-0162 | ¢ | Cent sign |
| Alt-0169 | © | Copyright |
| Alt-0174 | ® | Registered trademark |

*continues*

*Table 8.3    continued*

| ANSI Code | Character | Description |
|-----------|-----------|-------------|
| Alt-0177 | ± | Plus/minus sign |
| Alt-0178 | $^2$ | Small 2 |
| Alt-0179 | $^3$ | Small 3 |
| Alt-0182 | ¶ | Paragraph mark |
| Alt-0188 | $^1/_4$ | 1/4 |
| Alt-0189 | $^1/_2$ | 1/2 |
| Alt-0190 | $^3/_4$ | 3/4 |
| Alt-0247 | ÷ | Division sign |

# Creating Bulleted and Numbered Lists

One of the most effective ways to emphasize text in a list is to precede each list item with a bullet or a number. Normally, you'd use numbered lists to show the steps in the order in which you perform them to accomplish a task. Bulleted lists emphasize points that are in no particular order.

## *Creating a Bulleted List*

Word provides a shortcut way to create both bulleted and numbered lists using the Tools menu and the Bullets and Numbering command. Then, when you produce a bulleted list, you can use either a standard bullet from the Bullet Character box or a special bullet from the Symbol dialog box. For example, if you publish a newsletter for contract bridge players, you could use hearts, spades, clubs, or diamonds for bullets.

> Click on the Bulleted List button to create a bulleted list from one or more selected paragraphs. Each paragraph becomes an item in the list.

The following Quick Steps show you how to create bulleted lists.

 **Creating Bulleted Lists**

| | | |
|---|---|---|
| 1. | Select the part of the document that you want to have bullets. | Word highlights the selected text. |
| 2. | From the Tools menu, select the **B**ullets and Numbering command (Alt,O,B). | Word opens the Bullets and Numbering dialog box (Figure 8.12). |
| 3. | If the Bullets button is not filled in, select it. | If needed, Word changes the dialog box. |
| 4. | To select a standard bullet, select the type of bullet that you want from the Bullet Character box. Move the mouse pointer to the appropriate bullet or press ← or →. | Word highlights the selected bullet and changes the document in the Sample box. |
| 5. | To choose a special bullet, select **N**ew Bullet. | Word opens the Symbol dialog box. |
| 6. | Select a different bullet and then select OK or press Enter. | Word returns to the Bullets and Numbering dialog box. Your new bullet symbol is highlighted. |
| 7. | To change the size of the bullet, either enter a value in the Point Size box or use the arrow button to display the list from which you can choose. Valid values are from 4 to 127. | As you select a new point size, Word changes the illustration in the Bullet Character box. |
| 8. | Check or clear the **R**eplace Only Bullets box. | To replace bullets in previously bulleted lists, place a check in the box. To place bullets in front of text that you selected, clear the box. |
| 9. | To format each list item with hanging indents (a good option for bulleted lists), check the **H**anging Indent box. | Word shows the format in the Sample box. |

**223**

**10.** To adjust the amount of indentation, either enter a value in the By box or use the arrow buttons to cycle through valid values (from −22 through +22).

Word shows the format in the Sample box.

**11.** Select OK or **R**emove.

Word returns to the current document. If you have selected OK, Word applies the bullets; if you have selected Remove, Word removes the bullets from the selected text. □

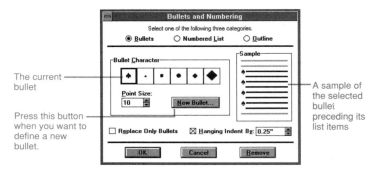

The current bullet

Press this button when you want to define a new bullet.

A sample of the selected bullet preceding its list items

*Figure 8.12    The Bullets and Numbering dialog box from which you can define bulleted and numbered lists as well as special bullet characters.*

## Creating a Numbered List

To create a numbered list, use **T**ools **B**ullets and Numbering. This time, however, fill in the Numbered List button. When Word displays the Bullets and Numbering dialog box for a Numbered List (shown in Figure 8.13), you can select a numbering format from the Format box. To change the Separator, which is the symbol between the number and the beginning of the list item, select from the list. To start the numbering at a specific number, enter a value in the **S**tart At box (Word's default is 1). To replace numbers in previously numbered lists, place a check in the Replace Only Numbers box. To place numbers in front of text that you selected, clear the box. To format each list item with hanging indents (a good option for numbered lists), check the Hanging Indent box. Every time you change a format, Word shows the format in the Sample box. If you select OK, Word returns to the document and applies the bullets. If you select **R**emove, Word removes the bullets from the selected text.

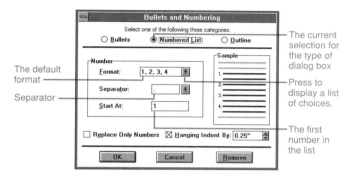

*Figure 8.13   The Bullets and Numbering dialog box for a Numbered List.*

Click on the Numbered List button to create a numbered list from one or more selected paragraphs. Each paragraph becomes an item in the list.

# Using Multiple Columns in a Document

Not every document consists of text that extends between the margins. Just think of your favorite newspaper or the last brochure you received. To create a newsletter or any document with multiple columns of equal width, you'll have to know how to use columns. The columns that Word creates are called *snaking columns,* which means the text continues from the bottom of one column up to the top of the next.

If you are combining single-column format, which is the format you've used so far (one line of text stretching from left to right margin), and multiple columns, insert a section break between the two types of column format. Type and correct all your text before formatting columns so that you can see how the column width and spacing looks on the page without worrying about the content of each column. Then, with Format Columns, select the number of columns.

 Click on the Text Columns button to define the number of columns (from one to six).

While the Columns dialog box (shown in Figure 8.14) is displayed, fill in the Apply To box with information about how you wish to apply the format: to the whole document, to selected sections (if you have selected text), or from the insertion point through the rest of the document (if you have not selected text).

To start a new column at the insertion point, select Selected Text in the Apply To box. Then check the Start New Column box.

Use the following Quick Steps to add columns to a document and to change the column formats.

 **Adding Columns to a Document**

1. Select a section of text to become columns or move the insertion point to the section in which you want to create columns.

   Word highlights the selected text.

2. Select the Format menu and the Columns command (Alt, T,O) or double-click on the section marker.

   Word displays the Columns dialog box (Figure 8.14).

3. Enter a value in the Number of Columns box or use the arrow keys to cycle through the valid values (from 1 to 100).

   Word changes the document in the Sample box and calculates the width of the columns and the space between the columns.

4. Enter a value in the Space Between box or use the arrow keys to cycle through the valid values (from 0 to 22 inches).

   Word changes the document in the Sample box.

5. To insert a vertical line between the columns, check the **L**ine Between box.

   Word changes the document in the Sample box.

6. Select how to apply formatting in the **A**pply To box.

   Depending on your selection, Word changes the document in the Sample box.

7. If you have completed filling in the box, select OK or press Enter.

   Word returns to your document and creates the columns as you desire. If you have checked Start New Column for selected text, Word places section marks at the beginning and end of the selected text. □

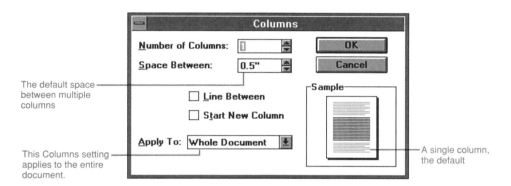

**Figure 8.14**  *The Columns dialog box, which allows you to define the number of columns for this section of your document.*

> ✎ **Note:** In Normal or Draft modes, you won't be able to see multiple columns; you'll have to use Page Layout mode or Print Preview to see the result.

## Changing Column Widths

While you are looking at your columns and text in Page Layout mode, you might decide that the lines of text are not long enough (generally, there should be at least 20 characters on a line), and you may want to make the columns wider. The easiest way to change the column widths and the spacing between columns is to use the Ruler. Since Word formats columns in equal widths, changing one of the columns will change all of them. However, you can use the Table menu to create columns of uneven widths. You'll learn about setting up tables in Chapter 10.

## Changing Column Width

1. Select the **V**iew menu and **P**age Layout to ensure that you are in Page Layout mode. If you don't see the Ruler, turn it on by selecting **V**iew and making sure that there is a check mark next to **R**uler.

   Word returns to the current document, displays columns (if you have defined columns) and displays the Ruler.

2. Click on the Margin Scale Symbol on the left side of the Ruler.

   Word changes the Ruler to show the margins of all columns (Figure 8.15).

3. Move the mouse pointer to one of the inner column marks and drag it to a new position on the Ruler.

   Word adjusts all column widths to match the new width.

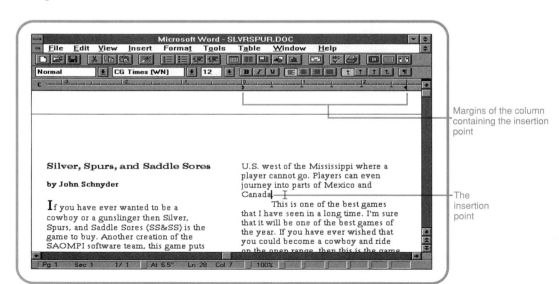

Margins of the column containing the insertion point

The insertion point

*Figure 8.15   The Ruler with two columns defined.*

## *Breaking Columns*

If you want to end one column (perhaps because the subject matter changes) and start a new one, you can enter a column break. When the insertion point is at the location where you want to end a column, select the Insert menu and the Break command (Alt,I,B). Fill in the Column Break button, and select OK or press Enter.

# What You Have Learned

▶ Through the **E**dit **F**ind command and the **E**dit **R**eplace command, you can not only search for and replace text but also search for and replace character and paragraph formatting and special symbols.

▶ Word provides shortcut keys so that you can find and replace character formats. Word also provides key codes so that you can find and replace characters, formats, and special symbols.

▶ There are two ways to insert special symbols in a document—via the **I**nsert menu and **S**ymbol command or by pressing the Alt key and numeric keypad keys.

▶ You can also emphasize text by converting it to a bulleted or numbered list. Either select the Bulleted List or Numbered List button from the Toolbar or use the **T**ools **B**ullets and Numbering command.

▶ To define snaking columns, use Forma**t C**olumns, click on the Text Columns button from the Toolbar, or double-click on the section marker. You can combine single-column and multiple-column formats by inserting a section break.

# Previewing and Printing Documents

## In This Chapter

- ▶ *Defining the active printer*
- ▶ *Previewing and realigning a document before printing*
- ▶ *Zooming a document*
- ▶ *Printing part or all of a document on a printer or to a file*
- ▶ *Learning about Word for Windows' printing options*
- ▶ *Solving common printer problems*

In Chapter 2, you learned how to view your document using the **F**ile Print Pre**v**iew command. Once you were satisfied with the document, you could print it with the **F**ile **P**rint command. In this chapter, we will go into further detail about both these commands and related options and features.

In this chapter, you will learn about changing the current active printer. This is done via *printer drivers,* which are files that contain information about how a specific printer works with Word.

The Print Preview feature enables you not only to view a document's format but to change positions of margins, headers and footers. When you change the appearance of a document in this way, you can immediately see the results.

Word provides several print options that allow for customization of the print job. For example, you can print just the information associated with a document, a range of pages within a document, or multiple copies of a document (either collated or not), or you can print to a file. In addition, you can customize other printer and printing options via the **Tools Options** command and the Options dialog box for the Print category.

This chapter concludes with a short troubleshooting guide. If your printer does not print, refer to this checklist for solutions to most common printing problems.

# Defining the Active Printer

**232**

At installation, you informed Word for Windows about your printers. (You had already installed the printers under Windows.) Word then installed the necessary printer drivers, telling Word how to communicate with the printer. If you have more than one printer installed, you can check to see which printer is active by selecting the **P**rint Setup command from the **F**ile menu. The highlighted printer is active. To verify, select Setup from the Print Setup dialog box. The name of the active printer is displayed in the Printer box.

You may want to change the active printer from one printer to another. For example, you may change from a dot-matrix printer, on which you print draft copies, to a laser printer, on which you print the final draft of a document. Or, you may want to change from a laser printer to a dot-matrix printer loaded with continuous-feed paper so that you can print forms on the printer having the continuous-feed paper.

To select a printer, you don't have to have an active document. Select File Print Setup (Alt,F,R). When Word displays the Print Setup dialog box, shown in Figure 9.1, all the printer drivers—active and inactive—are listed. When you select a printer, Word also shows you its *printer port*, the place in the back of your computer where you plug in your printer. Ports are communications gateways through which information from one part of the computer system flows to another part. There are two types of printer ports: parallel (designated as LPT, which stands for *line printer*) and serial (called COM, which stands for *communications*). Most laser printers can use either type of port.

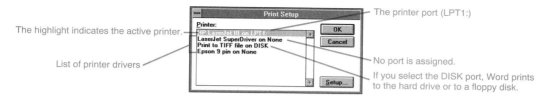

*Figure 9.1   The Print Setup dialog box with a list of
available printer drivers.*

Word also supports the port DISK, which enables document files (along with all formats) to be "printed" to the hard drive so that they can be printed later. Printing to files is covered later in this chapter.

Your computer can have more than one of each type of port. Multiple ports are referred to as LPT1, LPT2, COM1, COM2, and so on. Word allows you to connect multiple printers to multiple ports. You can also assign more than one printer to the same port, but only one of the printer drivers for that port can be active at a time.

**233**

To display or change options for the active printer, select the Setup button in the Print Setup dialog box. The Setup dialog box, shown in Figures 9.2 and 9.3, enables you to customize the printer driver to better serve your needs. See your printer manual for information about the options you can select for your printer.

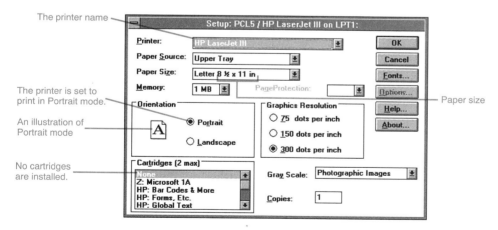

*Figure 9.2   The Setup dialog box for a Hewlett-Packard
LaserJet III printer.*

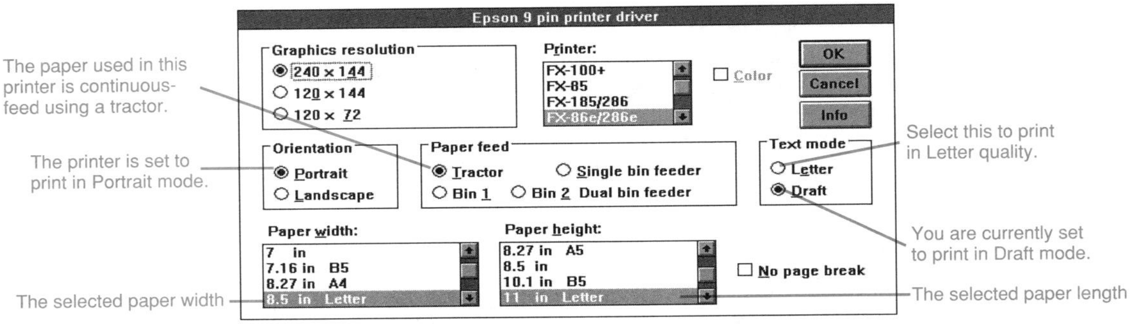

The paper used in this printer is continuous-feed using a tractor.

The printer is set to print in Portrait mode.

The selected paper width

Select this to print in Letter quality.

You are currently set to print in Draft mode.

The selected paper length

**Figure 9.3** *The Setup dialog box for an Epson FX 86E 9-pin dot-matrix printer.*

If you have more than one printer driver installed, you can select the printer that you want to use when you print. Use the following Quick Steps to select an active printer driver.

**234**

 **Selecting an Active Printer Driver**

1. From the File menu, select Print Setup (Alt,F,R).

   Setup dialog box, which lists all the available printer drivers. Note that the highlighted driver indicates the active printer. None indicates that no port is assigned to this printer.

2. To replace the current active printer with another, select its name. If the list of printers is too long to be displayed in the box, click on the up and down arrows on the scroll bar to move through the list.

   Word highlights your selection.

3. To display or change options for the selected printer, select Setup.

   Word displays a Setup dialog box for the printer you have just selected. Your Setup dialog box may look different from the examples in this book.

4. Select OK or press Enter.

   Word returns to the Print Setup dialog box.

5. Select OK or press Enter.　　Word returns to the
　　　　　　　　　　　　　　　　document window.　　　☐

　　　To install, configure, or remove a printer, refer to your Windows documentation. All these actions take place from within the Windows Control Panel.

# Previewing Your Document Before Printing

As you learned in Chapter 2, the **File** Print Preview command lets you look at your document's format before you print. Word reduces the page so that it fits on your computer screen. You may not be able to recognize words and characters, but you can see the page's format—how paragraphs, titles, headers, footers, and other parts of the document are positioned on the page. Print Preview lets you adjust margins and the position of headers and footers, but it doesn't let you format or edit text. You can also access some commands from within the **File**, **V**iew, Forma**t**, **T**ools, and **H**elp menus. For example, select Format Page Setup to set specific margin dimensions.

　　　To display the Print Preview window, select File Print Preview (Alt,F,V). Depending on the way the last document was viewed in Print Preview mode, Word displays one or two pages of your document, as shown in Figure 9.4.

　　　At the top of the Print Preview window are command buttons, which you can use to work on the document. Click on a button with the mouse, or, from the keyboard, press Alt and the underlined letter displayed with the command. For example, to print the document, click on the Print button or press Alt-P. Here is an overview of the command buttons in the Print Preview window:

　　　*Print*—Click on this button to print a document from this window. This **Print** command is the same command as that on the **File** menu.

　　　*Margins*—Click on this button to change positioning of headers, footers, and margins. For a complete description, see the next section of this chapter.

*One Page/Two Pages*—Click on this button to display either one page or two pages of your document. Depending on the way you are viewing your document in Page Preview, the button is either labeled Two Pages (if you are looking at a single page) or One Page (if you are looking at two pages at a time).

*Cancel/Close*—The Cancel button returns you to your document. When you have made changes to the document using the Margins command (see the following discussion), this button changes to a Close button. You also have limited access to several of the commands from the menus. The options that aren't available to you are shown dimmed.

Next to the Cancel/Close button is the current page number. And on the right side of the Print Preview window is a vertical scroll bar, which you can use to display the previous page or the next page in the document. You can also press PgUp or PgDn to move through the document.

**236**

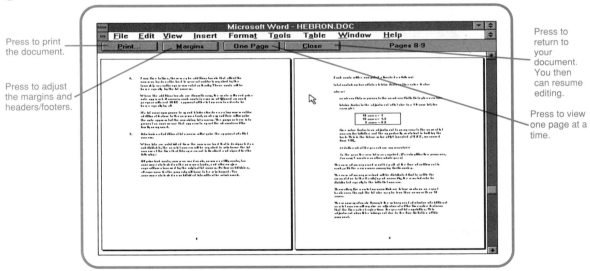

Press to print the document.

Press to adjust the margins and headers/footers.

Press to return to your document. You then can resume editing.

Press to view one page at a time.

*Figure 9.4    A sample Print Preview display of two pages of a document.*

## Changing Margins, Headers, and Footers in Print Preview Mode

While you're in Print Preview mode, you can change the positions of headers, footers, and margins. This is a good way to look at the formats of a document as you change them. When you select **M**argins, you'll see lines (representing margins) and rectangles (representing headers and footers) on the page being displayed (see Figure 9.5). If Print Preview is displaying two pages, only one page will have lines and/or rectangles. Press PgUp or PgDn to move the lines to the previous or next page, respectively.

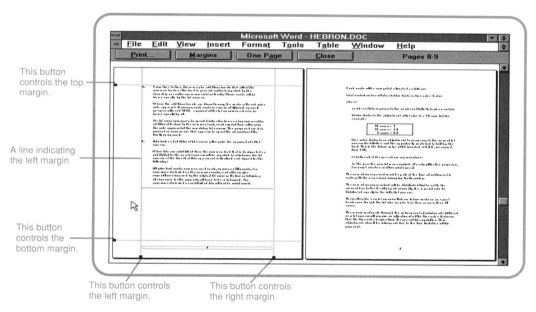

This button controls the top margin.

A line indicating the left margin

This button controls the bottom margin.

This button controls the left margin.

This button controls the right margin.

*Figure 9.5    Margins displayed in Print Preview mode.*

237

To make an adjustment, point at the block at the end of the line or anywhere within a rectangle. When the mouse pointer looks like two crosshairs, drag the line or rectangle to a new location. Alternatively, press the Tab key repeatedly until the mouse pointer (crosshairs) is positioned over the line or rectangle that you want to move. Then press any combination of arrow keys to move the line or rectangle. When you have completed the changes, remain in Print Preview mode and select the Tools menu and the Repaginate Now command (Alt,O,A) to repaginate.

Use the following Quick Steps to adjust margins, headers, and/or footers for the current document while in Print Preview mode.

### Q Changing Margins, Headers, and Footers in Print Preview Mode

1. From the File menu, select the Print Preview command (Alt,F,V).

   Word displays the current document in Print Preview mode.

2. Select Margins.

   Word adds lines and rectangles to one page of the document.

3. Move the mouse pointer or press Tab to select a line or rectangle.

   If you use the mouse pointer, its shape changes to crosshairs (Figure 9.6). If you press Tab, Word changes the color of the margin lines to white, making the margin lines match the background of the screen. Although you can't see the lines, the rectangles and the crosshairs mouse pointer remain their original colors. This color change ensures that you know the "active" margin line. When you move the selected margin line, it changes back to its original color.

4. Either drag the mouse pointer or press any combination of arrow keys to move the selected object to its new position.

   Word changes the appearance of your document.

5. Repeat steps 3 and 4 until you have completed changing the margins, headers, and footers. Then select Margins again.

   Word leaves Margins mode, removing the lines and rectangles from the display.

   □

**238**

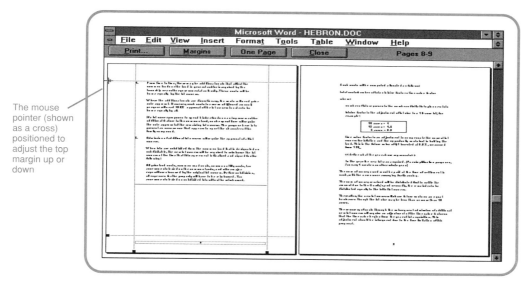

The mouse pointer (shown as a cross) positioned to adjust the top margin up or down

**Figure 9.6    The mouse pointer positioned to change a margin.**

**239**

# Zooming a Document

Another way of previewing your document is to use the **View Z**oom command. You can view your document up to twice its normal size, down to one-quarter its size, and many sizes between these two extremes. Word's default zoom setting is 100%.

Word also offers options to zoom the document based on its widest line or to display another version of Print Preview. However, unlike Print Preview, the Zoom Whole Page button on the Toolbar allows you to edit your document.

> Click on the Zoom Whole Page button to display a document, page by page, on the screen. Although this looks like Print Preview, you can edit the document and change the left and right margin settings.

Click on the Zoom 100 Percent button to display a document in normal view and at full size. This is the default zoom setting.

Click on the Zoom Page Width button to display the width of a page in this document.

Table 9.1 presents Word's zoom options and describes how to get them.

*Table 9.1   Magnification options.*

| Select | Description |
| --- | --- |
| Page Width button | Displays the widest line within the dimensions of the document window. |
| Whole Page button | Displays the entire page within the document window. This is the counterpart to **File** Print Preview. |
| 200% option button | Displays the document at twice its normal size. |
| 100% option button | Displays the document in its normal size. This is the default. |
| 75% option button | Displays the document at three-quarters its normal size. |
| 50% option button | Displays the document at half its normal size. |
| Custom box | Displays the document in a size that you determine. Select any size from 25% to 200%. |

# Printing Your Document

After using **File** Print Preview to view your document (and possibly to change its margins, header, and footers), you can print it.

In Chapter 2, you learned about Word's printing options and how to print a document using the defaults. Now you'll review that procedure and learn several ways to customize printing. First, select either the File-Print command (Alt,F,P or Ctrl-Shift-F12) or the Print button from the Print Preview window. Word displays the Print dialog box, shown in Figure 9.7, from which you can change the options described in the next sections.

> **Tip:** If the **P**rint and the Print Preview commands are dimmed, check to make sure that you have an active printer.

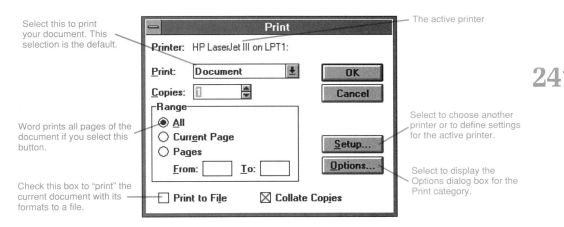

Select this to print your document. This selection is the default.

The active printer

Word prints all pages of the document if you select this button.

Select to choose another printer or to define settings for the active printer.

Check this box to "print" the current document with its formats to a file.

Select to display the Options dialog box for the Print category.

*Figure 9.7    The Print dialog box with the default options.*

At the top of the dialog box, Word displays the name of the active printer and the port to which it is attached. You learned at the beginning of this chapter how to define an active printer.

## *Printing Selected Parts of Your Document*

In Chapter 2, you learned how to print an entire document using the defaults. In this section, you'll see how to print information that is attached to your document, selected pages or ranges of pages, or multiple copies of the document. This is useful when you are testing the format or layout of one or two pages in a long document. Why print the entire document when a range of pages will do?

241

### Printing the Entire Document or Information About a Document

Using the Print box in the Print dialog box, you can choose to print either the entire document or information that is attached to the document. The default selection is Document—for printing the entire document. Select the down arrow to see the other choices: summary information, annotations (comments about a document), styles (paragraph formats covered in Chapter 11), glossary entries, and key assignments (macro names, the keys they're assigned to, and a description). For a description of annotations, see the *Microsoft Word for Windows User's Guide.* For glossaries and macros, see Chapter 12. Click on the list arrow to open the Print list box and make a selection. Then select OK or press Enter.

### Printing Multiple Copies of a Document

In the Copies box, click on the up or down arrow to cycle through the values (between 1 and 32767), or type a value in the box. Then select OK or press Enter.

When you print more than one copy of a document, Word's default is to print an entire document from the first page through the last and then start all over again with the next complete document. If you clear the Collate Copies check box, Word prints all the copies of the first page, then all the copies of the second page, and so on until it has printed all the copies of the last page.

> **FYIdea:** To save time when printing multiple copies on some printers (such as laser printers), rather than typing the number of copies in the Copies box, follow this procedure: Select File Print Setup. When Word displays the Print Setup dialog box, select Setup. At the bottom of the box, type the desired number of copies in the Copies box. Then select OK or press Enter. This procedure downloads only a single copy rather than multiple copies. However, Word prints multiple copies of the first page, then multiple copies of the second page, and so on. This procedure ignores the Collate Copies check box setting.

### Printing a Range of Pages

You can print the entire document, the current page, selected text, or a range of pages. To print the entire document, you don't have to make any changes, because All is the default.

To print just the page in which the insertion point is located, select Current Page. If you selected text to print, instead of Current Page, you'll see Selection. Select the circle next to Selection, and select OK or press Enter to print selected text.

To print specific pages, follow this procedure: In the From box, type the number of the first page to be printed. In the To box, enter the number of the last page to be printed. Select OK or press Enter to start printing. To print just one page, you can select Current Page to print the current page; otherwise, enter the number of the page that you want to print in both the From and To boxes. To print from a specific page to the end of the document, fill in the From box with the number of the first page to be printed and leave the To box blank. To print from the beginning of the document to a specific page, fill in the To box with the number of the last page to be printed.

### Printing to a File

Check the Print to File box to print this document to file rather than to the printer. This means that you have saved the document with its print format and can print it at a later time. This topic is described in detail later in the chapter.

**243**

## *Additional Printing Options*

Remember that Word provides an Options dialog box for the Print category, which is shown in Figure 9.8. From the File menu, select Print (Alt,F,P or Ctrl-Shift-F12). When Word displays the Print dialog box, select Options. You won't use the options on the Options dialog box as much as the options in the Print dialog box. You'll be more likely to set these just once or rarely. For example, in Chapter 5, you saw how Widow/Orphan Control works. You'll probably want this setting for every document, and once you've set it, you won't have to change it again.

The options on the Options dialog box for the Print category are:

***D**raft Output*—If you check this box, Word prints a document without graphics or text formatting, such as italics or boldface. Because Word doesn't need to spend processing time on text formatting, printing is usually faster, depending on the printer you are using. Experiment to see if this option is faster for your active printer.

*Reverse Print Order*—If you check this box, Word prints the document from the last page to the first. When you are using a printer that stacks pages face up after printing, select this option to save yourself the trouble of reordering your document.

*Update Fields*—If you check this box, Word updates field results in the document before printing occurs. For example, if you embed the system date in a header, a check means that Word always embeds the current system date. *Field Codes* prints field codes (for example, {DATE}) instead of field results (for example, February 17, 1992). The Insert Field command lists all Word field codes. For more information, refer to the *Microsoft Word for Windows User's Guide.*

*Summary Info* prints a separate page of information about the document. Note that this information is the same as that resulting from the File Summary Info command and the Summary Info option in the Print box of the Print dialog box.

*Annotations* prints annotations (comments or notes that are added to a document) after printing the document.

*Hidden Text* prints the document, including the hidden text.

If you have installed an envelope feeder for the active printer, place a check in the Printer's Envelope Feeder has been Installed check box. Otherwise, leave the check box clear. Chapter 14 describes printing envelopes.

244

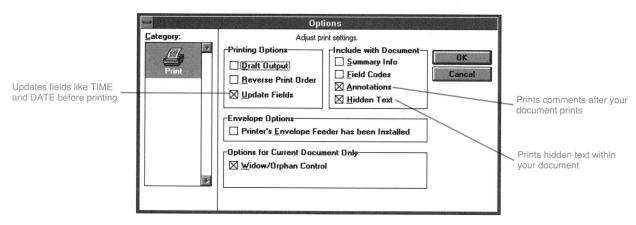

*Figure 9.8    The Options dialog box for the Print category.*

## *Printing to a File*

Most times, you'll print a document on a printer. However, there are times when you'll want to print a document, including all its print formats, to a file. For example, you might be working on several files that you want to print at the same time. If you are visiting a site that doesn't have the same brand of printer that you normally use or has no printer at all, save the print file and copy it onto a floppy disk. When you get back to your office, print on your own printer. Conversely, if you create a document to be printed at a remote site, save your document to a floppy disk and print it later.

Use the following Quick Steps to print the current document to file.

 **Printing to a File**

| | |
|---|---|
| 1. From the File menu, select the Print command (Alt,F,P or Ctrl-Shift-F12). | Word displays the Print dialog box. |
| 2. Select the print options you desire and place a check in the Print to File box. | Word places a border around the last option that you select. |
| 3. Select OK or press Enter. | Word returns to your document, displays a message that it is printing to file, and then asks you for an output file name in the Print To File dialog box (Figure 9.9). |
| 4. Type a unique file name that is one to eight characters in length plus an extension. | If you try to use the current name, Word displays an error message. |
| 5. Select OK or press Enter. | Word displays status information and then returns to the current document. |

**245**

Now you have a file that you can print anytime. To print this file, either exit Windows or double-click on the DOS icon from within Windows. Then type a DOS command to print. Examples of DOS commands that can be used to print this file are:

```
COPY filename.ext PRN
TYPE filename.ext > PRN
TYPE filename.ext > LPT1:
```

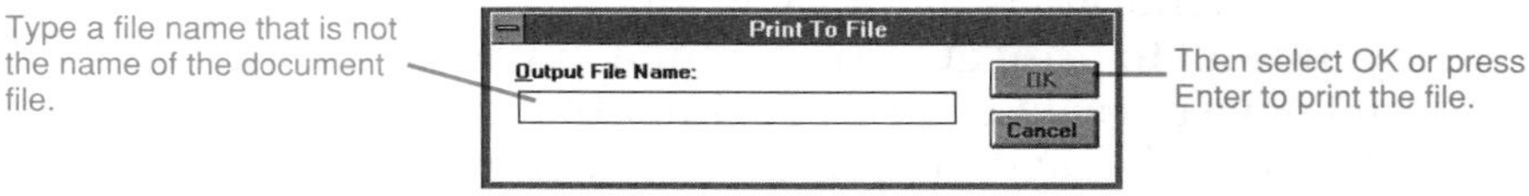

Type a file name that is not the name of the document file. ⟶

Then select OK or press Enter to print the file.

*Figure 9.9    The Print To File dialog box.*

# Troubleshooting Common Printer Problems

**246**

Although Word for Windows problems are rare, many are related to the printer. If Word displays the message that it is printing but does not print, give it a chance to print. Some printers are slower than others to print. Some documents or pages take longer to print, particularly if they contain graphics. If your printer does not print after a reasonable time, refer to this checklist:

1. Make sure that your printer is plugged in and turned on.
2. Try turning your printer off and on. Sometimes this clears a buffer that might be causing a problem. You can also try rebooting your computer.
3. If Word has been trying to print for a long time, it may display a message stating that it cannot print. Check the printer using the remaining items on this checklist and then answer the prompt.
4. Make sure all cables connecting your computer and printer are plugged in and that the appropriate cables are attached to the appropriate ports.
5. The printer's On-line light should be on. You might have to press a button.
6. Make sure that there is paper in the printer and that it is properly aligned (that is, not jammed).

7. Check that you are using the correct printer driver for the active printer.

8. Close all covers. Some printers cannot print unless every component is in its correct place. If you are using a laser printer, make sure the toner cartridge is correctly installed.

9. If the active printer is not attached to a port (that is, its port is NONE), it won't work.

10. Try running a self test on your printer.

11. See if the printer works when you enter a DOS print command. For example, TYPE DIR > PRN to print the current directory.

12. If your dot-matrix printer prints from DOS but not from Word for Windows, try changing to either the LPT1.OS2 or LPT2.OS2 port from the Printers - Configure dialog box in the Windows Control Panel. The OS/2 port sends documents through DOS to your printer.

13. Have someone evaluate your AUTOEXEC.BAT and CONFIG.SYS files. There may be a missing line or an incorrect line in one of these files.

**247**

---

**Caution:** If you edit AUTOEXEC.BAT, which is a text format (ASCII) file with Word, be sure to keep the file in the text format. If AUTOEXEC.BAT is not in ASCII format, it will contain extra formatting characters that your computer will misinterpret.

---

If this list does not prompt you to solve your problem, refer to your printer's manual.

## What You Have Learned

▶ Although printers are installed under the Windows program, Word provides a way for you to define the active printer using the **F**ile **P**rint Setup command. Windows defines all installed printers to ports, parallel (LPT) or serial (COM).

► The **F**ile Print Pre**v**iew command lets you look at your document's format before you print. You can use this command to adjust margins and the position of headers and footers.

► You can print by clicking on the Print button from the Print Preview screen or selecting the File Print command. Both methods display the Print dialog box.

► Word enables you to customize a print job or print settings by selecting print options from the Print dialog box and the Options dialog box for the Print category. Some of these options allow you to print a document or related information, selected pages or ranges of pages, or multiple copies of a document.

► You can "print" a document (along with its formats) to a file so that you can print at a later time. Use the **F**ile **P**rint command and then check the Print to File box. When it's time to print, use the DOS COPY or DOS TYPE command to direct the document to the printer.

# Creating Tables

## In This Chapter

**249**

> ▶ *Creating, editing, and formatting tables*
> ▶ *Manipulating cells, rows, and columns*
> ▶ *Navigating and selecting within a table*
> ▶ *Converting text to a table*
> ▶ *Sorting and calculating in tables*

Up to this point, you have learned how to create and format documents that consist of a single column of text, extending from margin to margin. In Chapter 8, you were introduced to the first multiple-column format, snaking columns. Remember that there is no way to make these columns unequal widths; every time you adjust the width of a column, all other columns assume the new width.

In this chapter, you will learn how to create, format, and edit another multiple-column format: *tables.* Unlike snaking columns, Word's table columns can be of unequal widths and can extend up to the full width of a page. You can select, edit, manipulate, and format tables and their contents in the same way that you work with other text in your documents.

# Creating Tables

A table is a good way to present information in an easy-to-read format. Unlike some word processors that have you create a table from scratch by using tabs, Word lets you create a table as if it were a spreadsheet. Like spreadsheets, Word's tables are made up of *cells,* arranged in rows and columns. With Word, it is easy to edit tables that you've created.

## *Inserting a Table in a Document*

Creating tables is similar to creating multiple columns. When you create a table using the Table menu and the Insert Table command, Word divides the space between the margins into equal columns. If you are working in a multiple-column format (such as snaking columns), the total width of the table is the width of the single column where the insertion point was located when you created the table. The height of a cell expands to hold all the text you have entered for that cell. The height of a row is the height of the largest cell in the row.

To create a table, select Table Insert Table (Alt,A,I). When Word displays the Insert Table dialog box (shown in Figure 10.1), define the size of the table. In the Number of Columns box, type a value or cycle through the range of values (from 1 to 31). In the Number of Rows box, type a value or cycle through the range of values (from 1 to 32767). To define the width of a column, type a value or cycle through the range of values (from 0 to 22 inches) in the Column Width box. You can also accept Word's column width, Auto, which is based on the width between the margins and the number of columns. Keep in mind that the ranges of values for the Insert Table dialog box are also affected by computer memory, paper width and height, and other factors. Therefore, you may not be able to use the full range of values that Word provides.

Define the number of
columns across the table.

**Insert Table**

Number of **C**olumns: 4

Number of **R**ows: 3

Column **W**idth: Auto

OK

Cancel

Define the number of rows
down the table.

Word sets the width of a column
based on the number of columns and
the width between margins.

*Figure 10.1   The Insert Table dialog box, which enables
you to define the columns and rows for a table to be
inserted in the current document.*

**FYIdea:** You can make a *Things to Do* page by using a table and a series of Word commands. First, create a table consisting of a single row. Select the table. Choose Forma**t** **B**order, select a single line, and then select OK or press Enter. Word surrounds the table with a single line. Making sure that the table is still selected, choose **E**dit **C**opy (Ctrl-Ins or Ctrl-C) and Edit Paste Row (Shift-Ins or Ctrl-V). Then select **E**dit **R**epeat (F4) to insert as many rows as you want (we used 48). You can create a header to hold the text *Things to Do*. Define a font, point size, and alignment. Then print the sheet.

**251**

Follow these Quick Steps to define a table and insert it into the current document.

### Defining a Table and Inserting It into a Document

1. Move the insertion point to the place in your document where you want to insert the table.

The insertion point flashes on and off.

2. From the Table menu, select the Insert Table command (Alt,A,I).

Word displays the Insert Table dialog box.

3. Type a number in the Columns, Rows, and Column Width boxes, or use the up and down arrow buttons to cycle through the values. The defaults are 2 columns, 1 row, and Auto.

As you insert values in the Numbers of Columns and the Number of Rows boxes, remember that you may not be able to use the full range of values because of computer limitations and other factors.

4. Select OK or press Enter.

Word returns to your document and inserts a blank table template with the characteristics that you specified (Figure 10.2). ☐

**252**

A table 4 columns wide and 3 rows down

End-of-cell mark

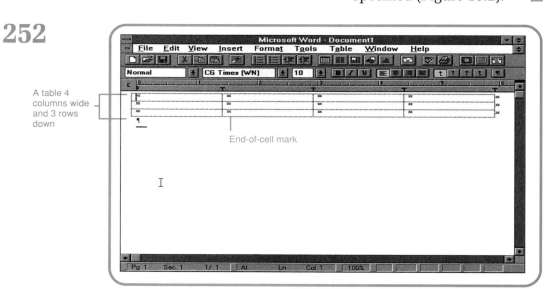

*Figure 10.2   A table template created by using the Table menu and the Insert Table command.*

Click on the Table button to insert the table template into the document at the insertion point. When Word displays the table template, drag the mouse to define the number of rows and columns in the table. Drag to the left or right to determine the number of columns, drag up or down to set the number of rows, or drag diagonally to change both rows and columns. If the insertion point is not moved, Word displays the Insert Cells dialog box the next time you click on this button.

When a table is inserted in your document, notice that dots surround each cell. The dots show the boundaries of the cell and do not print. To turn off the dots, select the Tools Options command (Alt,O,O), and select the Options dialog box for the View category. Then clear the Table Gridlines check box. Another way to turn off gridlines is to select the Table menu and remove the check from the Gridlines command (Alt,A,G).

**253**

**Tip:** You can adjust the width of any column by moving the mouse pointer within the table to the vertical line to be moved. When the mouse pointer changes to a double-ended arrow, press and hold the left mouse button. Then drag the line to the left or the right until it is in its new location. At that point, release the left mouse button. Word adjusts the table width. Notice that columns that you have not adjusted remain the same width but change position to accommodate the changed column widths.

## Navigating a Table

You can use the keyboard or the mouse to move around a table. Note that you cannot move down to the next cell in a table by pressing Enter; when you press Enter, the cell containing the insertion point just gets larger.

The easiest way to get around a table is to use the mouse pointer. Move the mouse pointer where you want to add text and click the left mouse button to place the insertion point.

You may find it awkward to switch between the keyboard and the mouse. If you are adding text to a table, you may want to use only the keyboard. Table 10.1 provides a list of table-navigation keys.

*Table 10.1    Word's table-navigation keys.*

| Key | Description |
| --- | --- |
| ↓ | The insertion point moves down one line within the table or out of the table. |
| ↑ | The insertion point moves up one line within the table or out of the table. |
| → | The insertion point moves to the next cell. |
| ← | The insertion point moves to the previous cell. |
| Tab | The insertion point moves to the next cell. |
| Shift-Tab | The insertion point moves to the previous cell. |
| Alt-Home | The insertion point moves to the first cell in the current row. |
| Alt-End | The insertion point moves to the last cell in the current row. |
| Alt-PgUp | The insertion point moves to the top cell in the column. |
| Alt-PgDn | The insertion point moves to the bottom cell in the column. |

 **Note:** Use Ctrl-Tab to insert a tab in a table.

## *Converting Text to a Table*

If the current document contains text that would look better as a table, there is an easy way to convert that text into table format. When you select text to convert it to a table, make sure that the segments of text that will make up table cells are separated by paragraph marks, tabs, or commas. If there is a combination of tabs and paragraph marks, or commas and paragraph marks, Word treats each paragraph mark as the end of a row. If all three of these marks are used to divide the text, Word asks you to choose the mark that represents the division between cells.

To convert text to a table, select the text to be converted and then choose the Table menu and the Convert Text to Table command (Alt,A,T). If Word detects a combination of characters used to separate the text, it displays the Convert Text To Table dialog box; otherwise, it returns to your document and converts the text to a table. You can also select a table and convert it to text. When you select a table, Word changes the Convert **T**ext to Table command to Convert **T**able to Text.

Follow these Quick Steps to convert text in a document to a table.

 **Converting Text to a Table**

1. Select the text to be converted to a table.

   Word highlights the text (Figure 10.3).

2. Select the **T**able menu and the Convert **T**ext to Table command (Alt,A,T).

   If you have more than one type of separator (for example, commas and tabs) between units of text, Word displays the Convert Text To Table dialog box (Figure 10.4).

3. If the Convert Text To Table dialog box is displayed, select the mark that represents the division between cells. Then select OK or press Enter.

   Word returns to the current document and makes a table (Figure 10.5).

4. To adjust the width of a column, move the mouse pointer to the Ruler. Find the bold *T* located above the vertical line to be adjusted. Press and hold the left mouse button and drag the line to the left or right. When the column width is satisfactory, release the left mouse button. Alternatively, place the mouse pointer on the vertical line you want to move and drag the line to its new position.

   Word adjusts the column width as you wish (Figure 10.6).

□

**255**

Tab mark

Paragraph mark

Text to be turned into a table

Comma

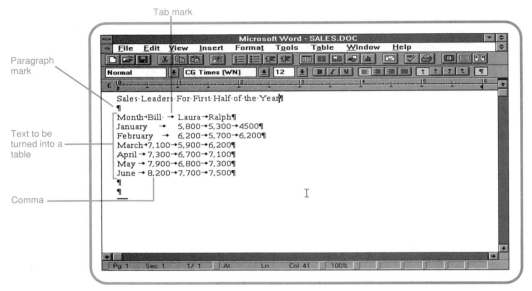

*Figure 10.3    Text before it is converted to a table.*

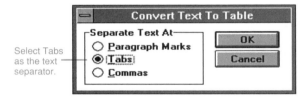

Select Tabs as the text separator.

*Figure 10.4    The Convert Text To Table dialog box from which you select the symbol that separates text.*

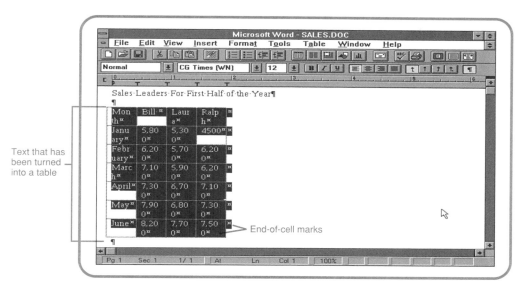

*Figure 10.5    Text converted to a table.*

**257**

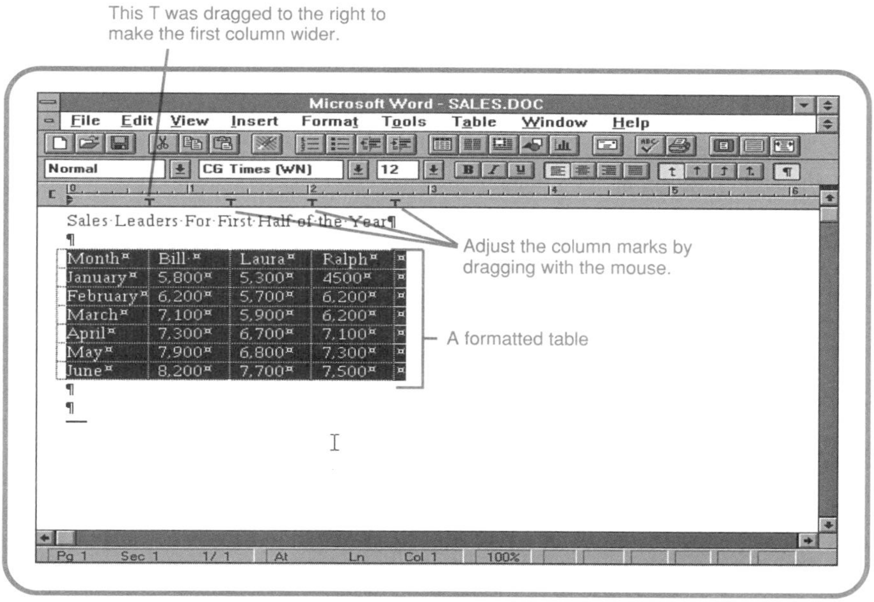

*Figure 10.6    The same table with adjusted columns.*

# Editing Tables

In this section, you'll learn how to select and manipulate text and the components of a table. You'll find editing tables almost the same as editing text in other parts of a document.

## Selecting Text in a Table

As you learned in Chapter 3, to copy or cut text when using Word, you must select the text first. Selecting text in a table is like selecting text anywhere else in your document. When you select text using any of the keys in Table 10.2, the selection starts at the location of the insertion point and extends from there. You can also turn Extend Selection mode on when selecting text in a table. In Chapter 3, you learned that you turn Extend Selection mode by pressing the F8 key. Remember that when Extend Selection mode is turned on, the only way to turn it off is to press Esc. Table 10.2 provides a list of table selection keys.

**258**

*Table 10.2    Word's table selection keys.*

| Key | Description |
| --- | --- |
| *In Standard Mode* | |
| Alt-5 (on the numeric keypad with Num Lock toggled off) | Selects the entire table |
| Shift-↑ | Selects the current cell and the cell above |
| Shift-↓ | Selects the current cell and the cell below |
| Shift-← | Selects the current cell one character at a time and then all of the adjacent cell to the left |
| Shift-→ | Selects the current cell one character at a time and then all of the adjacent cell to the right |
| Tab | Selects the contents of the next cell |
| Shift-Tab | Selects the contents of the previous cell |
| *In Extended Selection Mode* | |
| ↑ | Selects the current cell and the cell above |
| ↓ | Selects the current cell and the cell below |

| Key | Description |
|---|---|
| ← | Selects the current cell one character at a time and then all of the adjacent cell to the left |
| → | Selects the current cell one character at a time and then all of the adjacent cell to the right |

To select text with the mouse, click the left mouse button on specific cells, or click the left mouse button and drag the pointer across several cells of a table.

To select a row of cells, move the mouse pointer to the selection bar in the left margin. When the mouse pointer changes to an arrow pointing up and to the right, click the left mouse button. Word highlights the entire row.

There are two methods of selecting a column of cells: To use the first method, move the mouse pointer anywhere in the column and click the right mouse button. To use the second method, move the mouse pointer to the top border of the top cell. When the mouse pointer changes to a down arrow, click the left mouse button.

## *Editing Cells*

There are two aspects to manipulating cells; you can edit the text within a cell, or you can edit the cells themselves.

Cutting, copying, and pasting text from one cell to another is just like cutting, copying, and pasting in other parts of the document. Select all the text in a cell including the end-of-cell mark. Then use either the **E**dit **C**opy or **E**dit **Cu**t command. At this point the **E**dit **P**aste command becomes **E**dit **P**aste Cell. When you paste, the cell that you are pasting overwrites the cell to which you are pasting. When you copy or cut multiple cells, the area into which you paste must have the same row-by-column dimensions as the cut or copied cells. However, there is a way around this: you can use the insertion point to mark the upper left corner of the area into which the cut or copied cells are pasted.

**Tip:** To see the end-of-cell marks in a table, select the Show All button on the Ribbon. This displays all nonprinting symbols including the end-of-cell mark. See Figure 10.2 for an example of an end-of-cell mark.

You can also insert cells and shift selected cells at the same time. Select the location of the cells to be inserted. From the Table menu, select Insert Cells (Alt,A,I). When Word displays the Insert Cells dialog box (shown in Figure 10.7), select Shift Cells Right to insert cells and shift the selected cells one cell to the right; select Shift Cells-Down to insert cells and shift the selected cells one row down. You'll learn about the Insert Entire Row and Insert Entire Column options in the next section.

Select this button to insert cells and shift the selected cells one row down.

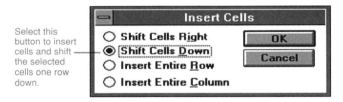

*Figure 10.7   The Insert Cells dialog box with Shift Cells Down selected.*

To delete cells and shift the remaining cells at the same time, select the cells to be deleted. From the Table menu, select Delete Cells (Alt,A,D). When Word displays the Delete Cells dialog box (shown in Figure 10.8), select Shift Cells Left to delete cells and shift the remaining cells one cell to the left; select Shift Cells Up to delete cells and shift the remaining cells one row up. To delete a row of cells, select Delete Entire Row, and to delete a column of cells, select Delete Entire Column.

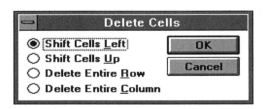

*Figure 10.8   The Delete Cells dialog box with Shift Cells Left selected.*

## *Editing Rows and Columns*

It is easy to add more rows and/or columns to a table. First, place the insertion point where the new row or column is to be placed. Select the Table Insert Cells command (Alt, A, I). When Word displays the Insert Cells dialog box, select the Insert Entire Row option to insert a row, or the Insert Entire Column option to insert a column.

Depending on the type of selection you have made (rows, columns, or cells), the command on the Table menu changes. If you select rows, you'll see the Insert Rows command. If you select columns, the command on the menu is Insert Columns. If you do not select any cell, you'll see Insert Cells.

# Formatting Tables

Certain problems are typical of tables. For example, information in some tables is hard to read because cells and text are squeezed together. Or one cell may contain too much text, resulting in a row that is half a page high and a table that looks lopsided. If the table is long, important information may be lost in it if pertinent facts aren't highlighted. The upcoming sections will show you how to use formatting to call attention to your table and its components, solve typical problems, and make the table easier to read.

There are two methods for formatting a table: You can use the Menu bar (specifically, the Format and Table menus) or a combination of the Ruler and Ribbon. In the upcoming sections on table formatting, you'll learn about both methods.

## *Changing the Width of a Column or Cells*

If you need to change the width of a column, you can use several methods. The first method relies on the mouse, the second uses the mouse with the Ruler, and the third is a command in the Table menu. When you change the size of a column, you can also decide whether to let that change affect the overall width of the table.

To change the size of a column using the mouse in the table, move the mouse pointer to the border of the cell that you would like to move. When the mouse pointer changes to two parallel lines with arrows pointing left and right, click the left mouse button and drag the border to its new location. This technique works only on vertical (width) lines and not on horizontal ones.

If you hold down the Shift key while you resize a table using the mouse, the table keeps its original width. If you hold down the Ctrl key while resizing a column with the mouse, not only will the table remain its original width but the space to the right of the resized column will be equally divided among the remaining columns in the table.

To use the mouse with the Ruler, first make sure that the insertion point is within a table or that cells are selected. If the Ruler does not display the Column Width markers, click on the Ruler Scale symbol to the left of the Ruler (shown in Figure 10.9) until the Column Width markers (which look like boldface *T*s) appear on the Ruler. Don't click too fast, or you'll open the Paragraph dialog box. To increase or decrease the size of a column, locate on the Ruler the Column Width marker that is directly above the corresponding vertical column line in the table. Then drag the marker to a new location on the Ruler.

The Ruler Scale symbol

*Figure 10.9    The Ruler with the Ruler Scale symbol. Click on this symbol to display the Ruler with column marks.*

To change the cell widths of certain rows in a table, select those rows. When you see the Column Width markers on the Ruler, drag them to a new location to increase or decrease the size of a column.

You can use the Table Column **W**idth command to change the width of columns in a table. With this method, the changes made to a column affect the entire width of the table. You can also change the width of certain cells in a table by selecting only the cells that you want to change.

Use the following Quick Steps to change the width of columns or cells with the Table Column **W**idth command.

## Q Changing the Widths of Columns or Cells

1. Select the column or cell whose width you want to change.

   Word highlights the selection.

2. Select the Table menu and the Column Width command (Alt,A,W).

   Word displays the Column Width dialog box (shown in Figure 10.10).

3. Enter a new width for the selected column or press the up or down arrow to cycle through the valid values (.17" through 17.49").

   Depending on the limitations of your computer system, paper dimensions, and other factors, Word may not allow the width that you entered.

4. To change the width of any other columns, select the Previous Column or Next Column button.

   Word changes the column width you just set, highlights the new column in the document, and displays the column number of the column that you are changing in the dialog box.

**263**

5. Repeat steps 3 and 4 until you have changed all the columns widths that you want. Select OK or Close, or press Enter.

   Word closes the dialog box and returns to the document.

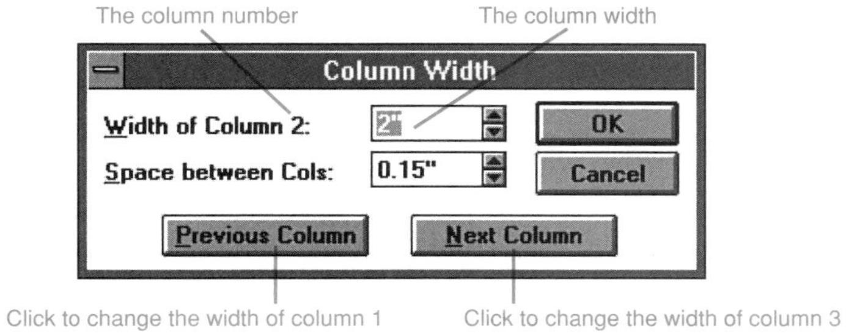

□

The column number  The column width

```
┌──────────────────────────────────────────┐
│ ▬         Column Width                     │
│                                            │
│ Width of Column 2:   [2"] ▲▼    [  OK  ]   │
│ Space between Cols:  [0.15"] ▲▼ [ Cancel ] │
│                                            │
│   [ Previous Column ]   [ Next Column ]    │
└──────────────────────────────────────────┘
```

Click to change the width of column 1   Click to change the width of column 3

*Figure 10.10   The Column Width dialog box.*

## *Adjusting the Space Between Columns*

To increase or decrease the space between columns, select any column in the table and select Table Column Width (Alt,A,W). Type the value of the space between columns (ranging from 0" to .98"), and select OK or press Enter. When you return to the document, all the columns in the table have the new spacing. You can also change the spacing of one row by selecting the row (or any cell in that row). When you change the spacing, only that row changes.

When you change the spacing between rows, you affect the width of the text area in a column. Thus, a column with a width of two inches and space between columns of 0.25 inch has a text area of 1.75 inches.

## *Changing the Height of a Row*

The height of a row is normally determined by the height of the tallest cell in a row. With the Row **H**eight command of the **Ta**ble menu (Alt,A,H), you can adjust the height of a row automatically (Word's default), or you can adjust a minimum height or a fixed height. If you use a fixed height, some items in large cells may be clipped on-screen and when the table is printed. A row height can be between 0 and 132 lines.

To change the height of a selected row, select the Row Height command from the Table menu (Alt,A,H). In the Row Height dialog box (shown in Figure 10.11), select Auto, At Least, or Exactly from the Height of Row list box. Auto is the default selection for all the rows in your table; this selection sets the height of each row using the highest cell of that row. When you want a row height to start at a minimum size but be larger, if needed, select At Least. To set a fixed row height, choose Exactly. If you select either At Least or Exactly, you will have to select a size in the At list box.

Notice that the Row Height dialog box has two buttons: Previous Row and Next Row. Choosing one of these buttons moves you either one row up or one row down from your current selection. You'll learn about the rest of the options in the Row Height dialog box later in this chapter.

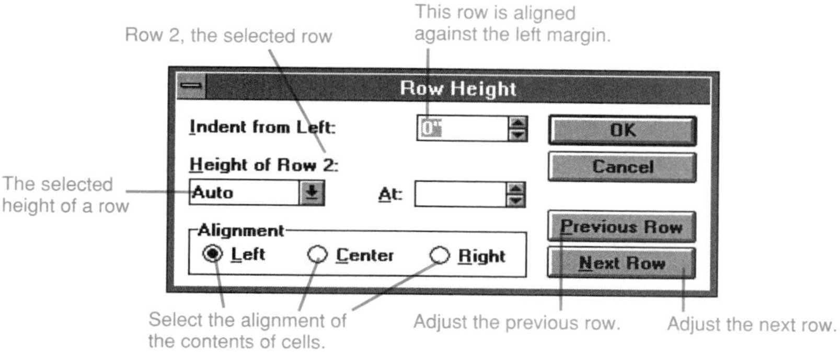

*Figure 10.11    The Row Height dialog box, from which you change the height of a row or alignment of the contents of cells.*

**265**

## Indenting and Aligning Rows in a Table

You can change the indentation of rows or an entire table in order to enhance the appearance of one or more tables or to align text in a table with other text in the document.

To change the alignment of rows, first select one or more rows to be changed. Then, select Table Row Height (Alt, A, H). In the Row Height dialog box, select one of the alignment buttons to align the cells' contents against the left or right margin or to center them between the margins. Use the Indent from Left box to define the distance (ranging from –22" to 22") from the left margin to the left edge of the selected row. Remember that the value that you select, even if it is within the range of valid measurements, is also affected by factors such as your computer system's limitations and paper dimensions.

## Adding Borders to a Table

To give a table or selected cells extra emphasis, add borders or lines. Use the same procedures described in Chapter 6 for surrounding paragraphs with borders and lines.

To place a border around a table, select the entire table. Next, select Format Border (Alt,T,B). In the Border Table dialog box (shown in Figure 10.12), select the type of box and the type of line that form the border. Then select OK or press Enter.

To place a border around selected cells, first select one or more cells. Next, select Format Border (Alt,T,B). In the Border Table dialog box, select the type of box and the type of line that form the border. Then select OK or press Enter.

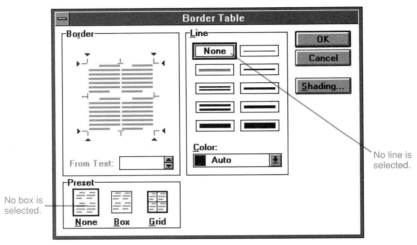

*Figure 10.12    The Border Table dialog box with its default settings.*

## Merging and Splitting Cells in a Table

If you want a cell to extend the width of a table or to be a combination of two cells, you can merge cells. For example, to include a long title at the top of a table, combine cells until the merged cell is the width that you want. Start by selecting the cells to be merged. Then select Table Merge Cells (Alt,A,M). Word returns you to your table and merges the selected cells. Once you have merged a cell, you can't merge it with another cell.

If you change your mind about cells that you have merged, Word provides the means to split the merged cells. Start by selecting the cell to be split. Then select Table Split Cells (Alt,A,P).

## *Formatting Text in a Cell*

One thing to keep in mind is that each cell in a table is like a miniature document; each cell has its own margins and format. Text within cells follows the cell format, not the document format. Just as you would format the text in a document, you can format cells or the contents of cells in a table.

Select the entire cell or the text within a cell to be formatted. Then use the formatting commands you learned in Chapter 6, 7, and 8. For example, to apply bold to selected text or cells, use the Format Character command or select the Bold button from the Ribbon. To change the alignment of the text in a cell, use the Format Paragraph command or select the appropriate button from the Ribbon. You can use the Ruler to change the margin settings for selected text. Click on the symbol to the left of the Ruler until the Ruler displays a *T*. Then drag the margin triangles to format text the way you want.

**267**

# Sorting Items in a Table

When creating tables, you might like to order the information within the table—alphabetically, numerically, or by date. Select the Tools menu and the Sorting command (Alt,O,I) to sort selected information. Word displays the Sorting dialog box, which is shown in Figure 10.13. Word ignores blank spaces, tabs, and indents; it sorts by the first alphanumeric character that it finds.

The selected sort order is from the lowest value to the highest value.

The dimmed area is ignored.

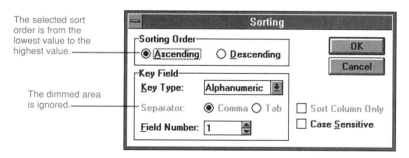

*Figure 10.13    The Sorting dialog box with its default settings.*

There are two different sort orders—Ascending and Descending—available in the Sorting dialog box. Ascending sorts from the lowest to the highest alphanumeric character; Descending sorts from the highest to the lowest alphanumeric character.

Normally, Word treats lowercase and uppercase letters as the same. However, if you are sorting a table alphabetically and you check the Case Sensitive box, Word puts uppercase letters before lowercase (for example, *S* before *s,* but not before *B* or *b*).

For Word to sort by dates, it must be able to recognize dates in the table. The date formats in Table 10.3 are the only formats that Word recognizes as dates; all other text is ignored.

*Table 10.3   Word's date formats.*

| Format | Example |
| --- | --- |
| MM/DD/YY | 04/17/67 |
| MM-DD-YY | 04-17-67 |
| Month Day, Year | April 17, 1967 |
| | Apr 17, 1967 |
| DD-Mon-YY | 17 April 67 |
| | 17 Apr 67 |
| Month-YY | April-67 |
| | Apr-67 |
| MM-DD-YY hh:mm PM\|AM | 04-17-67 08:55 PM |

The Numeric option sorts by number, regardless of where the number is in the paragraph; all characters that are not numbers are ignored. Select Sort Column Only to sort only the columns that you have selected.

# Performing Calculations

With the **T**ools **C**alculate command, Word makes it easy for you to perform calculations within tables or in regular text. Simply type in the numbers and the mathematical operators to make a calculation. You can use the regular keyboard, the numeric keypad, or a combination when you type your expression. Numbers that are not separated by a mathematical operator are added, which is the default.

> **Note:** When you perform a calculation, do not use an equal sign. If you do, Word displays a message stating: The result of the calculation is: `!Unexpected. End of Expres-sion`.

When you want Word to perform the calculation, just highlight the expression and select the Tools Calculate command (Alt,O,C). Word briefly displays the result in the Status bar, as shown in Figure 10.14, and pastes the result into the Clipboard. Then, if you want, paste the answer anywhere in the document. Table 10.4 lists Word's mathematical operators.

*Table 10.4   Word's mathematical operators.*

| Operator | Operation | Example | Result |
|----------|-----------|---------|--------|
| − | Subtraction | 500 − 50 | 450 |
| (nnn) | Subtraction | 500 (50) | 450 |
| / | Division | 500/50 | 10 |
| * | Multiplication | 500*50 | 25,000 |
| + | Addition | 500+50 | 550 |
| (space) | Addition | 500 50 | 550 |
| % | Percentage | 500*5% | 25 |
| ^ | Exponentiation | 5 ^ 3 | 125* |
|   |   | 125 ^ (1/3) | 5* |

*In the example, 5 cubed is 125. To derive radicals, use the inverse power; in the example, the cube root of 125 is 5.

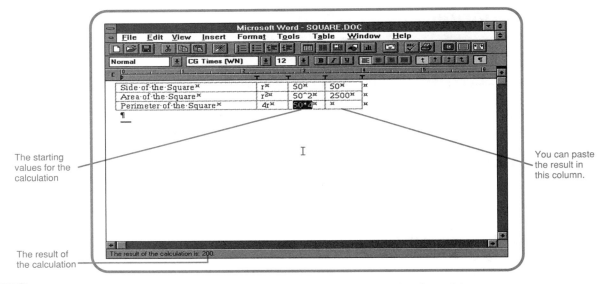

The starting values for the calculation

You can paste the result in this column.

The result of the calculation

*Figure 10.14   The result of a calculation is displayed in the Status bar and is added to the Clipboard.*

# What You Have Learned

▶ A table is a good way to present information in an easy-to-read format. Create a table using the Table Insert Table command (Alt,A,I), or use the Table button on the Toolbar.

▶ You can use the keyboard or the mouse to navigate a table. To use the keyboard, use Word's table-navigation keys. To use the mouse, move the mouse pointer where you want to start typing and click the left mouse button to place an insertion point.

▶ To convert text to a table, select the text and, from the Table menu, select the Convert Text to Table command (Alt,A,T). To convert a table to text, select the table and, from the Table menu, select the Convert Table to Text command (Alt,A,T).

▶ There are two aspects to manipulating cells; you can edit the text within the cell, or you can edit the cells themselves. Copying, cutting, and pasting text from one cell to another is the same as copying, cutting, and pasting in other parts of a document. Use the **C**opy, **C**ut, and **P**aste commands from the **E**dit menu.

▶ Word provides two ways to format a table. You can use the Menu bar (the Forma**t** and T**a**ble menus) or a combination of the Ruler and Ribbon. Use Forma**t** **P**aragraph and Forma**t** **C**haracter to format text in a table just as you use these commands in other parts of a document.

▶ You can sort within tables by using the T**o**ols Sor**t**ing command to sort selected information alphabetically, numerically, or by date. You can sort in ascending or descending order.

▶ To perform calculations in a table, type numbers separated by mathematical operators. Highlight the expression and select Tools Calculate (Alt,O,C). Word displays the result in the Status bar and pastes the result into the Clipboard.

**271**

# Working with Styles

## In This Chapter

▶ *Creating, changing, deleting, and renaming styles*

▶ *Defining a style based on an existing style*

▶ *Specifying the next style*

▶ *Applying a style*

▶ *Viewing style names and printing a list of styles*

In Chapters 6 and 7, you learned how to format paragraphs and characters. To make your formatting job easier, you can define various formats (character, paragraph, tabs, border, frame, and language), save them as a Word for Windows *style*, and then apply that style to selected paragraphs. This means that instead of formatting one or more selected paragraphs step-by-step, you can quickly format selected paragraphs by calling the style by name or by using a unique key combination that you have "linked" to the style. Once you've saved a style, you can use it again and again.

If your company has standards for all documents, styles make it easy for anybody creating a document to use the correct formats on a paragraph-by-paragraph basis. However, be aware that any character formatting is applied to all the text in a paragraph. For example, to apply italics to one word in a paragraph, you cannot use a style; you must use the Format Character command, the Ribbon, or shortcut keys instead.

The default style, Normal, which is displayed in the Style list box on the Ribbon (shown in Figure 11.1), is applied to every paragraph in Word for Windows. The Normal style formats are left-aligned text with block indentation, no spaces before or after, single line spacing, and a 10-point Times Roman font. Three other Word styles (heading 1, heading 2, and heading 3) are listed in the Style list box. Many other Word styles serve as defaults for such features as headers and footers, footnotes, headings, and so on, but these are not normally listed in the Style list box. (You'll see how to display them later in this chapter.)

The current style is
Normal, the default.

Other styles that
Word provides

The Style
list box

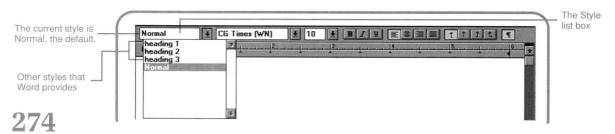

*Figure 11.1    The Style list box on the Ribbon.*

## Defining a Style by Recording a Paragraph's Formats

You can create a new style by using either the Ribbon or the Format Style command. The quickest way to define a style is to format an existing paragraph and then save the formats as a style using the Style list box on the Ribbon.

As with the Ribbon, you can select an existing paragraph with the formats you want and give it a style name with the Format Style command. However, you can also define additional formats for a style or create a new style using all the options available from the Style dialog box, which is shown in Figure 11.2.

Follow these Quick Steps to define a style by using the Ribbon.

 **Recording and Defining a New Style by Using the Ribbon**

1. Select a paragraph that contains all the formats you want in the style.

   Word highlights the paragraph.

| 2. Click on the Style list box or press Ctrl-S. | Word moves the insertion point to the word `Normal` in the Style list box. |
| 3. Type the style name in the Style list box. | As you type, Word scrolls the first characters off the left side of the Style list box. The maximum number of characters and spaces for a style name is 24. |
| 4. Press Enter or click anywhere outside the Style list box. | Word creates the style and adds its name to the list in the Style list box. □ |

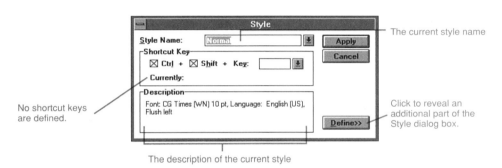

*Figure 11.2    The Style dialog box, displayed as a result of selecting the Style command from the Format menu.*

## About the Style Dialog Box

Although using the Ribbon is the easiest method for defining a style, the Format Style command (Alt,T,Y or press Ctrl-S twice) provides a wider variety of options. You can accept the current formats, build on those formats by making additional changes, or define all new formats. Another advantage to using the Format Style command is that you can link a key combination to a particular style as you create the style. The Style dialog box (Figure 11.2) displays the current style name and its description. Here is an overview of the options available in the Style dialog box:

The *Style Name box* displays the current style name, Normal, when the dialog box is first displayed. You can type a new name, or you can open the list in order to select an existing style name.

The *Shortcut Key box* enables you to specify a key or key combination for a style. If the key or key combination you select is already assigned, the current assignment appears next to the title Currently; otherwise, the word unassigned is displayed after the word Currently. In addition to Ctrl and Shift, available keys are A–Z, 0–9, F2–F12, Ins, and Del.

The *Description box* contains a description of the formats associated with the style named in the Style Name box.

The *Define button* adds a new section to the Style dialog box, with additional formatting options. See Figure 11.3.

Click on the *Character, Paragraph, Tabs, Border, Frame,* or *Language* button to display a dialog box in order to add formatting to the style. You can define character or paragraph formats; set tab positions and alignment; add borders, lines, and shading; define a frame; or indicate the character set for the language used in the selected paragraph.

The *Based On box* names the current style, which can be the style on which several other styles can be based.

The *Next Style box* names the style for the paragraph that follows the current paragraph. For example, headings are normally followed by body text. Use the Next Style box to ensure this.

The *Add to Template check box* indicates whether this style is added to the template attached to this document or is used just for this document. Chapter 12 describes templates.

Click on the *Apply button* to apply the style to the selected paragraph.

Click on *Cancel* to return to the current document without applying the style.

Click on *Change* to apply the formats you have just defined to the current style. When you type a new style name in the Style Name box, Change becomes Add. Click on *Add* to add the style to the list of styles.

Click on *Delete* to remove the current style from the list of styles.

Click on *Rename* to rename the current style.

Click on *Merge* to merge styles from a document or template to another document or template.

>  **Tip:** One reason to open the Style dialog box is to display the description of a style so that you can use some of the same settings for another style or a format.

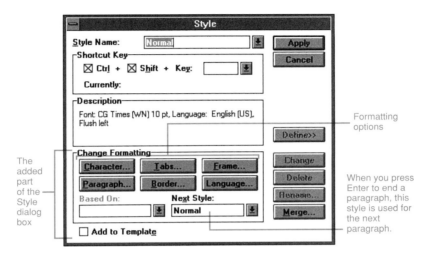

The added part of the Style dialog box

Formatting options

When you press Enter to end a paragraph, this style is used for the next paragraph.

**277**

*Figure 11.3    The Style dialog box with additional formatting options.*

## Defining a Style by Using the Format Style Command

Remember that you can use the Format Style command to create a new style without formatting an existing paragraph. You can select a paragraph that has formats that you can start with and then add and/or change more formats.

Use the following Quick Steps to define a new style with the Format Style command.

### Recording and Defining a New Style by Using the Format Style Command

1. Select a paragraph that is formatted the way you want.

Word highlights your selection.

2. From the Format menu, choose Style (Alt,T,Y or press Ctrl-S twice).

   Word displays the Style dialog box (Figure 11.2).

3. In the Style Name box, type the name for your new style.

   When you type the first letter of the style name, the Description box changes to read `Description (by example)`. Word enters the style name in the Description box.

4. To define a shortcut key, select Ctrl and/or Shift, and, in addition, select a keyboard key that is currently un-assigned. To select Ctrl or Shift, check or clear the appropriate box. In the Key box, type the keyboard key that you wish.

   If you select an assigned shortcut key, Word displays its current usage next to the title `Currently`.

5. Select Define.

   To the Style dialog box, Word adds a section in which you can define formats and dims the Define button.

6. In the Change Formatting box, select one of the six buttons.

   Word displays the Paragraph dialog box (Figure 11.4).

7. Change or add formats and click on OK.

   Word adds each new format to the Description box.

8. Repeat steps 5 and 6 until you have added all the formats you want. Then select Apply.

   Word adds the new style to the style list in the Ribbon, returns to the current document, and changes the selected paragraphs. ☐

## *Basing a New Style on an Existing Style*

Another way of defining a new style is to base it on an existing style. For example, the Normal style is a good starting point. Using the formats of the Normal style, add more formats for the new style. For example, you might want to highlight a paragraph by making it all bold. You can keep the Normal formatting and just add bold to the style.

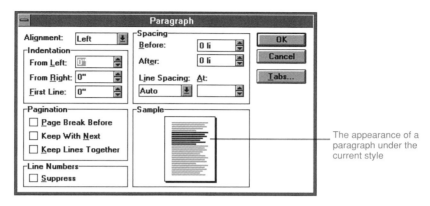

The appearance of a paragraph under the current style

*Figure 11.4    The Paragraph dialog box—one of the formatting dialog boxes that you can use to define formats for a style.*

**279**

When you create a style this way, you have to keep track of the new style as well as the style on which it is based. When either style is changed, it affects the formatting of the paragraphs that use either style. For example, if you use a style called B-Body1 as the basis for a style called Body1 Plus, whenever you change B-Body1, you automatically cause paragraphs formatted with Body1 Plus to change as well. It's a good idea to assign a character to all base styles so that you can track them. In our example, we used *B-* to indicate a base style.

To base a new style on an existing style, follow these Quick Steps.

 **Basing a New Style on an Existing Style**

1. From the Format menu, choose Style (Alt,T,Y or press Ctrl-S twice).

   Word displays the Style dialog box (Figure 11.2).

| | |
|---|---|
| 2. In the Style Name box, type the name for your new style. | When you type the first letter of the style name, the Description box changes to read `Description (by example)`. Word enters the style name in the Description box. |
| 3. Select **Define**. | To the Style dialog box, Word adds a section in which you can define formats. Word also dims the Define button. |
| 4. In the Based On box (located at the bottom of the Change Formatting box), type the name of the style on which you want to base the new style. | Word changes the description in the Description box. |
| 5. In the Change Formatting box, select one of the six buttons. | Word displays the Character dialog box (Figure 11.5). |
| 6. Change or add formats and click on OK. | Word adds each new format to the Description box. |
| 7. Repeat steps 5 and 6 until you have added all the formats you want. Then select Apply. | Word adds the new style to the style list in the Ribbon, returns to the current document, and changes the selected paragraphs. □ |

**280**

You can also create a base style on which other styles will build. When you define a base style, define only those formats that every style will use. For example, you might want to create a base style for body text. You might define a font and point size in the base style, but to have several types of paragraph formats (for example, hanging indents or block formats and so on), build those formats into the styles based on the base style.

## *Specifying the Next Style*

As you add text to a document with or without styles, the paragraph format of the preceding paragraph is applied to the following paragraph whenever you press Enter. However, some of Word's default styles are automatically followed by other styles. For example, if you define a paragraph as heading 1, the next paragraph is automatically Normal. (If a paragraph is defined with the Normal style, the next style is also Normal, since that is the default.) You can also define the style that follows the current style by typing a style name in the Next Style box. The paragraph in which the insertion point is located has the style on which the next style will be based.

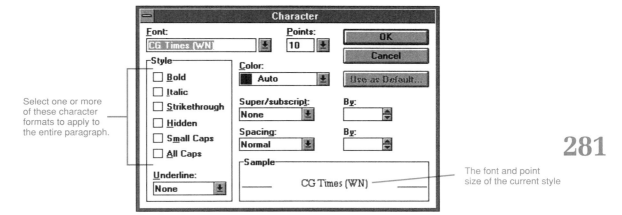

Select one or more of these character formats to apply to the entire paragraph.

The font and point size of the current style

**281**

*Figure 11.5    The Character dialog box—another dialog box that you can use to add formatting to a style.*

Use the following Quick Steps to designate the next style.

 **Specifying the Next Style**

1. Choose the Format Style command (Alt,T,Y or press Ctrl-S twice).

   Word displays the Style dialog box.

2. In the Style Name list box, name a style that will be followed by the next style.

   When you type the first letter of the style name, the Description box changes to read `Description (by example)`. Word enters the style name in the Description box.

3. Select Define.

   Word displays the rest of the Style dialog box.

4. In the Next Style list box, select or type the name of the next style.

As you type, Word scrolls the first characters off the left side of the Style list box. The maximum number of characters and spaces for a style name is 24.

5. Select Apply.

Word closes the Style dialog box and returns to the document. When you press Enter to indicate the end of the current paragraph, the text that follows assumes the style that you defined as the next style.  □

## 282 *Applying Styles*

You can apply any style, whether Word has defined it or you have, to one or more selected paragraphs. You can also apply a style to a paragraph that you have not typed. Just move the insertion point to the paragraph mark and start typing.

There are three ways to apply a style—from the Ribbon, by pressing the shortcut keys that you have defined, or by using the Format Style command. The fastest way to apply a style is by pressing shortcut keys. To apply a style from the Ribbon, select the style from the Style list box on the Ribbon. Select the Style list box and click on the list arrow to display the list of available styles. Either use the scroll bar or press any combination of ↑or ↓ to select the desired style. Press Enter or click the left mouse button to apply the style that you have chosen.

If you choose the Format Style command, Word displays the Style dialog box. Select the style name from the Style Name list box and select OK or press Enter. An advantage of displaying the Style dialog box is that you can use this opportunity to modify the formatting for the selected style.

Suppose that you have applied formatting to several paragraphs in a document. To change a format in one paragraph, it's probably not worth defining a new style (unless you know that you'll use this change in the future). You can use Format **P**aragraph or

Format Character to format a paragraph after you've applied a style. This overrides the formats defined using the style.

>  **Tip:** Press Ctrl-Q to remove all formats from a highlighted paragraph (including fonts and point sizes). Press Ctrl-Spacebar to remove all character formats. You then can reapply any styles and/or formats that you wish.

You can repeat a style by pressing F4 or selecting Edit Repeat. Remember that in order to repeat, you must not have performed any more actions since the actions that you want to repeat.

Word does not save a new style that you have applied to a document until you save or close the document or exit Word. When you take one of these actions, Word displays a small dialog box asking if you want to save changes to your document. If you answer Yes, Word saves your document and any changes to styles.

**283**

## *Viewing Style Names in the Document Window*

There are two ways to view the names of the styles that have been applied to paragraphs in a document. You've already seen that the current style name is always displayed in the Ribbon. You can also have Word display the style name in the style area near the left margin.

To display the style area, its width must be greater than 0 but no more than 3.34 inches. For example, to display the name Normal, the style area must be .4 inch or greater. Use the following Quick Steps to display the style area.

### Displaying the Style Area

1. From the Tools menu, select the Options command (Alt, O,O).

   Word displays the Options dialog box that you last used in this session of Word.

2. In the Category column, select View.

   Word displays the Options dialog box for the View category (Figure 11.6).

3. Type a value between 0" and 3.34" in the Style Area Width box.

The insertion point remains in the Style Area Width box in case you need to change the width.

4. Select OK.

Word returns to the current document and displays the style names for each paragraph next to the left edge of the document. □

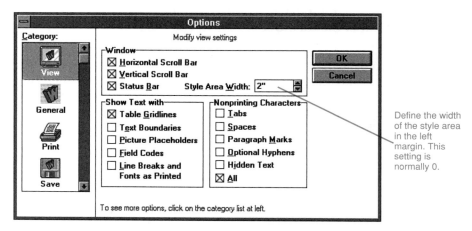

Define the width of the style area in the left margin. This setting is normally 0.

*Figure 11.6  The Options dialog box for the View category.*

Once you have set a size for the style area by using the Tools Options command, you can use the mouse pointer to readjust its width. When you move the mouse pointer to the vertical line representing the left edge of the paper, its shape changes to a double vertical line with two arrows pointing left and right, as shown in Figure 11.7. Press and hold the left mouse button and drag the vertical line so that the style area takes more or less room on the left side of the screen. You can drag the line about halfway across the computer screen. When you have found the ideal width, release the mouse button. To close the style area, drag the vertical line all the way to the left side of the screen.

## Changing a Style

When you use the Format Style command to change the formats for a style, every paragraph using that style automatically assumes the new formats. If other styles are based on the changed style, the paragraphs on which those styles are based also change to reflect the new formats.

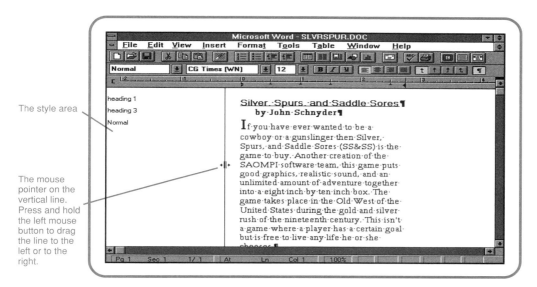

The style area

The mouse pointer on the vertical line. Press and hold the left mouse button to drag the line to the left or to the right.

*Figure 11.7    The mouse pointer on the line between the style area and your document.*

285

You can also change any of Word's default styles with the Format Style command. With the Style dialog box displayed, press the list arrow to the right of the Style Name box. When Word displays a list of styles, press Ctrl-Y to display all of Word's default styles (such as all levels of headings and index entries, footnotes, headers and footers, and so on). Ctrl-Y is a toggle key, so you can switch between the display of all styles and the ones that you usually see displayed in the Style list box. Changing the Normal style is a quick way to change the default paragraph format for the current document. For example, to change from the default Times Roman font to Century Schoolbook, select the Format Style command and then choose the Define button. Select the Character button and enter the new font in the Font box. Select OK or press Enter.

> **Tip:** If you don't like one of the settings in the Normal default style, you can change it globally. For example, if you always change the font from its default setting, you can make a permanent change by selecting Format Style. Select Define and make the appropriate change in format. When you select OK or press Enter and then choose Apply, Word asks if you want to change the properties of the standard style. Answer Yes to change to Normal, or No to return to the current document.

## Deleting and Renaming Styles

Although you cannot rename or delete a Word default style, you can rename or delete any style that you have defined. If a style is deleted, paragraphs that have been formatted with that style assume the formats of the Normal style. If a style is renamed, paragraphs that have been formatted with that style assume the new style name but keep the same formats. One reason to rename a style is to better reflect the purpose of the style. For example, you could rename a base style with a code (such as *B*-) that reminds you when you view the style list that this is a base style.

To rename or delete a style, select Format Style (Alt,T,Y or press Ctrl-S twice). When Word displays the Style dialog box, select the style name in the Style Name box that you want to rename or delete. Select the Define button. To rename that style, select Rename. In the Rename Style dialog box, shown in Figure 11.8, type a new style name and select OK or press Enter. To delete the specified style, select Delete. Word displays a dialog box that asks you to answer **Y**es to delete the style, **N**o to return to the Style dialog box without deleting the style, or **H**elp to display an explanation of your choices (see Figure 11.9). You can't delete or rename a Word Default style; if you try to delete a Word default style, both the Delete and Rename buttons are dimmed.

## Printing a List of Styles

With the **F**ile **P**rint command, you can print an alphabetized list of styles for a document. The list includes the Word default styles in the Style list box, the styles that are attached to the document, and a description of the formats for each style. When you print a document for your files, you can also save the style list as a reference. Then, when you want to copy the format of a paragraph in a new document, you can use this list as a guide.

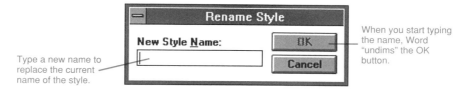

Type a new name to replace the current name of the style.

When you start typing the name, Word "undims" the OK button.

*Figure 11.8    The Rename Style dialog box.*

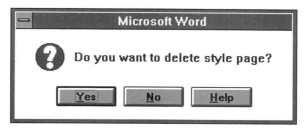

*Figure 11.9    A message dialog box that asks you to verify deletion by selecting Yes.*

**287**

To print a list of styles, open the document containing the styles you want to print. Select File Print (Alt,F,P or Ctrl-Shift-F12). When Word for Windows displays the Print dialog box, select the list arrow next to the Print box. From the list of print options, select Styles, as shown in Figure 11.10. Select OK or press Enter to print the style list.

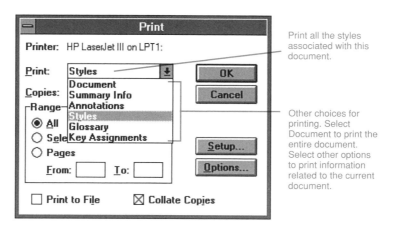

Print all the styles associated with this document.

Other choices for printing. Select Document to print the entire document. Select other options to print information related to the current document.

*Figure 11.10    The Print dialog box with the list of print options displayed.*

# What You Have Learned

- ▶ You can create a new style by using the Ribbon or the Format Style command. If you use the Ribbon, select an existing paragraph and give it a style name in the Style list box. If you use Format Style, you can select an existing paragraph, define a new style from scratch, or define a shortcut key for applying the style.

- ▶ Using the Style dialog box, you can base a new style on an existing style. When you then use the new style to format a paragraph, that paragraph is formatted with both styles' formats. You can create several styles based on one style.

- ▶ Some of Word's default styles are automatically followed by other styles. You can also define the style that follows another by typing a style name in the Next Style box of the Style dialog box.

- ▶ There are three ways to apply a style—from the Ribbon, by pressing defined shortcut keys, or by using the Format Style command (Alt,T,Y or press Ctrl-S twice). The fastest way to apply a style is by pressing shortcut keys. However, when you select Format Style, Word displays the Style dialog box so that you can change formats.

- ▶ Word provides two ways to display a style name for the current paragraph: in the Style list box in the Ribbon and, optionally, on the left side of the screen. To display the style name on-screen, select the Tools Options command (Alt,O,O). Then select the Options dialog box for the View category and type a value between 0" and 3.34" in the Style Area Width box.

- ▶ Although you cannot rename or delete a Word default style, use the Format Style command to rename or delete any style that you have defined. If you rename a style, the paragraphs that have been formatted with that style assume the new style name, but all formats remain the same. If you delete a style, the affected paragraphs assume the formats of the Normal style.

# Using Word's Advanced Features

## In This Chapter

- ► *Using glossaries*
- ► *Changing, deleting, and printing glossary entries*
- ► *Recording, running, deleting, and renaming macros*
- ► *Using Word's automatic macros*
- ► *Creating templates from documents, from templates, and from scratch*
- ► *Editing and changing templates*

As you learned in Chapter 11, Word for Windows provides styles as a shortcut method of storing and applying paragraph and character formats. Word provides three other methods for saving time and improving your efficiency. *Glossaries* enable you to store often-used text and graphics. *Macros* allow you to record and reuse command and keystroke sequences. *Templates* act as built-in guides for document formats. In this chapter, you'll also see how styles are related to glossaries, macros, and templates, and how to use each one of these Word features to make creating documents easier. For more information about all the topics covered in this chapter, see the *Microsoft Word for Windows User's Guide*.

# Connecting Glossaries, Macros, Styles, and Templates

A template, which is made up of glossaries, macros, and styles, provides Word with document-formatting guidelines. A template is a pattern or foundation for creating a particular type of document, such as a memo or a report. Every document in Word for Windows is based on a template—either the default NORMAL, a predefined template, or a custom template. Word's default template, NORMAL, provides default settings, such as margins, page dimensions, and character and paragraph formats. All templates, whether they are Word defaults or custom-made, have the extension .DOT.

Word makes features available to you in three ways: global, template, and document. When you use the default template, NORMAL, any glossaries, macros, and styles saved in this template are available globally—to all Word documents. When you use any other template, any glossaries, macros, and styles saved are available only to documents based on that template. Finally, you can tie styles, but not glossaries and macros, to an individual document.

# Using Glossaries to Save Time

In Chapter 3, you learned about the Spike, a permanent storage facility that is related to the glossary. Remember that you use the Spike to accumulate pieces of text and/or graphics from several locations. In contrast, a glossary entry is one piece of text and/or graphics from a single location. However, the single location from which you get a glossary entry can be the Spike.

If the glossary (including the Spike) is empty, the Glossary command on the **E**dit menu is dimmed, meaning that the command is not available. To activate the **E**dit Gl**o**ssary command, select text or graphics in the current document.

The glossary can store various types of text and graphics. For example, you can store a logo or other image that you insert at the bottom of every letter; your name and title or distribution lists; or a product name, including its registered trademark symbol. Using the glossary for these purposes means that you only have to create these items once. The glossary can hold up to 150 entries, but it's best to delete entries that you don't plan to use again. The larger your glossary, the longer Word will take to retrieve an entry. Use the **E**dit menu and Gl**o**ssary command to save, delete, and insert glossary entries.

To save selected text or graphics as a glossary entry, select Edit Gl**o**ssary (Alt,E,O). When Word displays the Glossary dialog box (shown in Figure 12.1), type a name for the glossary entry to be saved. Glossary entry names can include up to 31 characters and spaces. However, keep in mind that the longer the glossary entry name, the more characters you have to type when you insert an entry into a document. Don't make a glossary entry name so short that you can't remember its purpose. When saving a glossary entry, give it a name that will jog your memory. For example, if you are saving a command called CREATE, name the glossary entry `create`.

**291**

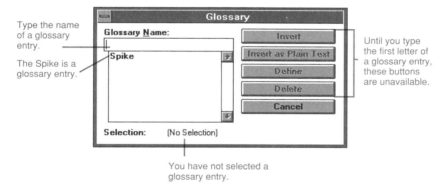

*Figure 12.1   The Glossary dialog box. Notice that there is some text or graphics saved in the Spike.*

Use the following Quick Steps to save selected text or graphics as a glossary entry.

 **Saving Text or Graphics as a Glossary Entry**

1. Select the text and/or graphics to be saved. You can also select special and nonprinting symbols.

   Word highlights the selection.

**2.** From the Edit menu, select the Glossary command (Alt,E,O).

Word displays the Glossary dialog box.

**3.** In the Glossary Name text box, type a name for the new glossary entry.

Word displays as many characters at the selected text as it can fit at the bottom of the dialog box (Figure 12.2). If the text or graphics selection is greater than can fit at the bottom of the dialog box, Word displays a line of text and an ellipsis ( . . . ). If you store a graphic, you'll see an ellipsis at the bottom of the dialog box.

**4.** Click on the Define button or press Enter.

Word returns to the current document. When you save the document and its template, Word automatically saves glossary entries.  □

If you are using the Word default template, NORMAL.DOT, Word will not ask you to specify a storage location for a glossary entry. However, if you've defined and attached a custom template to the current document, Word may ask where you want to store the glossary entry. If you select As Global, the glossary entry is available to all documents, no matter what template a document uses. To limit this glossary entry to only documents associated with a custom template, select In Template.

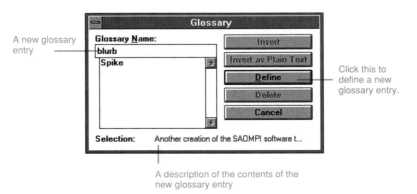

A new glossary entry

A description of the contents of the new glossary entry

Click this to define a new glossary entry.

*Figure 12.2    The Glossary dialog box with a glossary entry.*

You can also specify where glossary entries are stored by using the **F**ile **T**emplate command. In the Template dialog box, you have three storage choices: Global, With Document Template, and Prompt for Each New Save. Select Global to make glossary entries available to all new documents. Select With Document Template to make glossary entries available to only those documents associated with the current template. Select Prompt for Each New Save to specify a storage location every time you add an entry to the glossary.

It's a simple procedure to insert a glossary entry into a document, and you can insert an entry in as many locations as you want. When you insert a glossary entry, you can insert it as it was saved (including formatting), or you can insert it without any formatting. Click on the Insert button to insert the entry with its original formats; click on Insert as Plain Text to insert the entry without formats.

To insert a glossary entry in the current document, use the following Quick Steps.

 **Inserting a Glossary Entry into Your Document**

| | |
|---|---|
| 1. Place the insertion point where you want to insert a glossary entry. | The insertion point flashes on and off at its location. |
| 2. From the Edit menu, select the Glossary command (Alt,E,O). | Word displays the Glossary dialog box. |
| 3. Select a glossary entry from the Glossary Name list by moving the mouse pointer or pressing ↓ or ↑. | Word highlights your selection. |
| 4. Select Insert (or press Enter) or Insert as Plain Text. You can combine the actions of steps 3 and 4 by double-clicking on the glossary entry name of your choice. | Word inserts the contents of the glossary entry into the current document, starting at the location of the insertion point. □ |

To insert the same entry elsewhere in the document, place the insertion point at a new location and press F4 or select the Edit Repeat command (Alt,E,R). To undo the insertion, press Ctrl-Z or select Edit-Undo (Alt,E,U). Because Undo and Repeat remember the most recent action performed, execute either of these commands before performing any other action.

> **Tip:** To insert a glossary entry whose name you know, move the insertion point where you want the entry placed, type the name of the glossary entry, and press F3. If Word displays an error message, try typing a space, and then retype the entry name and press F3.

## Changing, Deleting, and Printing Glossary Entries

When you know that you have completed a document, you no longer need glossary entries that are specifically saved for that document. You can either delete an entry outright or save a new entry and give it the old entry name.

You can print a list of glossary entries and their contents to keep track of the entries for a particular document or for all documents. This is helpful when you can't remember the contents of a glossary entry. To print a list of glossary entries, select the File Print command (Alt,F,P or Ctrl-Shift-F12). When Word displays the Print dialog box, select Glossary from the Print list box, and select OK or press Enter. Word prints each glossary entry name and its contents.

To delete a glossary entry, select Edit Glossary (Alt,E,O). When Word displays the Glossary dialog box, select the glossary entry name from the Glossary Name list box and select Delete. Word deletes the entry and dims the Delete button. To return to the current document, select Close or press Enter. You cannot undo the deletion of a glossary entry, and Word does not ask you to confirm a deletion, so be very careful before you delete a glossary entry.

To change a glossary entry, insert the entry into your document and edit it there. Then select the changed entry and select Edit Glossary (Alt,E,O). When Word displays the Glossary dialog box, select from the Glossary Name list box the name of the entry that you changed. Then select Define. When Word displays a dialog box asking if you want to redefine the glossary entry, select Yes. Word replaces the entry's contents and returns to the current document.

# Using Macros

Macros are the means by which you can record command and keystroke sequences that you use often. To run a macro after you have recorded it, simply select one command or press a shortcut key. Word then executes all the commands or keystrokes that you have recorded, saving you time and effort.

Word provides two ways of creating macros: using the macro recorder and using the macro language. Since the macro recorder is easier to learn and to use, this section will focus only on the macro recorder. For information about using Word's WordBasic macro language, see the *Microsoft Word for Windows User's Guide*.

## *Recording a Macro*

**295**

When you turn on the macro recorder, it accumulates each command or keystroke as you enter it. After you have recorded a sequence, you can repeat the series of commands and keystrokes by running the macro.

To start recording, select the Tools menu and the Record Macro command (Alt,O,R). When Word displays the Record Macro dialog box (shown in Figure 12.3), type a macro name in the Record Macro Name box. Macro names may be one to 33 characters long; they may not contain spaces and must start with an alphabetic character. You can select Word's choice, Macro1, but it's best to relate a macro name to the actions that you're recording. For example, if you're recording a series of actions that turn on the Ruler, Ribbon, and Toolbar, and select the viewing mode, you could call the macro DOCSETUP. After entering the macro name, type a description (up to about 150 characters) in the Description box.

If you know that you will use this macro often, you can specify a shortcut key for running the macro by making a selection in the Shortcut Key box. Keep in mind that there is a limited combination of keys available to you, so don't assign shortcut keys to every macro you create. To select an unassigned key combination, select the Ctrl and/or Shift check boxes; then open the Key list box and select from the list of keys. If the key combination is already assigned, Word displays the command or macro with which it is associated. Otherwise (unassigned) is displayed. You are more likely to find an unassigned shortcut key starting with both Ctrl and Shift. For that reason, Word starts with both keys checked in the Record Macro dialog box.

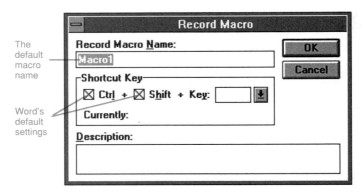

The default macro name

Word's default settings

*Figure 12.3   The Record Macro dialog box.*

After you have completed the dialog box, select OK or press Enter. Word displays REC in the Status bar. This indicates that the macro recorder is turned on and will record every action or command that you use. To turn off the macro recorder, select Tools Stop Recorder (Alt,O,R).

When the macro recorder is turned on, the mouse pointer changes. Instead of looking like an I-beam, the pointer looks like a transparent arrow, as shown in Figure 12.4. This is a reminder that the macro recorder cannot record mouse actions in the text area. You can still use the mouse pointer to select commands and options.

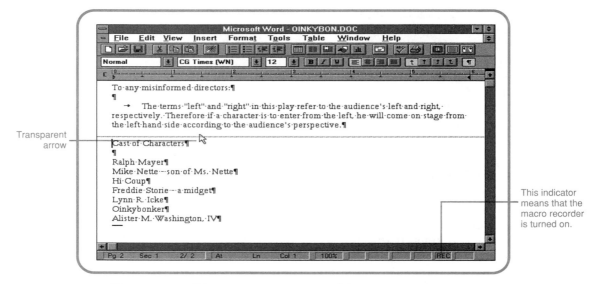

Transparent arrow

This indicator means that the macro recorder is turned on.

*Figure 12.4   The computer screen with a transparent arrow and the REC indicator. This means that the macro recorder is turned on.*

To record a macro, use the following Quick Steps.

 **Recording a Macro**

| | |
|---|---|
| 1. From the Tools menu, select Record Macro (Alt,O,R). | Word displays the Record Macro dialog box. |
| 2. In the Record Macro Name box, type a macro name. | As you type, Word scrolls characters off the left side of the Record Macro Name Box. |
| 3. In the Description box, type a description. | Word displays the description in the Macro Run dialog box. This helps you to select the appropriate macro. |
| 4. In the Shortcut key area, specify keys to be used to start the macro. | If you have selected a key combination that is already assigned, Word displays the name of the action. Otherwise, Word displays (unassigned). |
| 5. Select OK or press Enter. | Word returns to the document window and displays REC in the Status bar. The mouse pointer turns into a transparent arrow. |
| 6. Perform commands or press keys that you want recorded. | The macro recorder accumulates the actions as you perform them. |
| 7. From the Tools menu, select the Stop Recorder command (Alt,O,R). | Word stops the macro recorder. □ |

Storing a macro is the same as storing glossary entries. If you are using the Word default template, NORMAL, you don't have to specify a storage location. However, if you have defined and have attached a custom template to the current document, Word may ask where you want to store the macro. To access the macro for all documents regardless of the template to which they are attached, select As Global. To limit this macro only to documents attached to the custom template, select In Template.

Word also provides a command that you can use to specify where macros will be stored. Select File Template (Alt,F,T). In the box labeled Store New Macros and Glossaries as, you have three choices: Global, With Document Template, and Prompt for Each New Save. Select Global to make macros available to all new documents. Select With Document Template to make macros available to only those documents associated with the current template. Select Prompt for Each New Save to specify a storage location every time you create a new macro.

## Using Word's Auto Macros

Not only can you run macros by using certain keystrokes but you can also create macros that run whenever you select certain commands or when you start or exit Word. These special macros are known as *automatic macros* and have reserved names. When an action like starting Word or opening a document is performed, you can have a special macro automatically perform a series of actions. The procedure for recording an automatic macro is the same one described in the preceding Quick Steps, "Recording a Macro."

As an example of an automatic macro, you could create a macro named AutoExec, which would run a series of actions that you wanted Word to perform automatically when you started the program. Table 12.1 lists the reserved macro names and gives a description for each.

*Table 12.1   Word's automatic macro names.*

| Reserved Name | Description |
| --- | --- |
| AutoExec | A macro with this name automatically runs when you start Word. |
| AutoNew | A macro with this name automatically runs when you create a new document. |
| AutoOpen | A macro with this name automatically runs when you open a document. |
| AutoClose | A macro with this name automatically runs when you close a document. |
| AutoExit | A macro with this name automatically runs when you exit Word. |

## Running a Macro

Once you have created a macro, you can run it by selecting the Tools Macro command (Alt,O,M). When Word displays the Macro dialog box (shown in Figure 12.5), you can select from three lists. Note that you must have defined a macro for these lists to appear. You can display a list of macros available for all documents by selecting Global Macros in the Show box. If you are working with a template other than NORMAL, you can display a list of macros available for documents associated with the active template by selecting Template Macros in the Show box. You can also display and/or run Word commands by selecting Commands. In the Macro Name box, either type or select a macro name. Then select Run.

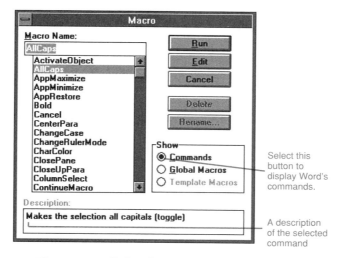

299

*Figure 12.5    The Macro dialog box enables you to display macros and Word commands. Here, Word commands are selected and listed.*

## Deleting and Renaming Macros

To change the name of a macro that you have created, select Tools Macro (Alt,O,M). When the Macro dialog box appears, display either Global Macros or Template Macros. Type a macro name or select one from the list. Then select Rename. When Word displays the Rename dialog box, type a new macro name into the New Macro Name text box; then select OK or press Enter. Word renames the macro and returns to the Macro dialog box.

To delete a macro that you have created, select Tools Macro (Alt,O,M). When the Macro dialog box appears, display either Global Macros or Template Macros. Type the name of the macro that you want to delete, or select one from the list. Then select Delete. Word deletes the macro and returns to the Macro dialog box.

## Document Templates

As you know, all Word documents are built on structures known as templates. Templates contain glossary entries, macro keystrokes, and styles. Word's default template, NORMAL, is used as the basis for every document unless you attach or create a different template. In addition to NORMAL, Word provides many predefined templates that you can use to set up documents (for example, letters, memoranda, reports, or even a fax cover sheet). For a list of predefined templates, select File New (Alt,F,N) to display the New dialog box. You can also create custom templates from scratch or based on other templates or documents. You'll learn about predefined and custom templates in this section.

You can define templates to standardize the appearance of your company's documents. For example, use the LETBLOCK template to create business letters with block paragraphs. Or, write all your business proposals using PROPOSAL.

Use the **File New** command to start a new document based on a predefined Word template or to create a new template. After you select **File New**, Word displays the New dialog box, shown in Figure 12.6. Word provides 19 predefined templates, including the default NORMAL.

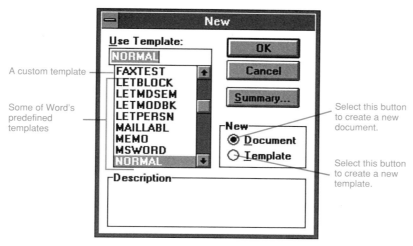

A custom template

Some of Word's predefined templates

Select this button to create a new document.

Select this button to create a new template.

*Figure 12.6    The New dialog box, which contains a list of Word's predefined templates along with one custom template (FAXTEST).*

**301**

## Creating a Template from a Document

The easiest way to create a template is to create and format a document. When you have the format just the way you want it, save the document along with its styles, glossary entries, and macro keystrokes. The following Quick Steps show you the procedure for creating a template from the current document.

 **Creating a Template from a Document**

1. From the **File** menu, select the **New** command (Alt,F,N).

   Word displays the New dialog box.

2. Select Template.

   Word displays the Use Template box.

3. Type the name of the existing document to be used as the basis for this template.

   Word adds the .DOC extension for you.

4. Select OK or press Enter.

   Word may display the Summary Info box.

5. Fill in as much information as you wish.

If you type anything in the Title box, Word uses the text as the template description.

6. Select OK or press Enter.

Word returns to the current document, and the Title bar includes the name Template1 (see Figure 12.7). □

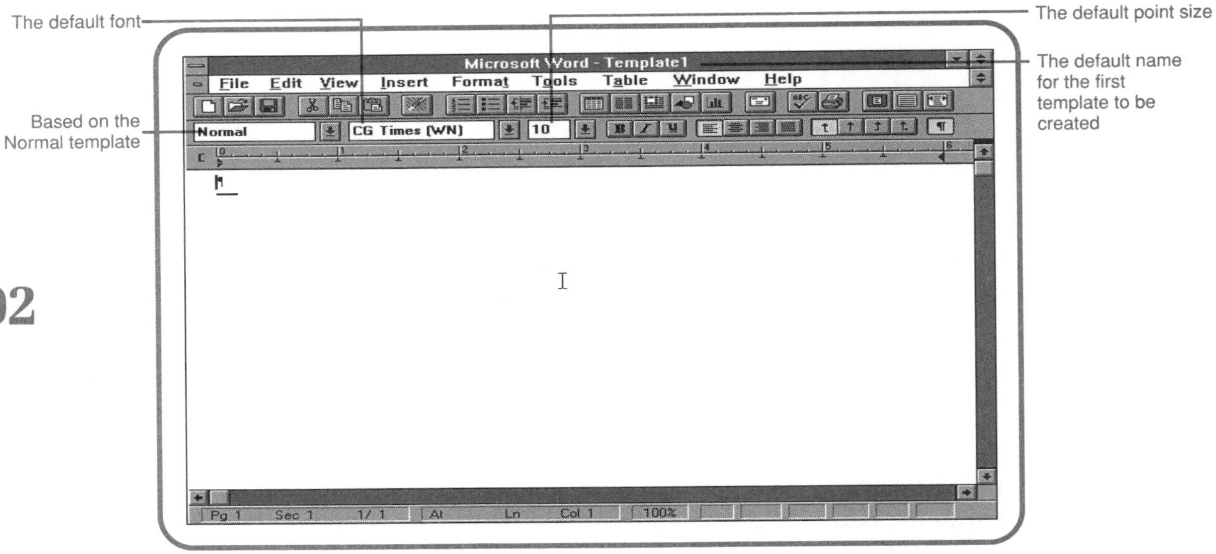

The default font — — The default point size

— The default name for the first template to be created

Based on the Normal template

*Figure 12.7    The Template1 name in the Title bar. Until you name a template, Word names it temporarily.*

## Creating a Template Not Based on a Document

To create a template that is not based on an existing document, select File New (Alt,F,N). When Word displays the New dialog box, select the Template button. Then select OK or press Enter. When you return to the document window, notice that Template1 is displayed in the Title bar.

You can now create styles, glossary entries, and/or macro keystrokes; define any type of format (ranging from document-wide through character); and type text that will become a permanent part of this template.

When you have completed the template design, select File Save (Alt,F,S or Shift-F12). Notice that when Word displays the Save As dialog box (shown in Figure 12.8), all the files listed in the File Name box have a .DOT extension. Type a template name from one to eight characters long, and select OK or press Enter. You don't have to type the .DOT extension; Word does it for you.

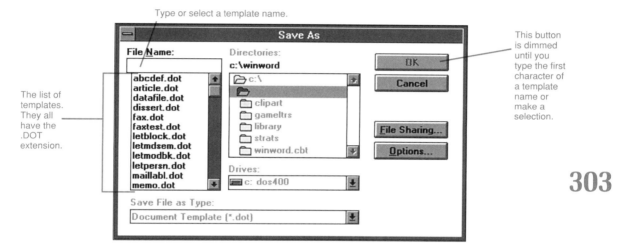

Type or select a template name.

The list of templates. They all have the .DOT extension.

This button is dimmed until you type the first character of a template name or make a selection.

**303**

*Figure 12.8    The list of current template files in the Save As dialog box.*

If Word displays the Summary Info dialog box, fill in any information you want. Anything you type in the Title box serves as the description in the New dialog box. Select OK or press Enter. Word returns to the document window and displays the name of the template in the Title bar.

## Creating a Template Based on an Existing Template

Rather than define a new template for a document, consider using one of Word's predefined templates. You can use the template as is, or you can customize it for your own needs. If you plan to customize a predefined template, first save it under a new name and then edit it. This way the original template remains untouched.

Creating a new template based on an existing template works in much the same way as creating a new style based on an existing style, which is covered in Chapter 11. When you base a new template on an existing template, Word uses the information in both templates for a document based on the new template. For example, you might start with the FAX.DOT template (shown in Figure 12.9), which is a fax cover sheet, and create a new template to add a message to the bottom of the cover sheet. The new template combines the contents of both templates.

Some of the text in the FAX template

304

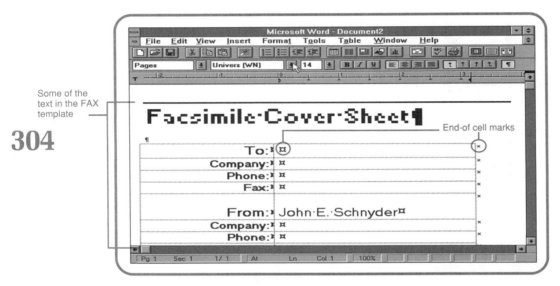

*Figure 12.9    The FAX fax cover sheet, one of Word's predefined templates.*

To create a template based on an existing template, select File New (Alt,F,N). When Word displays the New dialog box, select the Template button. In the Use Template list box, type or select the name of the existing template that will be the foundation for the new template. Select OK or press Enter. Word returns to the document window and displays any text in the template. After editing the template, select File Save As (Alt,F,A or F12), and type a template name in the File Name box. Then select OK or press Enter.

If Word displays the Summary Info dialog box, fill it in as you wish. Anything in the Title box serves as the description. Once again, select OK or press Enter.

## *Editing a Template*

Edit a template as you would a document. Be aware, however, that when you edit a template, any documents that are based on this template don't automatically change to fit the new version; they are based on the older version of the template. If you change the default template NORMAL, you'll permanently change Word's defaults. This affects future documents only.

## *Assigning or Changing the Template for a Document*

To open a new document based on any template, including NORMAL or one of Word's predefined templates, select File New (Alt,F,N). When Word displays the New dialog box, select a template from the Use Template box. Select OK or press Enter. Word returns to the document window and opens a new document based on the selected template. For a list of predefined templates, see the *Microsoft Word for Windows User's Guide,* the New dialog box, or the list of templates found in the Help facility under the heading `Templates That Come with Word`.

> **Tip:** You can sometimes use one of Word's predefined templates as a shortcut for document creation. For example, to create a document with landscape orientation, select REPLAND. Edit it as you wish and then save it using **File Save As**.

When you start working on a new document, it is automatically based on the NORMAL template unless you specifically selected another template from the New dialog box. To take advantage of the macros, glossary entries, and custom keys and menus of another template, you can change to that template. However, you will not be able to apply any of the formats, styles, or text associated with that template.

To change from the current template, display the document and select File Template (Alt,F,T). When Word displays the Template dialog box, type the name of the template that you wish to attach in the Attach Document to box, or select the list arrow to open a list of templates from which you can choose. Then select OK or press Enter.

You can also merge styles from two templates. You can keep using the current template but take advantage of the options associated with another template. You'll see how to merge styles in the following section.

## Adding or Merging Styles to a Template

Normally, Word saves styles to the current document rather than to the current template. However, you can add a style to the current template so that it becomes available to all documents based on that template. Keep in mind that if you apply styles to NORMAL, these styles are available for all Word documents. You can also merge a style from one template into another template or document, thereby making the style available for the template in which it was originally located and the template or document into which it was merged.

To add a style to the template associated with the current document, select Format Style (Alt, T, Y or press Ctrl-S twice). In the Style Name box of the Style dialog box, select the name of a style and select Define. Select the Add to Template check box. Select Change and then Close.

To merge all the styles from one template into another template or document, first open the document or template into which you want to merge the styles and make sure that the document or template is in the active window (refer to Chapter 13 if you need help to do this). Select Format Style (Alt, T, Y or press Ctrl-S twice). When Word displays the Style dialog box, select Define and then Merge. Word displays the Merge Styles dialog box, which is shown in Figure 12.10. To merge styles to the template of the current document, you do not need to select that document; just select the To Template button. To merge styles to another document or to another template, first select the document or template in the File Name box. Then select the To Template button. If there are duplicate file names, Word displays a message asking you to verify whether you want to replace the styles with merged styles of the same name. To merge styles from the selected document or template into the current document, select the From Template button. Then select the Close button.

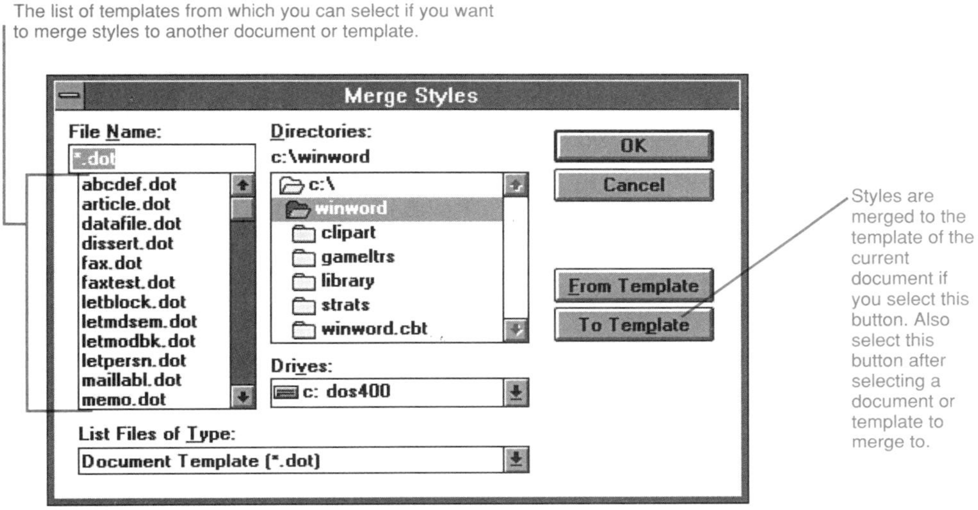

The list of templates from which you can select if you want
to merge styles to another document or template.

Styles are
merged to the
template of the
current
document if
you select this
button. Also
select this
button after
selecting a
document or
template to
merge to.

*Figure 12.10   The Merge Styles dialog box.*

**307**

# What You Have Learned

▶ Use glossaries to save text or graphics that you will use
repeatedly. To save a glossary entry, select the Edit Glossary
command (Alt,E,O). The Spike is a special type of glossary
entry.

▶ When you turn on the macro recorder, it starts accumulating
each command or keystroke as you enter it. To start recording, select Tools Record Macro (Alt,O,R). After accumulating
actions and commands, stop the recorder by selecting Tools
Stop Recorder (Alt,O,R).

▶ Word provides six automatic macros, which run automatically at certain times in a Word session. Word reserves
names for these automatic macros.

▶ To run a macro, select Tools Macro (Alt,O,M). You can run
macros available for all documents, macros associated with
the active template, or Word commands.

▶ Templates, which are made up of glossaries, macros, and styles, are document-formatting guidelines. You can create a template from a document, from a template, or from scratch. Use the File New command (Alt,F,N) to start a new document based on a template or to create a new template.

**308**

# Managing Documents, Windows, and the Word Program

## In This Chapter

▶ *Searching, deleting, copying, sorting, and displaying files with the Find File command*

▶ *Selecting, opening, and printing multiple files*

▶ *Converting documents to Word for Windows from other formats*

▶ *Manipulating windows*

▶ *Customizing the Toolbar*

This chapter begins with an explanation of the handy **F**ind File command, which allows you to manage your documents. It lets you search your list of files in order to copy, delete, open, or print several documents at a time. Next you'll learn how to open several windows at once or to manipulate a single window so that you can split that window.

Finally, you'll learn how to customize the Toolbar. The Toolbar is a new and exciting feature of Word for Windows. Twenty-two default buttons give you easy point-and-click access to many commonly used commands and procedures. Additional buttons can be customized so that if you have tasks that you perform often, you can do so with a click of a button.

# Using the Find File Command

The Find File command is an all-purpose command that allows you to copy, print, open and delete documents. In addition, you can search for specific documents using information from the Summary Info box, and you can view the contents of a file.

When you select the Find File command from the File menu, Word displays the Find File dialog box, which is shown in Figure 13.1. The Find File dialog box lists the files in the current path. The Content box shows the top of the first page of the highlighted file in the File Name list box.

**310**

Selected
document file

The contents of
the selected file

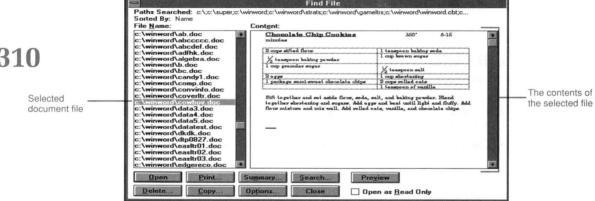

*Figure 13.1    The Find File dialog box.*

## Searching for Files

If you are looking for a particular file and remember only sketchy information about it (such as the approximate date it was created, its title, any keywords, or its author), select the Search button to narrow your choice of files.

When you select the Search button in the Find File dialog box, Word displays the Search dialog box (shown in Figure 13.2), in which you can specify the file's location, the file type, the time period during which the file was created and/or saved, and information like title, subject, keywords, author, who saved the file, or text strings that might appear in the document itself.

When you enter text strings to search for documents, whether they are in a title search or a keyword search, you can use special characters to enhance your search. Table 13.1 lists the special characters available for a document search.

*Figure 13.2   The Search dialog box.*

**311**

*Table 13.1   Word's special search characters.*

| Character | Description |
|---|---|
| * | Searches for any number of characters (for example, ABC*.* finds ABC001.DOC and ABCDEF.DOC). This is known as a *wildcard character*. |
| ? | Searches for one character (for example, ABC??F.DOC finds ABCDEF.DOC but not ABC001.DOC.) This is known as a *wildcard character*. |
| ^ | Enables Word to recognize a special character (for example, ^? identifies the question mark as punctuation, not a wildcard character). |
| & | The summary information must match every criterion listed. This symbol represents a logical AND. |
| , | The summary information must match at least one criterion listed. This symbol represents a logical OR. |
| ~ | The summary information must not match this criterion. This symbol represents a logical NOT. |

## Sorting and Displaying Documents

To display your documents in a given order in the Find File dialog box or to display the files according to some particular criterion, select the Options button. When Word displays the Options dialog box (shown in Figure 13.3), you can determine how files will be sorted in the File Name list box and how those documents are displayed.

By default, contents of files are displayed in the Find File dialog box. If you have many documents that use text with a small point size, reading each document can be difficult. For this reason, consider displaying document file names with the summary information that Word finds for each document. You can display files by the title, author, summary information, or document statistics. You can also display the summary information for the selected file by choosing the Summary button.

In order to view a graphic, it must be embedded in a document. However, if it is not embedded, use the Preview button to view it.

You can find sort options in the Sort Files By box. You can sort by Author, Creation Date, Last Saved By, Last Saved Date, Name, and Size.

**312**

Sort files alphabetically by name and place the result in the File Name box.

The default displays the contents of the file.

*Figure 13.3    The Options dialog box from the Find File command.*

## Selecting and Opening Multiple Files

The file that will be selected is highlighted in the File Name list box. To select a group of contiguous files, hold down the Shift key and click the left mouse button on the first file in the group. Then (still holding down Shift) click on the last file in the group. All files in the group should then be highlighted. To select files that are not contiguous, hold down the Ctrl key while clicking with the left mouse button on the desired file names.

You can open a document from the Find File dialog box the same way you would open a document using the File Open command. Double-click with the left mouse button on the document name, or highlight it and select the Open button.

You can open more than one file at a time (as long as the files are listed consecutively) by selecting all the files to be opened and choosing the Open button.

If you want to look through the contents of a file but you don't want to make any changes to it, select the Open as Read Only check box. You cannot save a file that is opened while this box is checked. To save changes that you have made, use the Save **As** command and save the document under a different name.

## *Printing Multiple Files*

The Print button lets you print one or more highlighted files. You can select the custom printing options (described in Chapter 9) when Word displays the Print dialog box.

## *Deleting and Copying Files*

**313**

Whether you select one file or multiple files, you can delete or copy the selection. When you select the Delete button, Word displays a small dialog box, which asks you to confirm your actions.

To copy selected files to a disk or to another directory on your hard disk drive, use the **C**opy command. Select one or more files and then choose the Copy button. The Copy dialog box prompts you to enter the path (the drive and directory) in which you want to store the copies. You can type the path name, or you can use the Drives and Directories list boxes to create a path to which the copies will be copied.

# Converting Documents to Different File Formats

You won't always have the luxury of working with Word for Windows document formats. If a coworker or client uses some other program (including word processors, spreadsheets, and so on) to create documents, you may need to convert a file from that format to the Word for Windows format. Conversely, you may have to convert a file from Word for Windows format to a foreign format. Word provides conversion utilities for both types of conversions.

---

> ✏️ **Note:** In order to use the Word conversion utilities described in this section, you must install them either at the original installation or at a later time. See Appendix A for a description of Word for Windows' installation.

---

When you open a document that is not in a Word for Windows format, Word recognizes that the format is different and prompts you with the Convert File dialog box. Select the file format of the non-Word document to be converted, and select OK or press Enter; Word converts the file to Word for Windows format.

To convert a Word for Windows document to another format, select File Save As (Alt,F,A). When Word displays the Save As dialog box, open the Save File as Type list box and select the format to which you wish to convert the file.

For a list of the different document formats, see the Word for Windows help facility for the Save As dialog box.

# Manipulating Application and Document Windows

An important feature of Windows (and applications like Word for Windows) is that you can switch between applications and documents without having to open and close them. To use Windows most effectively, learn how to manipulate application and document windows. In Chapter 1, you learned a little about using the components of the Windows screen. Now you'll learn about them in more depth.

When you first open Word, both the Word application window and the document window are *maximized*—they take up the entire screen. In the maximized mode, the two windows appear as one, but they are actually two distinct windows, one superimposed on the other. Figure 13.4 shows the starting Word window.

Like any other Windows application, you can resize the Word window so that other applications are visible. Even though you can use only one application at a time, it is easy to switch from one to another. You don't have to start an application every time you want to use it; just activate that application's window. Windows lets you display up to nine windows at a time. The document window can be manipulated just like the application window, and you can have up to nine document windows open at a time.

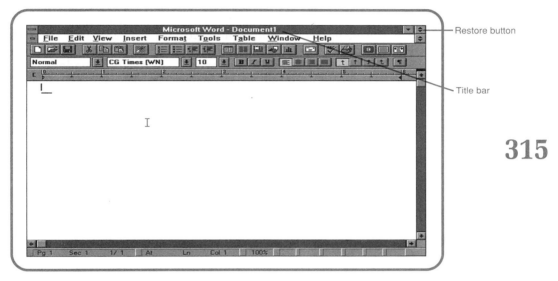

*Figure 13.4    Word's starting window.*

315

The following sections describe the commands commonly used to manipulate windows. For more information about manipulating windows, refer to your Windows and Word for Windows documentation.

## Restoring and Maximizing a Window

When you open Word, the application window fills the entire screen. To shrink this application window but not totally remove it (in order to look at other applications), select the Restore button on the right side of the Title bar. You can restore either the Word program window or a document window.

When you restore a window, the Restore button changes from double triangles to an up triangle. When you click on this button, you maximize the window, which means that the window takes as much room on-screen as it possibly can.

## Resizing a Window

Once you have restored an application or document window, you can resize it. Move the mouse pointer to any location on the border of the restored window. The mouse pointer changes to a double-headed arrow. Click the left mouse button and drag the border to a new location. Notice that, near the corners, the double-headed arrow points diagonally. This means that you can change both the horizontal and vertical sides at one time while keeping the starting proportions of the window. Anywhere else on the borders, you can change either the horizontal or the vertical sides but not both.

**316**

## Moving a Window

When a window is restored, you can move it around on-screen by moving the mouse pointer to its Title bar, clicking the left mouse button, and dragging the window to a new location.

## Navigating and Activating Multiple Document Windows

Up to this point, you probably have worked with only one document in one window at a time. At times, working in only one window can limit you. Suppose you are working in one document, and you need to check some facts in another document or even another program. With a Windows-based application (like Word for Windows), you can have all your facts accessible in other windows. The next sections will explain how to work with several documents in several document windows.

Remember that you can use the **File Find File** command to open multiple documents. There are several ways to navigate multiple document windows and to make a particular window the active window. You can press Ctrl-F6 to scroll forward through the multiple windows, or press Ctrl-Shift-F6 to scroll back through the windows. You can also use the **W**indow menu, which is shown in Figure 13.5, to select an active window. Either select a number or click next to the document to be activated. You can move the mouse pointer within the window that you want to activate; then click the left mouse button.

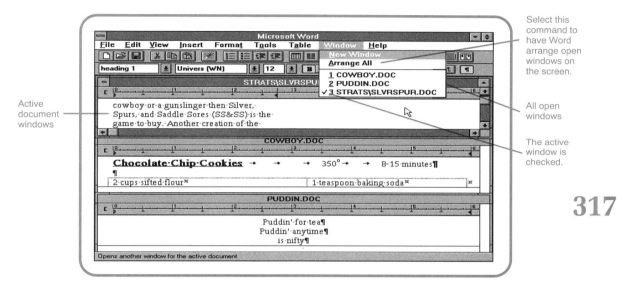

Select this command to have Word arrange open windows on the screen.

Active document windows

All open windows

The active window is checked.

**317**

*Figure 13.5    The open Window menu from which you can select a window or arrange multiple windows.*

## Arranging Multiple Document Windows

Use the **W**indow menu and the **A**rrange All command to divide the available space on the computer screen among all the open documents. Word determines how the windows are arranged. The window that is active at the time of the command is at the top of the screen.

## Closing a Document Window

Close a document window by opening the Document Control menu and selecting Close. A shortcut method is to press Ctrl-F4 or double-click on the Document Control button.

## *Splitting a Document Window*

When you are working on a document, and you need to refer to some text in another part of the same document, Word provides a tool that splits your document window, allowing you to view and work on two parts of your document.

At the top of the vertical scroll bar (immediately above the up arrow) is a small rectangle. To split a document window, move the mouse pointer to the rectangle. When the mouse pointer changes to two horizontal lines with up and down arrows, click the left mouse button and drag down. Word displays a faint line stretching the width of the screen. Drag the line until it is located at the place where you want to split the screen. Then release the left mouse button. Word displays two vertical scroll bars—one for each part of the document window. The blinking insertion point indicates the active part of the window. The two parts of the document window are actually two views of the same document, so that any change you make in one part is reflected in the other part as well. Figure 13.6 shows a split document window.

**318**

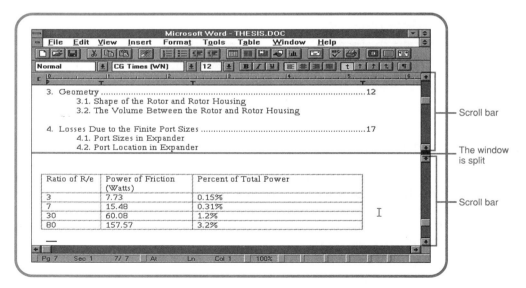

*Figure 13.6    A split document window.*

## *Switching to Other Windows Applications from Word*

You can switch to other Windows applications without closing Word. Simply open the Application Control menu and select Switch To (Alt,space bar,W or Ctrl-Esc). Windows displays the Task List (shown in Figure 13.7), which shows all the programs that are open. To switch to one of the listed programs, select it.

The list of
open programs

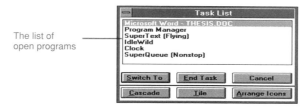

**Figure 13.7** **The Windows Task List, which shows open programs.**

319

# Customizing the Toolbar

The Toolbar is a new Word for Windows feature. It is located just below the Menu bar (and above the Ribbon) on your screen. Its 22 default buttons cover many of Word's commonly used commands and procedures, including opening and saving a document; cutting, copying, and pasting text and graphics; undoing your last action; formatting numbered and bulleted lists; and printing. All of the default buttons are shown on the inside back cover of this book.

As you become more comfortable with Word, you'll find that you use certain commands more than others. Chances are these commands are already on the Toolbar, but if they aren't, there is a way to customize the Toolbar by adding more buttons or by replacing some of the default buttons. The upcoming sections will explain how to add or delete buttons and restore or reassign buttons.

## *Adding a Button to the Toolbar*

If you want to add a button to the Toolbar, Word provides a variety of options. You can define the button for all documents or for only those documents associated with a specific template. You can display either a list of Word commands or a list of macros that you have created. There are 22 default Toolbar buttons. Since you insert a button into a space between the default buttons, you can add about five buttons before some of the default buttons are squeezed off the right side of the Toolbar.

To add a button to the Toolbar, use the following Quick Steps.

 **Adding a Button to the Toolbar**

1. From the Tools menu, select Options (Alt,O,O).

   Word displays an Options dialog box.

2. Select Toolbar in the Category box.

   Word displays the Options dialog box for the Toolbar category (Figure 13.8).

3. In the Show box, select Commands or Macros.

   Word displays a list of choices from which you can select. The box is titled either Commands or Macros, depending on your selection.

4. In the Context box, select Global to make this Toolbar button available to all documents, or select Template to make this button available only to documents associated with a specific template.

   Word surrounds your choice with a dotted-line border.

5. Choose from the list in the Commands/Macros box.

   Word describes your selection in the Description box.

6. Select a button in the Button box.

   The first nine buttons displayed are the Word default buttons.

7. In the Tool to Change box, select the button to be replaced or a space into which your selection will fit.

   Word highlights your selection.

8. Select Change.

    Word adds the defined button to the Toolbar.

9. Repeat steps 3 through 8 until you have finished making your selection. Then select Close.

    Word closes the Options dialog box and returns to the document window.

☐

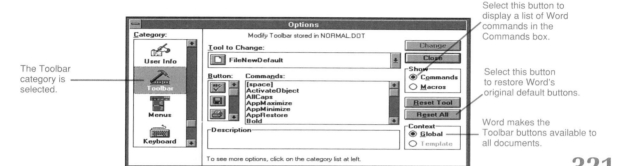

The Toolbar category is selected.

Select this button to display a list of Word commands in the Commands box.

Select this button to restore Word's original default buttons.

Word makes the Toolbar buttons available to all documents.

*Figure 13.8    The Options dialog box for the Toolbar category.*

321

> ✎ **Tip:** Word provides an alternative way to zoom using the Toolbar. Normally, the ViewZoom100 command (displayed in the Options dialog box for the Toolbar category) is assigned to the Zoom 100% Toolbar button. ViewZoom100 displays a document at 100% size, as does the Zoom 100% button on the Toolbar. By assigning the ViewZoom command (instead of the ViewZoom100 command) to the Toolbar button, you can choose from a range of zoom percentage. When you press the Zoom 100% Toolbar button (now reassigned to the ViewZoom command), Word allows you to scale from 25% to 200% by sliding the mouse pointer along a displayed arrow.

## Deleting a Button from the Toolbar

If you have a seldom-used button on the Toolbar, you can remove it in order to make room for a button that you'll use more often. Follow these Quick Steps to remove a button from the Toolbar.

**Removing a Button from the Toolbar**

| | |
|---|---|
| 1. From the Tools menu, select Options (Alt,O,O). | Word displays an Options dialog box. |
| 2. Select Toolbar in the Category box. | Word displays the Options dialog box for the Toolbar category. |
| 3. In the Show box, select Commands or Macros. | Word displays a list of choices from which you can select. The box is titled either Commands or Macros, depending on your selection. |
| 4. In the Tool to Change box, select the button to be removed from the Toolbar. | Word highlights your selection along with its associated button, closes the list, and displays the selection at the top of the box. |
| 5. In the Commands (or Macros) box, select [space], which is at the top of the list. | Word highlights your selection. |
| 6. Select Change. | Word removes the button from the Toolbar and displays [space] in the Tool to Change box. Word dims the Change button. |
| 7. Repeat steps 3 through 6 until you have removed all the buttons that you want. Then select Close. | Word closes the Options dialog box and returns to the document window. □ |

**322**

## *Restoring or Reassigning Buttons*

To restore the default buttons to the Toolbar, select Reset All. To return a specific button to its default setting on the Toolbar, select it in the Tool to Change box. If the button is a default, it remains on the Toolbar in its original position. If you have added the button to the Toolbar, Word removes it and restores the original button.

## **Q** Reassigning a Command or Macro Button

| | |
|---|---|
| 1. From the Tools menu, select Options (Alt,O,O). | Word displays an Options dialog box. |
| 2. Select Toolbar in the Category box. | Word displays the Options dialog box for the Toolbar category. |
| 3. In the Show box, select Commands or Macros. | Word displays a list of choices from which you can select. The box is titled either Commands or Macros, depending on your selection. |
| 4. In the Commands or Macros box, select the command or macro to be added to the Toolbar. | Word highlights your selection and "undims" the Change button. |
| 5. In the Tool to Change box, select the button to be changed. | Word highlights your selection. |
| 6. Select Change. | On the Toolbar, Word replaces the original button with your new selection. The Options dialog box remains on display. |
| 7. Select Close. | Word returns to the document window. □ |

**323**

# What You Have Learned

▶ The **F**ind File command on the **F**ile menu is an all-purpose command that allows you to review the contents of documents before you open them. Use this command to search through a list of files in order to open or print one or more files.

▶ You can use the File Find File command to open multiple documents in multiple windows. To move among multiple windows to activate one, press Ctrl-F6 or Ctrl-Shift-F6, move the mouse pointer to a window and click the left mouse button, or open the **W**indow menu and select a window.

▶ Word provides utilities to convert from other file formats to Word for Windows formats and also to convert from Word for Windows formats to other file formats. When you open a file in a foreign format,if you have installed the conversion utilities, Word asks you whether it should convert the file. When you save a file, you can select a specific file format.

▶ As a Windows application, Word's windows can be restored, maximized, resized, and moved by using the mouse or keystrokes. Using the mouse to restore a window, move the mouse pointer to the Restore button and click the left mouse button. To resize a window, move the mouse pointer to the window border, click the left mouse button, and drag the border to its new location. To move a window, move the mouse pointer to the Title bar, click the left mouse button, and drag the window to its new location.

**324**

▶ You can switch to other Windows applications from Word by opening the Applications Control menu and selecting Switch To (Alt,space bar,W or Ctrl-Esc). When Windows displays the Task List, select a program.

▶ Word allows you to customize the buttons on the Toolbar so that the commands you use most often are available to you. To define, remove, or restore a Toolbar button, select the Tools Options command and display the Options dialog box for the Toolbar category.

# Creating Form Letters, Labels, and Envelopes

## In This Chapter

► *Creating form letters by merging main documents and data files*

► *Creating data files and header records*

► *Sorting records in a data file*

► *Printing form letters on a printer and to a file*

► *Producing and printing mailing labels and envelopes*

Word enables you to produce documents that are custom-made for each member of your audience. By using a main document and a data file, you can mention each recipient by name, refer to his or her address, and incorporate special messages in selected letters. In addition, you can send your letter to selected segments of your audience.

In this chapter, you'll learn the basics of creating and printing form letters, mailing labels, and envelopes. Refer to the *Microsoft Word for Windows User's Guide* for advanced features.

# Creating and Printing Form Letters

The basic components of a form letter are a main document and a data file. Once you have opened these documents, you must link them. The linking, or merging, process is what actually creates a form letter.

The *main document* is like any other letter, with one exception. It includes all the text that you plan to send to your audience as a whole but omits the information unique to each individual. For example, a main document might include an invitation to a grand opening, a plea for a donation, or a cover letter for an enclosed brochure but would not include the name and address of any recipients. You can create a form letter using a brand-new or existing main document.

The *data file* contains the unique information about each recipient of your letter. A data file is a table that includes names, addresses, and information that might not even make its way into your letter. Information like the amount of the last donation, the money the recipient owes your company, or whether an individual pays with a check or a credit card might not appear in a letter but might trigger special messages in a letter (for example, "We appreciate receiving your check." or "You may have overlooked our last bill. Thank you for paying promptly."). The data file is made up of records (such as name, address, and telephone number) for each individual to whom you will send a letter. Records, in turn, are made up of fields, which consist of one piece of information about the individual.

The first record in a data file is the *header record,* containing all the *merge fields,* which identify or label the fields and tell Word what field goes where in a main document. Merge fields are between one and 31 characters long and can contain only letters, numbers, and underscores; no spaces are allowed. Examples of merge fields are First_Name, Last_Name, Address, and City. The remaining records in the data file contain the actual information about each individual. Examples are Mary, Smith, 123 Main Street, and Anytown. You can create a form letter by using a brand-new or an existing data file.

## *Creating and Linking a Main Document and a Data File*

The first step in creating a form letter is to open a main document. If you're starting with a new document, you don't need to enter text now. At this stage, you're just identifying the main document and the data file and creating a link between the two. If your main document does not exist, select the File New command (Alt,F,N) and select OK or press Enter. If your main document already exists, select File Open (Alt,F,O) and select the appropriate file name from the File Name box. Then select OK or press Enter.

You'll then attach a data file to the main document by selecting the Print Merge command from the File menu (Alt,F,M). Word displays the Print Merge Setup dialog box, which is shown in Figure 14.1. The Print Merge Setup dialog box is unique in that it not only has the buttons used to create a form letter but illustrates the creation of a form letter. When you view this box, the dimmed or undimmed state of the buttons serves as a reminder of what your next step is before you can merge the two documents.

**327**

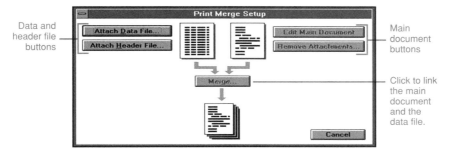

**Figure 14.1    The Print Merge Setup dialog box, which illustrates a print merge operation.**

Use the following Quick Steps to create and link a new main document with a new data file.

 **Creating and Linking a Main Document and a Data File**

1. To create a new main document, select the File menu and the New command (Alt,F,N).

   Word displays the New dialog box (Figure 14.2).

2. Select OK or press Enter.

Word displays a blank document window.

3. Select File Print Merge (Alt,F,M).

Word displays the Print Merge Setup dialog box.

4. Select the Attach Data File button.

Word displays the Attach Data File dialog box (Figure 14.3).

5. Select Create Data File.

Word displays the Create Data File dialog box (Figure 14.4).

6. Type the name of a merge field (for example, **First_Name**) in the Field Name box.

Word "undims" the Add button.

7. Select Add or press Enter.

Word adds the field to the Fields in Header Record box.

8. To delete a field, select Delete.

Word deletes the field from the Fields in Header Record box.

9. Repeat steps 6, 7,and 8 until you have added all the field names you want to the header record. Then select OK.

Word displays the Save As dialog box.

10. Enter the data file name in the File Name box. Then select OK or press Enter.

Word returns to the document window and displays the data file's header record on the screen. □

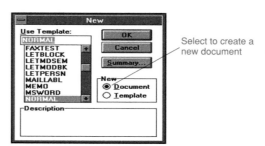

*Figure 14.2    The New dialog box, which enables you to create a main document.*

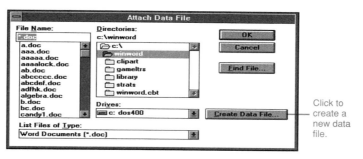

*Figure 14.3    The Attach Data File dialog box.*

*Figure 14.4    The Create Data File dialog box, in which you enter the names of the fields.*

There are two special features associated with a data file: custom buttons on the Toolbar, which are shown in Figure 14.5, and the Print Merge bar, shown in Figure 14.6. When Word displays a data file for the first time, new buttons are displayed on the Toolbar. If you press the button labeled M, Word clears the data file from the screen and displays the Print Merge bar, which enables you to insert a merge field into a document, check for errors, or print a form letter to the printer or to a file. On the Print Merge bar, you'll also find the Edit Data File button, which removes the Print Merge bar and returns to the data file. In other words, you can toggle between the Print Merge bar and the data file.

You have just learned about the M Toolbar button. Table 14.1 lists and describes all the data file Toolbar buttons.

*Table 14.1    Data file Toolbar buttons.*

| Button | Description |
| --- | --- |
| A | Inserts a new record before the current insertion point or after the last record in the data file |

*continues*

*Table 14.1    continued*

| Button | Description |
|--------|-------------|
| D | Deletes the record at the insertion point or deletes a record with a certain record number |
| E | Edits the record above the current insertion point or at the record that you go to |
| G | Goes to a record with a certain record number |
| F | Adds a new field to the data file |
| S | Sorts the entire file using up to three sort keys |
| N | Inserts record numbers in front of each record |
| C | Displays the Database Diagnostic Tools dialog box, so you can edit or check items in a data file |
| L | Manually creates a DDE* link |
| M | Displays the Print Merge bar and removes the data document file from the screen |

* DDE stands for Dynamic Data Exchange, an advanced Windows feature. DDE allows you to link the current document with either another application or the Clipboard. Then when you update text or graphics in the source document (the source of the text or graphics), the same text or graphics are updated in the document that is linked.

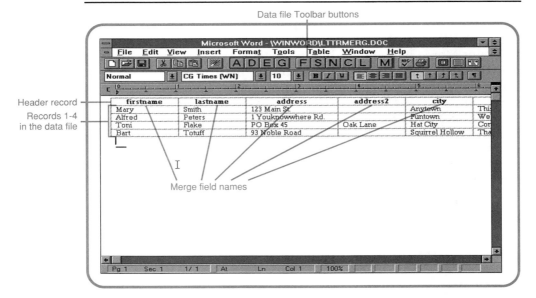

*Figure 14.5    The data file with its header record and the changed Toolbar.*

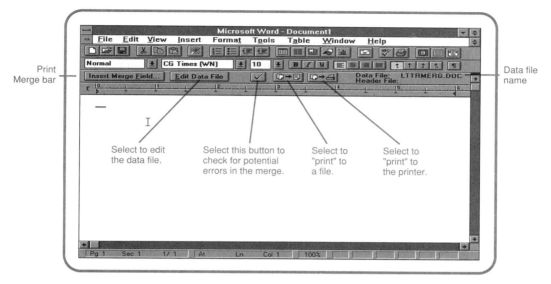

**Figure 14.6** **The Print Merge bar, which allows you to control form-letter creation on-screen.**

 **Tip:** Once the Print Merge bar is displayed, you can double-click on it to display the Print Merge Setup dialog box.

Complete the data file with the individual information for each record. In the column under each merge field name in the header record, type appropriate information. For example, under City, type the name of a city. You can edit the contents of a data file in the same way as you edit any Word document. In addition, you have the new Toolbar buttons to help you.

When you remove a data file from the screen and display the Print Merge bar, the link between the data file and the main document remains. To bring the data file back to the screen and remove the Print Merge bar, select Edit Data file from the Print Merge bar. You'll learn about the other options on the Print Merge bar later in this section.

## *Creating a Data File Using the Table Menu*

The previous section showed you how to create a new data file in conjunction with a new main document. However, there may be times when you need a data file that is independent of a main document or one that is used for several main documents. For example, perhaps you send out a form letter regularly; you may need to create only one data file (although you may have to edit it often to keep it updated).

In Chapter 10, you learned how to create tables. A data file is also a table, and you can create one by using the Table menu and the Insert Table command. This is the easiest way to create a data file.

To create a table, choose the Table Insert Table command (Alt,A,I). Word displays the Insert Table dialog box, shown in Figure 14.7. In the Number of Columns box, enter the number of fields in your data file; in the Number of Rows box, enter the approximate number of records required for the file. You don't have to be exact; you can use either Table menu commands or the data-file Toolbar buttons to add records. It's not important to define column width; select the default, Auto. Then select OK or press Enter.

**332**

---

Click on the Table button to insert the table template into the document at the location of the insertion point. When the table template is displayed, drag the mouse to define the number of rows and columns in the table. If you don't move the insertion point, the next time you click on this button, Word displays the Insert Cells dialog box.

---

To create a data file using the Table menu, follow these Quick Steps.

**Q** **Creating a Data File by Using the Table Insert Table Command**

| | |
|---|---|
| 1. From the Table menu, select the Insert Table command (Alt,A,I). | Word displays the Insert Table dialog box (Figure 14.7). |
| 2. Select the number of columns and number of rows. Then select OK or press Enter. | Word returns to the document window and creates a table.  □ |

Select the number
of columns for
merge field names.

| Insert Table | |
|---|---|
| **Number of Columns:** | 2 |
| **Number of Rows:** | 1 |
| **Column Width:** | Auto |

OK

Cancel

Select the number
of records in the
data file.

*Figure 14.7    The Insert Table dialog box, which enables
you to define the number of fields and the approximate
number of records in the data file.*

Once you have created a table, type merge field names in the
header record (the first row of the table). In each succeeding record,
enter information about each individual in the file. Keep in mind
that each cell in the table represents a field in the record, and that a
row is an entire record. To save the data file, Select File Save (Alt,F,S
or Shift-F12) and follow the prompts.

> **Tip:** When you name a data file, don't worry about typing
> an extension; Word uses the .DOC extension for data files.

**333**

In Chapter 10, you also learned how to convert existing text to
a table. Another way to create a data file is to enter text in a regular
document, separating the entries with tab marks or commas. End
each line with a paragraph mark. Then use the T**a**ble menu and the
Convert **T**ext to Table command.

If you already have a database file in another application (either
Windows- or non-Windows-based), you can import it into Word and
then convert it to Word for Windows format (provided that you have
installed the conversion utilities). Chapter 13 describes how to
convert documents to different formats. For more information, refer
to the *Microsoft Word for Windows User's Guide*.

## Using an Existing Data File to Create a Form Letter

In the first section of this chapter, you started out with a new main
document and a new data file. Remember that you also can link an
existing main document and an existing data file (or any combination of new and existing files) to produce a form letter. To create a
link between a main document and an existing data file, first open
the main document and then select File Print Merge (Alt,F,M). Select
the Attach Data File button and choose the data file from the File

Name list. Select OK or press Enter. Word displays the Print Merge bar between the Ribbon and the Ruler. The Print Merge bar enables you to control form-letter creation on-screen.

Select Edit Data File to display the data file. You can add or delete new merge field names in the header record by selecting Add or Delete. Within the rest of the data file, you can add, edit, or delete records. After editing, save the data file by choosing the File Save command (Alt,F,S) and selecting OK or pressing Enter.

## Sorting Records in a Data File

Before you print form letters, you may want to sort the records. Let's say that you want to send letters only to those people living in a certain city. Sort the records in the data file on the City field, identify the range of record numbers for the city, and then print the form letters. Word enables you to define up to three sort criteria, so you can refine a search for specific records. For example, you can sort to find the records for a certain ZIP code within a city, or even to find a specific street within a ZIP code within a city.

To start a sort, first select the S button on the Toolbar. When Word displays the Sort Records dialog box (shown in Figure 14.8), select one of the fields listed in the box under Sort Key 1, and choose either Ascending or Descending order. To sort within Sort Key 1, select a field and sort order in the Sort Key 2 box, and to sort within both Sort Key 1 and Sort Key 2, select a field in the Sort Key 3 box and choose the sort order. For example, to sort a city and then a ZIP code within that city, define City as Sort Key 1 and Zip Code as Sort Key 2. Then select OK. Word returns to the data file and sorts it as you specified. For more information about sorting within a document, see the *Microsoft Word for Windows User's Guide*.

**334**

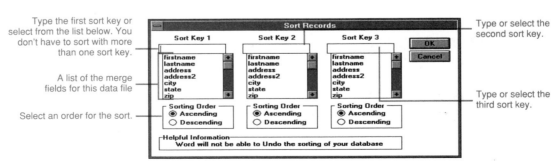

*Figure 14.8   The Sort Records dialog box.*

## *Creating a Header Record*

Occasionally, you'll want to create a header record that is not associated with a specific data file. For example, you may want to create a header file that you can use as the first record in several data files. This will allow you to keep separate databases of, say, clients and friends. If each database has an identical format, you can use the same header record for both.

Creating a header record is similar to creating a data file. You'll use buttons and dialog boxes that look identical to those you have used in the first Quick Steps in this chapter but that have different names.

First, select File Print Merge (Alt,F,M). Select the Attach Header File button in the Print Merge Setup dialog box. From the Attach Header File dialog box, select Create Header File. Word displays the Create Header File dialog box, which is shown in Figure 14.9. Complete this dialog box as you did the Create Data File dialog box. After entering the last merge field name, select OK or press Enter. Then save the header record.

**335**

Type the first merge field name.

Merge field names accumulate in this box.

Select this button to add a merge field name to the list.

*Figure 14.9    The Create Header File dialog box, which is similar to the Create Data File dialog box.*

After you attach the header file to a main document, attach a data file. If that data file already has a header record, it will be treated as a regular data record. There should just be one header record for each group of main documents and data files, so if there are two header records associated with a data file, make sure that you delete one.

## *Adding Merge Fields to a Main Document*

After creating and/or editing a data file, you are ready to work on the main document. First, you'll need to type the body of the letter if you haven't already done so. Then, to be able to get information from the data file, you'll have to insert merge fields.

To display the main document so that you can insert merge fields, select File Print Merge (Alt,F,M), or from the **W**indow menu, select the main document. The Print Merge bar is displayed on-screen between the Ribbon and the Ruler.

Start editing the main document. To insert a merge field at the insertion point location, select the Insert Merge Field button (Alt-Shift-F) on the Print Merge bar. Then select a print merge field from the list in the dialog box, and select OK or press Enter.

To check for any errors in the main document, select the Check button (Alt-Shift-K) on the Print Merge bar. If Word finds any discrepancies between the main document and the data file, it displays a dialog box explaining the error.

The following Quick Steps explain the procedure used to add merge fields to your main document.

**336**

 **Adding Merge Fields to the Main Document**

| | |
|---|---|
| 1. In your document, move the insertion point to the location in which you want to merge a field from the data file. | The insertion point flashes on and off. |
| 2. Select the Insert Merge Field button from the Print Merge bar between the Ribbon and the Ruler. | Word displays the Insert Merge Field dialog box (Figure 14.10). |
| 3. Select **P**rint Merge Field (the merge field from the data file), or **W**ord Fields, which are explained in the *Microsoft Word for Windows User's Guide* and in Word's help facility. | Word inserts the field name into the main document at the insertion point (Figure 14.11). |
| 4. Repeat steps 2 and 3 until you have completed the document. | Word places the insertion point after your last insertion in the main document. |

5. To check the document for errors, select the Che**c**k button on the Print Merge bar.

Word reviews your entries and displays a message.

6. After correcting any errors, save the main document by choosing **F**ile **S**ave (Alt,F,S or Shift-F12).

Word displays the Save As dialog box.

7. Type a file name in the File **N**ame box.

If this is the first time you have saved this file, Word prompts you for summary information.

8. Enter any summary information you wish and select OK or press Enter.

Word returns to the main document.

*Figure 14.10    The Insert Merge Field dialog box.*

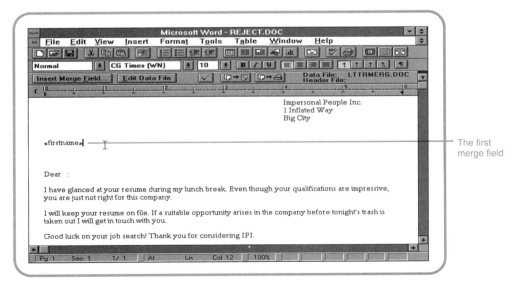

*Figure 14.11    A document with merge fields.*

## *Merging and Printing Form Letters*

After the process of creating and editing the main document and the data file, you are now ready to merge the two files into your form letter. There are two ways to do this: You can select a button from the Print Merge bar, or you can select the File Print Merge command (Alt,F,M). If you select a button from the Print Merge bar, Word displays the Print dialog box. This means that you must accept Word's merge defaults.

However, if you select **File** Print **M**erge and then select the Merge button, Word displays the Print Merge dialog box (shown in Figure 14.12), which enables you to customize the merge.

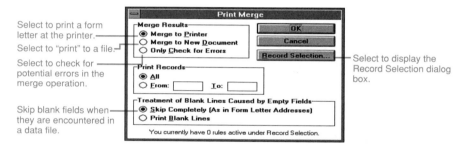

**Figure 14.12** *The Print Merge dialog box, which enables you to customize the merge.*

In the Merge Results box, you can choose to merge the main document and the data file into a form letter that is either printed or saved to a file for later printing. You can also check for potential errors in the merge without printing or saving. In the Print Records box, choose to print or save all the form letters, or choose selected form letters by specifying the numbers of the records to be printed.

To print a range of form letters, enter a starting number in the From box; if you leave the From box empty, Word prints from the first record. If you fill in the To box, Word prints to that record; if you leave the To box empty, Word prints through the last record.

You can also decide whether to print blank lines in your data file. For example, your data file might include two fields for street address, allowing for post office boxes and apartment or suite numbers. However, many of your records do not use both fields. Word's default, Skip Completely, fills in blank spaces with the next field. If you select the Print Blank Lines button, the empty second address field is printed as a blank space in the form letter.

To further refine your selection, from the Print Merge dialog box, choose Record Selection. Word displays the Record Selection dialog box, which is shown in Figure 14.13. In this box, you can define up to six *rules,* or criteria used to select the records for printing. For example, you can print only records in which City is equal to Cambridge, or Zip is greater than 02138. This feature is useful in directing a form letter to clients in that area only. For example, if your company has a new warehouse outlet opening in a certain city, you can send a special mailing to customers living in a particular area to announce the grand opening sale. Select a field from the Field Name box. In the Is box, select one of eight operators; then type a value in the Compared To box. For example, select City and Equal to, and type `Cambridge` in the Compared To box. This prints form letters for only those clients living in Cambridge. You can also select records based on a combination of conditions, joined by an And (for example, a certain city AND a certain ZIP code within that city), or based on one Or another condition (for example, Cambridge OR Boston OR Somerville). For more information about refining the records selected for a print merge, see the *Microsoft Word for Windows User's Guide.*

**339**

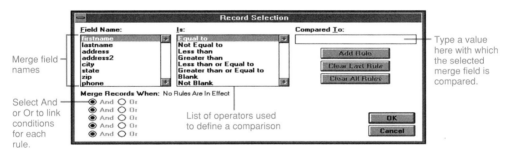

*Figure 14.13   The Record Selection dialog box.*

Use the following Quick Steps to merge the main document and the data file and print the resulting form letter.

 **Merging and Printing the Main Document and the Data File**

1. Make sure that your screen is displaying the main document to be merged and printed.

Word displays the current document on-screen.

2. From the **F**ile menu, select Print **M**erge (Alt,F,M).

Word displays the Print Merge Setup dialog box. If you have prepared the main document and the data file carefully, all buttons should be available for use.

3. Select the **M**erge button. (If the Merge button is dimmed, you have not yet attached a data file to the main document.)

Word displays the Print Merge dialog box.

4. Restrict the merge by checking buttons on this box. To further restrict the selection of records, select the **R**ecord Selection button.

Word displays the Record Selection dialog box.

5. In the Field Name list box, select a field to be restricted.

Word highlights your selection.

6. Select an expression in the Is box.

Word highlights your selection.

7. Type a value in the Compared To box.

Word "undims" the Add Rule box.

8. Select the **A**dd Rule button.

Word displays the new rule after the title Merge Records When. Word "undims" the first line of And and Or.

9. Repeat steps 5 through 8 for each criterion you want to add (up to five more). To remove the last rule you added, select the Clear **L**ast Rule button. To remove all rules, choose the Clear All **R**ules button.

Word changes the display after the Merge Records When box.

10. Under Merge Records When, select the available And and Or option buttons as you wish.

Word surrounds your last choice with a dotted-line border.

11. Select OK or press Enter.

Word returns to the Print Merge box.

12. Select OK or press Enter.

Word displays the Print dialog box.

13. Select the number of copies or the range of pages. Then select OK or press Enter.

Word starts the merge process.

□

## *Saving Merged Form Letters to a File*

Word also provides the means for you to save a merged document for printing at a later time. First, make sure that the main document and the data file are linked. Then on the Print Merge bar, select the Print to File button. Word then displays the form letter on-screen and assigns the name Form Letters 1, which is replaced when you save the file. At any time, you can print the form letters saved in this file. For example, if you prepare a form letter that can't be sent until a particular date, save the form letter file and then print and send it on the specified date.

**341**

## *Removing the Link Between a Main Document and a Data File*

After printing a form letter, you may never use it again as a form letter. However, you may want to keep it as a regular letter to send to others when needed.

To convert a main document back to a regular Word document, remove the link between the main document and its data file. Once you have removed the link, the Print Merge bar is removed from the screen.

### Q Removing the Link Between the Main Document and the Data File

1. Make sure that your screen is displaying the main document to be converted.

Word displays the Print Merge bar between the Ribbon and the Ruler.

2. Select the File Print Merge command (Alt,F,M).

Word displays the Print Merge Setup dialog box. Notice that all the buttons are available.

3. Select the **R**emove Attach-
ments button.

Word displays a message allowing you to verify that the main document will become a normal Word document.

4. Select **Y**es.

Word returns to the current document and removes the Print Merge bar from the screen. □

# Creating and Printing Mailing Labels

Mailing labels, which Word regards as a type of form letter, also result from the link between a main document and a data file. However, mailing labels use the MAILLABL template, which has an associated macro that guides you through the creation process.

Depending on your computer system, the MAILLABL template may ask you questions about your active printer, the type of label on which you wish to print, and then asks you to select fields to be printed. After each selection, choose Add To Label. Using the Special Character box, you can determine whether the next field prints on the same line or the next line, and you can separate fields with commas, colons, or periods. As you select fields, Word displays a sample mailing label layout so that you can correct any mistakes. If you need to correct the last entry, select Undo Last Add. When you have completed your selection, select Done.

To create and print mailing labels, use the following Quick Steps.

 **Creating and Printing Mailing Labels**

1. From the **F**ile menu, select the **N**ew command (Alt,F,N).

Word displays the New dialog box.

2. In the Use Template box, select the MAILLABL template. Select OK or press Enter.

Depending on your computer system, Word displays the Mailing Labels dialog box (Figure 14.14), which enables

3. Select the type of printer.

you to select whether to print on a laser or a dot-matrix printer.

If you select Laser printer, Word displays the product numbers for 47 Avery labels.

If you select a dot-matrix printer, Word displays a message and then displays the product numbers for 40 Avery labels.

4. Select the type of label. Select OK or press Enter.

Word opens a document based on the MAILLABL template and then runs the mailing label macro.

5. As Word displays each prompt, respond. The first prompt asks you to choose **S**ingle Label or **M**ultiple Labels.

Word displays a dialog box that asks whether the merge names and data are in a header file and a data file or not.

6. Respond to the prompt.

Word creates a main document using the information you provided and then displays the Attach Data File dialog box, from which you can select a data file.

7. Select a data file and select OK or press Enter.

Word displays the Layout Mailing Labels dialog box.

8. Select a field and the special character that follows it. Then select **A**dd To Label.

Word adds the field to the sample mailing label.

9. To undo the last field added to the label, select **U**ndo Last Add.

Word removes the field from the sample mailing label.

10. Repeat steps 8 and 9 until you have selected all the fields for the label. Then select **D**one.

Word calculates the number of labels needed and places the fields on each label in the position that you selected. Word then displays an informational dialog box.

**343**

11. Select OK or press Enter.　　　　Word returns to the main document.

12. Select the Print button from the Print Merge bar.　　　　Word displays the Print dialog box.

13. Select OK.　　　　Word prints the mailing labels.　　☐

Select if your printer is a laser printer.　　Select if your printer is a dot-matrix printer.

*Figure 14.14　The Mailing Labels dialog box.*

# Creating and Printing Envelopes

Although mailing labels are often used when you send form letters, envelopes provide a more personal touch. However, unless you use an envelope feeder or continuous form envelopes, you'll be sitting in front of your printer feeding envelopes manually. Unless you're mailing hundreds of letters, the extra effort is worth it.

Before getting started, if your printer has an envelope feeder, select the Printer's Envelope Feeder Has Been Installed check box. However, be aware that some printer drivers support envelope feeders in such a way that the Printer Envelope Feeder check box will be dimmed. Do this by selecting Tools Options (Alt,O,O). Under Category, choose Print. In the Envelope Options box, check the Printer's Envelope Feeder Has Been Installed option. Once you have done this, the setting remains in effect until you change it. Then insert the envelope in the envelope feeder. If your printer does not have an envelope feeder, clear the Printer's Envelope Feeder Has Been Installed check box in the Options dialog box for the Print category. Then insert the envelope into the manual feeder.

To create and print an envelope, select the Tools Create Envelope command (Alt,O,E). When Word displays the Create Envelope dialog box, type the Addressed To and Return Address envelope information. Then select Print Envelope.

If you have filled in the Mailing Address box in the Options dialog box for the User Info category, that information will automatically appear in the Return Address box in the Create Envelope dialog box.

---

[icon] Click on the Envelope button to display the Create Envelope dialog box in order to create an envelope for this document or to define envelope attributes.

---

To create and print an envelope, use the following Quick Steps.

## *Q* Creating and Printing Envelopes

1. Prepare your printer and insert an envelope into the feeder or tray for your printer (flap down, with the top of the envelope toward the right of the envelope feeder). From the Tools menu, choose Create Envelope (Alt,O,E).

   Word displays the Create Envelope dialog box (Figure 14.15).

**345**

2. In the Envelope Size box, select the appropriate envelope size.

   Word's default is Letter size.

3. Type a name and address in the Addressed To box. After typing each line, press Enter.

   Word provides a five-line address capacity.

4. If the Omit Return Address box is checked, the Return Address box is unavailable. Otherwise, if you haven't completed the Mailing Address box in the Options dialog box for the User Info category, enter a return address. Select Print Envelope.

   Word prints the envelope. If you haven't loaded an envelope, your printer prompts you to load an envelope.

   □

Fill in your recipient's name and address.

Fill in your address if needed.

Check to omit printing the return address.

Select to print an envelope.

Select to add the Addressed To and Return Address to the current document.

Select the size of the envelope.

*Figure 14.15    The Create Envelope dialog box.*

You can print an envelope and a document at the same time. First open the document. To print an envelope for that document, select Tools Create Envelope (Alt,O,E). Type the name and address in the Addressed To box, and select Add to Document. Word adds the name and address at the top of the document and inserts a section mark between the envelope and the document. You can copy the name and address to the document and then format it. To view the document and envelope before you print, select File Print Preview (Alt,F,V). When you are ready to print, insert an envelope and select Print from the Print Preview screen or select File Print (Alt,F,P).

You can print a series of envelopes when you print form letters. To the main document, insert name and address fields as you would address an envelope. Select Tools Create Envelope (Alt,O,E). When Word displays the Create Envelope dialog box, the fields are already entered in the Address To box. Select Add to Document. Word adds the name and address at the top of the document and inserts a section mark between the envelope and the document. At this point, you can continue to edit the document. When you are ready to print, insert an envelope in the feeder or tray and select Print from the Print Preview screen or select File Print (Alt,F,P).

# What You Have Learned

▶ The basic components of a form letter are a main document and a data file. Use the Print Merge command from the File menu to open both documents and then link them.

► Because a data file is a table, you can create a data file using the Table Insert Table command or the Table button on the Toolbar.

► To be able to get information from a data file to a main document, you must insert merge fields into the main document. To insert a merge field at the insertion point location in the main document, select the Insert Merge Field button (Alt-Shift-F) on the Print Merge bar.

► To print a form letter to the printer or to a file for later printing, you can use the File Print Merge command and select the Merge button in the Print Merge dialog box. You can also press one of the buttons on the Print Merge bar to print to the printer or to save the form letter to a file.

► Mailing labels also result from the link between a main document and a data file. However, mailing labels use the MAILLABL template, which has an associated macro that guides you through the creation process.

► To print envelopes, select the Tools menu and the Create Envelope command (Alt,O,E). You can print an envelope and a document at the same time by selecting the Add to Document button in the Create Envelope dialog box. To print a series of envelopes with form letters, fill in the Address To box with merge fields. After completing the Create Envelope dialog box, select Print Envelope.

**347**

# Installing Word for Windows

## Before Installing Word for Windows

You should have already installed Windows on your computer system and followed the Windows guidelines for hardware and software requirements. Here are some recommendations:

► Your computer system should be an IBM-compatible computer based on an Intel 80386 processor or greater.

► You should have installed Windows version 3.0 or above.

► You should have at least 2 megabytes of RAM on your computer. The more RAM you have, the better Windows runs.

 *Random-access memory* (*RAM*) is your computer's main memory; your computer uses RAM to run DOS, Windows, and applications software, and to temporarily store information. When you turn off your computer, the contents of RAM are deleted.

► Additional memory, in any combination of extended and expanded memory, also helps Windows run better.

 There are three types of RAM: conventional, extended, and expanded. *Conventional memory* (you can have as much as one megabyte) is the regular RAM that your computer uses. *Extended memory* is an extension to conventional memory.

*Expanded memory* requires special software and often re-quires a special board; it is separate from conventional and extended memory.

► Your color monitor and video card should support VGA.

*VGA* stands for Video Graphics Array, which produces high resolution and lets you have 16 colors at a time on your system.

► Although a mouse is not required to run Word for Windows, a Microsoft-compatible mouse is an invaluable asset.

► To get the most from Word for Windows, a printer (either laser or dot-matrix) should be part of your computer system.

 **Tip:** Before you install Word for Windows, make copies of the product disks and store them in a safe place.

## 350

# Installing Word for Windows

You can install Word for Windows from DOS or from Windows. The Setup installation program gives you many choices, which cannot be covered in this space. The two Quick Steps in this appendix show you the most common path through installation. If you aren't able to follow this installation path strictly, remember that the Setup program guides you carefully through every step of your installation.

 **Note:** If at any time during the installation, you don't want to continue, select Cancel or press F3.

## *Installing Word for Windows from DOS*

Use the following Quick Steps to install Word from DOS. If you want to install Word from Windows, skip to the next section.

**Installing Word for Windows from DOS**

1. At the DOS prompt, insert the diskette labeled Setup into the floppy drive. Type the appropriate floppy drive identifier (A: or B:) and `win setup` and press Enter.

Windows starts and loads the Setup program. The Setup program displays an installation screen and asks for your name and organization.

2. Enter your name, tab to Organization, and enter the name of your company. Select Continue (to continue the installation) or Exit (to leave the installation).

Setup asks you to verify the information you just entered.

3. Select either Continue or Exit.

Setup displays directory information and gives you a choice of the directory on which Word will be installed.

**351**

4. Accept the WINWORD directory. Then select Continue.

If Setup detects an old version of Word for Windows, it asks you whether you want to delete the old program files in the directory (your old documents will not be deleted).

5. To overwrite the old program files, select Continue.

Setup displays a menu giving you the following options: Complete Installation, which installs all Word's options; Custom Installation, which allows you to select the options that you want to install; and Minimum Installation, which installs the smallest possible version of Word.

**352**

6. Select Complete Installation to install all Word's options. Press Enter.

Setup asks you if you want the AUTOEXEC.BAT file updated (adding the new directory to your PATH and making sure that the SHARE utility, which installs the file sharing and locking capabilities of your system, is executed every time you start your computer).

7. Select either Update or Do Not Update.

Setup informs you that it is setting up the program. As it installs Word, Setup displays the percentage of installation completed, the file currently being installed, its destination, and its features. When Setup is finished installing from one floppy disk, it beeps.

8. Insert the next floppy disk and press Enter.

If you put the wrong floppy disk in the drive, Setup prompts you to insert the proper floppy disk.

9. Repeat step 8 until you have inserted all the program disks.

At the end of the installation, Setup updates files that help Word to run more efficiently, returns to Windows, displays the Word for Windows window, and informs you that Setup is complete. □

## *Installing Word for Windows from Windows*

Use these Quick Steps to install Word from Windows.

 **Installing Word for Windows from Windows**

1. Start Windows.

Windows goes through its regular startup routine.

2. At the DOS prompt, insert the diskette labeled Setup into the floppy drive. Type the appropriate floppy drive identifier (A: or B:) and `win setup` and press Enter.

Windows starts and loads the Setup program. The Setup program displays an installation screen and asks for your name and organization.

3. Choose Run.

Windows opens the Run dialog box.

4. In the Command Line box, type either `a:setup` or `b:setup`, depending on the disk drive selected in step 2. Press Enter.

The Setup program displays an installation screen.

5. Enter your name, tab to Organization, and enter the name of your company. Select Continue (to continue the installation) or Exit (to leave the installation).

Setup asks you to verify the information that you just entered.

## 353

6. Select either Continue or Exit. Remember, you can press F3 at any time to exit the installation.

Setup displays directory information and gives you a choice of the directory on which Word will be installed.

7. Accept the WINWORD directory and select Continue.

If Setup detects an old version of Word for Windows, it asks you whether you want to delete the old program files in the directory (your old documents will not be deleted).

8. To overwrite the old program files, select Continue.

Setup displays a menu giving you the following options: Complete Installation, which installs all Word's options; Custom Installation, which allows you to select the options that you want to install; and Minimum Installation, which installs the smallest possible version of Word.

9. Select Complete Installation to install all Word's options. Press Enter.

Setup asks you if you want the AUTOEXEC.BAT file updated (adding the new directory to your PATH and making sure that the SHARE utility, which installs the file sharing and locking capabilities of your system, is executed every time you start your computer).

10. Select either Update or Do Not Update.

Setup informs you that it is setting up the program. As it installs Word, Setup displays the percentage of installation completed, the file currently being installed, its destination, and its features. When Setup is finished installing from one floppy disk, it beeps.

**354**

11. Insert the next floppy disk and press Enter.

If you put the wrong floppy disk in the drive, Setup prompts you to insert the proper floppy disk.

12. Repeat step 11 until you have inserted the last floppy disk.

At the end of the installation, Setup updates files that help Word to run more efficiently, returns to Windows, displays the Word for Windows window, and informs you that Setup is complete. □

# Keystroke Shortcuts

This appendix contains a list of the most commonly used keystrokes in Word for Windows with a brief description of each.

| Keystroke | Description |
| --- | --- |
| ↓ | Decreases the value of a measurement; moves down in a list or in text; moves the split bar down; opens a list |
| ← | Moves one character to the left |
| → | Moves the insertion point to the next cell or moves one character to the right |
| ↑ | Increases the value of a measurement; moves one item up a list or up one line of text; moves the split bar up; moves the insertion point up one line within a table or out of a table |
| Alt | Highlights the Menu bar to make a selection |
| Alt-↓ | Displays or cancels a dialog box list |
| Alt-0*nnn* (num. keypad) | Inserts a special character (with Num Lock on) |
| Alt-5 (num. keypad) | Selects a table (with Num Lock off) |
| Alt-End | Moves the insertion point to the last cell in the current row of a table |
| Alt-Esc | Switches to other open applications |

*continues*

| Keystroke | Description |
|---|---|
| Alt-F1 | Equivalent to F11 |
| Alt-F2 | Equivalent to F12; saves a file (File Save As) |
| Alt-F4 | Exits Word for Windows, Help, or the Clipboard |
| Alt-F5 | Restores an application window |
| Alt-F6 | Goes to the next document window |
| Alt-F9 | Minimizes an application window |
| Alt-F10 | Maximizes the application window (if the application icon is selected on the desktop) |
| Alt-Home | Moves the insertion point to the first cell in the current row of a table |
| Alt-Hyphen | Opens the Document Control menu |
| Alt-PgDn | Moves the insertion point to the bottom cell in a column in a table |
| Alt-PgUp | Moves the insertion point to the top cell in a column in a table |
| Alt-Shift-5 (num. keypad) | Applies Normal style |
| Alt-Shift-D | Inserts the system date at the insertion point |
| Alt-Shift-F | Inserts a Merge field in a main document |
| Alt-Shift-F2 | Saves a file (**F**ile **S**ave) |
| Alt-Shift-F6 | Goes to the previous document window |
| Alt-Shift-P | Inserts the current page number at the insertion point |
| Alt-Shift-T | Inserts the system time at the insertion point |
| Alt-space bar | Opens the Application Control menu |
| Backspace | Deletes the character to the left |
| Caps Lock | Locks uppercase letters |
| Ctrl-= | Toggles between normal and subscript |
| Ctrl-↓ | Moves one paragraph down |
| Ctrl-← | Moves one word to the left |
| Ctrl-→ | Moves one word to the right |
| Ctrl-↑ | Moves one paragraph up |
| Ctrl-0 | Deletes an extra line before a paragraph |
| Ctrl-1 | Applies single-spaced lines to a selection |
| Ctrl-2 | Applies double-spaced lines to a selection |

| Keystroke | Description |
| --- | --- |
| Ctrl-5 | Applies one-and-one-half-spaced lines to a selection |
| Ctrl-5 (numeric keypad) | Selects a document (**Edit Select All**) |
| Ctrl-A | Toggles between normal and all caps |
| Ctrl-B | Toggles between normal and boldface |
| Ctrl-Backspace | Deletes the word to the left of the insertion point |
| Ctrl-C | Copies selected text to the Clipboard (**Edit Copy**) |
| Ctrl-D | Toggles between normal and double underline |
| Ctrl-Del | Deletes the word to the right of the insertion point |
| Ctrl-E | Centers a paragraph |
| Ctrl-End | Moves to the end of the document |
| Ctrl-Enter | Inserts a page break |
| Ctrl-Esc | Opens the Task List dialog box |
| Ctrl-F | Selects the Font box on the Ribbon |
| Ctrl-F (twice) | Displays the Character dialog box |
| Ctrl-F3 | Cuts a selected item and stores it in the Spike |
| Ctrl-F4 | Closes a document window (**File Close**) |
| Ctrl-F5 | Restores a document window to its prior size once |
| Ctrl-F6 | Goes to the next document window |
| Ctrl-F7 | Moves a document window |
| Ctrl-F8 | Resizes a document window |
| Ctrl-F10 | Maximizes the current document window |
| Ctrl-F12 | Opens a file (**File Open**) |
| Ctrl-G | Decreases hanging indent to the previous tab stop |
| Ctrl-H | Toggles between normal and hidden text |
| Ctrl-Home | Moves to the beginning of the document |
| Ctrl-I | Toggles between normal and italicized text |
| Ctrl-Ins | Copies selected text to the Clipboard (**Edit Copy**) |
| Ctrl-J | Justifies selected paragraph between the left and right margins |
| Ctrl-K | Toggles between normal and small caps |
| Ctrl-L | Aligns selected paragraph to the left |
| Ctrl-M | Unindents the selected paragraph by one tab stop |

**357**

*continues*

| Keystroke | Description |
|---|---|
| Ctrl-N | Indents the selected paragraph by one tab stop |
| Ctrl-O | Adds one line of space before a paragraph |
| Ctrl-P | Highlights the point size box on the Ribbon |
| Ctrl-PgDn | Moves to the bottom of a window |
| Ctrl-PgUp | Moves to the top of a window |
| Ctrl-Q | Removes all paragraph formatting from selected text |
| Ctrl-R | Aligns selected paragraph to the right |
| Ctrl-S | Highlights the style box on the Ribbon |
| Ctrl-S (twice) | Displays the Style dialog box |
| Ctrl-Shift-= | Toggles between normal and superscript |
| Ctrl-Shift-↓ | Selects to the end of a paragraph |
| Ctrl-Shift-← | Selects to the beginning of a word |
| Ctrl-Shift-→ | Selects to the end of a word |
| Ctrl-Shift-↑ | Selects to the beginning of a paragraph |
| Ctrl-Shift-8 | Displays nonprinting symbols |
| Ctrl-Shift-End | Selects from the insertion point to the end of a document |
| Ctrl-Shift-F3 | Empties the Spike into the document |
| Ctrl-Shift-F6 | Goes to the previous document window |
| Ctrl-Shift-F8 | Selects a column of text |
| Ctrl-Shift-F12 | Prints a document (**File P**rint) |
| Ctrl-Shift-Home | Selects to the beginning of a document |
| Ctrl-space bar | Returns selected text formatting to default normal text but not if applied with a style |
| Ctrl-T | Increases a hanging indent for the selected paragraph |
| Ctrl-Tab | Inserts a tab character in a table cell |
| Ctrl-U | Toggles between normal and underline |
| Ctrl-V | Pastes cut or copied text from the Clipboard (**Edit P**aste) |
| Ctrl-W | Toggles between word underline on and off |
| Ctrl-X | Cuts selected text to the Clipboard (**Edit C**ut) |
| Ctrl-Z | Undoes the last action, if allowed (**Edit U**ndo) |
| Del | Deletes the current character or field |
| End | Moves to the end of the current line |

| Keystroke | Description |
| --- | --- |
| Enter | Indicates that a command is complete (also ends paragraphs) |
| Esc | Cancels an action or closes a menu |
| F1 | Displays help |
| F2 | Moves text to a new location |
| F3 | Inserts a Glossary entry |
| F4 | Repeats the last action, if allowed (**Edit R**epeat) |
| F5 | Goes to a specified location in the current document (**Edit G**o To) |
| F7 | Checks spelling of a selected word |
| F8 | Extends a selection—from word, sentence, paragraph, section, to document |
| F8-*x* | Extends a selection to *x* (where *x* represents a character or symbol) |
| F10 | Activates the Menu bar |
| F12 | Saves a file (**File Save A**s) |
| Home | Moves to the beginning of the current line |
| Ins | Switches between Insert and Overtype modes |
| Num Lock | Enables the numeric keypad for entry of numbers |
| PgDn | Moves down one screen |
| PgUp | Moves up one screen |
| Shift-↓ | Selects one line or file name down |
| Shift-← | Selects one character or graphic to the left |
| Shift-→ | Selects one character or graphic to the right |
| Shift-↑ | Selects one line up |
| Shift-Del | Cuts text (**Edit C**ut) |
| Shift-End | Selects to the end of a line |
| Shift-Enter | Inserts a newline mark within a paragraph (soft carriage return) |
| Shift-F1 | Displays help on the item at the insertion point |
| Shift-F2 | Copies text |
| Shift-F3 | Changes case of selected characters |
| Shift-F4 | Displays Find dialog box |
| Shift-F5 | Goes back to the last three editing locations |

**359**

*continues*

| Keystroke | Description |
|-----------|-------------|
| Shift-F7 | Selects the Thesaurus |
| Shift-F8 | "Deselects" from a selected paragraph, a sentence, down to a word |
| Shift-F12 | Saves a file (**File S**ave) |
| Shift-Home | Selects to the beginning of a line |
| Shift-Ins | Pastes text from the Clipboard (**Edit P**aste) |
| Shift-PgDn | Selects one screen down |
| Shift-PgUp | Selects one screen up |
| Shift-Tab | Moves to the previous field, box, cell, button, or option; selects the contents of the previous cell |
| Tab | Moves to the next field, cell, box, button, icon, term, or option; selects contents of next cell; inserts a new row in a table if you are in the last cell in a row |

# Index

**Symbols**

↓ key, 19, 41, 355
← key, 41, 355
→ key, 41, 355
↑ key, 19, 41, 355

**A**

active printers, defining, 232-235
active window, 25
aligning paragraphs, 143-146
Alt key combinations, 355-356
320-323, 344
Always Create Backup Copy
    feature, 53-54
annotations, 9
ANSI special characters, 221-222
Application Control menu, 5
Application Control, Switch To
    command, 319

applications, switching, 319
ascenders, 147
asterisk (*) wild card, 56
automatic
    macros, 298
    page breaks, 151
Autosave feature, 50-51

**B**

backing up files, 52-54
Backspace key, 356
bit-mapped fonts, 195
blocks (of text), 62
Border command, 159-168
borders
    adding to tables, 266
    placing around paragraphs,
        160-162
Break command, 129-130, 229

bulleted lists, creating, 222-224
buttons, 12

**C**

Caps Lock key, 356
cartridge fonts, 195
cells, 250
  changing width in tables, 261-263
  editing in tables, 259-260
  merging/splitting in tables, 266
centered
  alignment, 30, 145
  indents, 155
Character command, 178-180, 191-192
Character dialog box, 179
characters, 35, 175
  formats, finding/replacing, 212-216
  formatting, 108, 176
    with Format Character command, 178-180
    with Ribbon, 177
  kerning, 183-185
  point size, 176
  special
    adding, 219-222
    ANSI, 221-222
  superscript/subscripts, 180-182
  wildcard, 311
check boxes, 15, 18
clicking, 13
Clipboard, 73-74
  versus Spike, 72-73
  viewing/deleting contents of, 75-76

closing
  custom dictionaries, 93
  pull-down menus, 8
  windows, 317
columns
  adding to documents, 225-227
    breaking columns, 229
    changing column widths, 228
  adjusting space between, 264
  changing width in tables, 261-263
  selecting in documents, 65
command buttons, 15, 18
commands
  accessing with Toolbar, 19
  Application Control, Switch To, 319
  context-sensitive, 77
  Document Control, Close, 317
  Edit, Copy, 68-70, 259
  Edit, Cut, 68-72, 259
  Edit, Find, 68, 78-80, 205-206, 209, 214
  Edit, Glossary, 69, 290-294
  Edit, Go To, 68
    navigating documents, 42-43
  Edit, Links, 69
  Edit, Object, 69
  Edit, Paste, 68-70
  Edit, Paste Special, 68
  Edit, Repeat, 68, 77, 293
  Edit, Replace, 68, 78, 81-83, 205-206, 210-212, 215-216
  Edit, Select All, 68
  Edit, Undo, 68, 72, 77-78, 144, 293
  File, Find File, 310-311, 316
  File, New, 300-306, 327, 342
  File, Open, 312, 327

File, Print, 58, 188, 241, 245,
  286-287, 294, 346
File, Print Merge, 327-328,
  333-341
File, Print Preview, 34, 123,
  235-236, 346
File, Print Setup, 232-235
File, Save, 45-49, 303, 333
File, Save As, 45, 304, 314
File, Summary Info, 103
File, Template, 293, 298
Format, Border, 160, 163, 166,
  266
Format, Character, 178-180,
  191-192, 273, 282-283
Format, Columns, 225-227
Format, Page Setup, 112-114
Format, Paragraph, 144-146,
  149-152, 156-158, 282
Format, Section Layout, 137
Format, Style, 273-287, 306
Format, Tabs, 168-172
Help, Getting Started, 21
Help, Learning Word, 21
in menus, 9-11
  selecting with mouse, 13-14
Insert, Break, 129-130, 229
Insert, Symbol, 206, 219-222
selecting with keyboard, 16-17
Table, Column Width, 261-264
Table, Convert Text to Table,
  254-257, 333
Table, Delete Cells, 260
Table, Gridline, 253
Table, Insert Cells, 260
Table, Insert Table, 250-251,
  332-333

Table, Merge Cells, 266
Table, Row Height, 264-265
Table, Split Cells, 266
Tools, Bullets, 222-225
Tools, Calculate, 269
Tools, Create Envelope, 344-346
Tools, Grammar, 96-102
Tools, Macro, 299-300
Tools, Numbering, 222-225
Tools, Options, 28, 109-111, 131,
  186, 232, 253, 283-284, 320-323,
  344
Tools, Record Macro, 295-298
Tools, Repaginate Now, 131
Tools, Sorting, 267-268
Tools, Spelling, 86-88
Tools, Stop Recorder, 296
Tools, Thesaurus, 94-96
Undo, 72, 77-78, 358
View, Header/Footer, 125-129
View, Normal, 126
View, Page Layout, 228
View, Zoom, 239-240
Window, Arrange All, 317
context-sensitive commands, 77
conventional memory, 349
copying
  files, 313
  fonts from one port to another,
    203
  text, 69-70
Ctrl key combinations, 356-358
custom dictionaries
  adding words to, 93-94
  creating, 91-92
  CUSTOM.DIC dictionary, 86-90
  opening/closing, 93

**363**

**364**

# D

data files, 326
   creating form letters from existing
      data files, 333-334
      using Table menu, 332-333
   linking with main documents,
      327-331
   merging with main documents,
      339-341
   removing link to main
      documents, 341-342
   sorting records in, 334
   special features, 329
   Toolbar buttons, 329-330
default names (documents), 26
defining styles
   basing on existing styles, 279-280
   with Format, Style command,
      277-278
   with Ribbon, 274-275
Del key, 73, 358
deleting
   buttons from Toolbar, 321-322
   contents of Clipboard, 75-76
   files, 313
   fonts, 199
   macros, 299-300
   styles, 286
   text, 69-72
dialog boxes, 2
   Character, 179
   Find File, 310-312
   General, 28
   Glossary, 291
   Grammar, 29
   Keyboard, 29
   Macro, 299-300

Menus, 29
navigating
   with keyboard, 17-19
   with mouse, 14-15
New, 300
Options, 36, 90-91, 243-244,
   282-283, 319-323
Page Setup
   for Margins, 112-119
   for Size and Orientation,
      119-122
Print, 29, 57, 313, 338
Print Merge, 338
Print Merge Setup, 327
Record Macro, 295-298
Rename Style, 286
Save, 29
Save As, 314
Section Layout, 137
Spelling, 29, 87-88
Style, 274-281
Template, 293
Toolbar, 29
User Info, 29
View, 28
WIN.INI, 29
dictionaries, 86-90
   custom
      adding words to, 93-94
      creating, 91-92
      opening/closing, 93
   exclude, creating, 94
direction keys
   navigating through tables, 254
   selecting text, 258-259
Document Control menu, 5
   Close command, 317

document window, 25
document-wide formatting, 107,
111-112, 141
documents
    adding
        columns, 225-229
        special characters, 219-222
        tables, 250-253
    assigning/changing templates,
        305-306
    converting to different file
        formats, 314
    creating
        new paragraphs, 30
        templates from, 301-302
    default names, 26
    editing
        with Grammar command,
            96-102
        with Thesaurus command,
            94-96
    elements, 35-36
    footers, 124-129
    formatting
        adjusting line spacing, 146-149
        characters, 108
        controlling page breaks,
            151-152
        controlling widows/orphans,
            132
        customizing pagination,
            133-134
        document-wide, 107, 111-113,
            141
        enhancing paragraphs, 159-160
        indenting paragraphs, 153-159
        inserting page breaks, 129-130
        one page versus two pages at a
            time, 113-114

        options for units of
            measurement, 109-111
        paragraphs, 108, 141-146
        placing borders around,
            160-162
        placing lines around
            paragraphs, 163-164
        sections, 107, 134-138
        setting margins, 114-119
        setting page orientation,
            122-123
        setting paper size, 119-122
        setting paragraph spacing,
            149-151
        shading paragraphs, 164-167
        tabs, 168-173
        turning off automatic
            pagination, 131
        viewing changes made, 123
    headers, 124-129
    inserting glossary entries,
        293-294
    main, 326
        adding merge fields, 335-337
        linking with data files, 328
        merging with data files,
            339-341
        removing link to data files,
            341-342
    naming, 47
    navigating, 38
        with Go To command, 42-43
        with keyboard, 41-42
        with mouse, 38-41
    previewing before printing,
        235-236
        changing margins/headers/
            footers, 237-238

**365**

zooming, 239-240
printing, 57-58, 241
    print options, 243-244
    selected parts of documents,
        241-243
    to files, 245
retrieving, 54-56
saving, 45-49
    Autosave feature, 50-51
    Fast Save feature, 52
selecting text, 62
    with keyboard, 65-67
    with mouse, 62-65
sorting/displaying, 311
spell checking, 86-90
statistics, 103
DOS
    installing Word for Windows
        from, 350-352
    prompt, starting Word for
        Windows from, 4
.DOT extension, 290
double-clicking, 13
downloading fonts to printer,
    199-203
dragging, 13
    and dropping (moving text),
        71-72


E

Edit menu, 9, 68-69
    Copy command, 68-70, 259
    Cut command, 68-72, 259
    Find command, 205-206, 209,
        214
    Glossary command, 69, 290-294
    Go To command, 42
    Links command, 69
    Object command, 69
    Paste command, 68-70
    Paste Special command, 68
    Repeat command, 68, 77, 293
    Replace command, 68, 78, 81-83,
        205-206, 210-212, 215-216
    Select All command, 68
    Undo command, 68, 72, 77-78,
        144, 293
editing
    tables, 258
        cells in tables, 259-260
        rows/columns, 261
        selecting text, 258-259
    templates, 305
End key, 41, 358
endmark, 7
Enter key, 19, 359
envelopes, creating/printing,
    344-346
Esc key, 359
exclude dictionaries, creating, 94
expanded memory, 349
extended memory, 349


F

F1 key, 20, 359
F2 key, 359
F3 key, 73, 359
F4 (Repeat command) key, 77, 359
F5 (Go To command) key, 41, 359
F7 key, 89, 359
F8 key, 359
F10 key, 359

F12 (Save As command) key, 304,
  359
Fast Save feature, 52
field codes, 9
File menu, 9, 43
  Find File command, 68, 78-80,
    310-311, 316
  New command, 300-306, 327, 342
  Open command, 312, 327
  Print command, 58, 188, 241,
    245, 286-287, 294, 346
  Print Merge command, 327-342
  Print Preview command, 34, 123,
    235-236, 346
  Print Setup command, 232-235
  Save command, 45-49, 303, 333
  Save As command, 45, 304, 314
  Summary Info command, 103
  Template command, 293, 298
files
  backing up, 52-54
  copying, 313
  data, 326
      creating Table menu, 332-333
      linking with main documents,
        327-331
      merging with main documents,
        339-341
      removing link to main
        documents, 341-342
  deleting, 313
  printing documents to, 245
  saving form letters to, 341
  searching for, 310-311
  selecting/opening multiple files,
    312

Find File dialog box, 310-312
finding/replacing
  formats, 206-218
  symbols, 218-219
first-line indents, 154
fonts, 175-176
  adding, 197-198
  bit-mapped, 195
  cartridge, 195
  changing, 191-194
  copying from one port to another,
    203
  deleting, 199
  downloading to printer, 199-203
  monospace, 190-191
  permanent, 199-200, 203
  point size, changing, 191-194
  printer, 194
  proportional, 190-191
  sans serif, 190-191
  scalable, 192, 195
  screen, 194
  selecting, 194-195
  serif, 190-191
  soft, 195
  viewing, 196-197
footers, 124-129, 237-238
footnotes, 9
form letters
  creating, 325-327
      basing on existing data file,
        334
      linking main documents with
        data files, 327-331
  merging/printing, 338-341
  saving, 341

**367**

Format menu, 9
  Border command, 160, 163, 166, 265-266
  Character command, 178-180, 191-192, 273, 283
  Columns command, 226-227
  Page Setup command, 112-114
  Paragraph command, 144-146, 149-152, 156-158, 282
  Section Layout command, 137
  Style command, 274-279, 282, 306
  Tabs command, 168-172
formats
  converting, 314
    text to table formats, 254-257
  finding/replacing, 206-219
formatting, 35
  accessing features with Ribbon/Ruler, 19
  characters, 108, 175-176
    with Format Character command, 178-180
    with Ribbon, 177
  document-wide, 107, 112, 141
  documents
    controlling widows/orphans, 132
    customizing pagination, 133-134
    viewing changes made, 123
  one page versus two pages at a time, 113-114
  paragraphs, 108, 141-142
    adjusting line spacing, 146-149
    aligning paragraphs, 143-146

368

    controlling page breaks, 151-152
    enhancing paragraphs, 159-160
    indenting paragraphs, 153-159
    placing borders around, 160-162
    placing lines around, 163-164
    setting paragraph spacing, 149-151
    shading, 165-167
    tabs, 168-173
  section, 107, 134-138
  symbols, 36-37
  tables, 261
    adding borders, 266
    adjusting row height, 264
    adjusting space between columns, 264
    changing column/cell widths, 261-263
    indenting/aligning rows, 265
    merging/splitting cells, 266
    text in tables, 267
full
  justification, 30
  screen window, 5

G

General dialog box, 28
Getting Started command, 21
glossaries, 289-290
  deleting/changing entries, 294
  inserting glossary entries into documents, 293-294
  printing entries, 294

saving text/graphics as glossary entries, 292
Glossary dialog box, 291
Grammar command, 96-102
Grammar dialog box, 29
gutter margins, 112

## H

hanging indents, 154
hard page breaks, 151
hardware recommendations for Word for Windows, 349-350
header records, 326
  creating, 335
headers, 124-129
  changing, 237-238
help, accessing, 20-21
Help menu, 9
  Getting Started command, 21
  Learning Word command, 21
hiding text, 185-186
  printing hidden text, 187-189
highlighting, 38
Home key, 42, 359

## I-J

icons, 12
  reducing Word to, 21
indenting paragraphs, 153-159
Ins key, 359
Insert menu, 9
  Break command, 129-130
  Symbol command, 206, 219-222
Insert mode, 31

insertion point, 7
  versus mouse pointer I-beam, 11
installing Word for Windows
  from DOS, 350-352
  from Windows, 352-354

justifying text, 145

## K

kerning, 183-185
key combinations, 16, 355-360
key successions, 16
keyboard
  indenting paragraphs, 158-159
  navigating
    documents, 41-42
    Word for Windows, 15
  selecting
    menus/commands, 16-17
    text, 65-67
  starting Word for Windows, 3-4
  working with dialog boxes, 17-19
Keyboard dialog box, 29
keys
  ↓, 19, 41, 355
  ←, 41, 355
  →, 41, 355
  ↑, 19, 41, 355
  Alt, 355
  Backspace, 356
  Caps Lock, 356
  Del, 73, 358
  direction
    navigating through tables, 254
    selecting text, 258-259
  End, 358

Enter, 19, 359
Esc, 359
F1, 20, 359
F2, 359
F3, 73, 359
F4 (Repeat command), 77, 359
F5 (Go To command), 41, 359
F7, 89, 359
F8, 359
F10, 359
F12 (Save As command), 304, 359
for Clipboard/Spike, 73
Home, 42, 359
Ins, 359
navigation, 41
Num Lock, 359
PgDn, 42
PgUp, 42
PrtSc, 73
shortcut, 218
Tab, 19, 360
toggle, 31

**L**

landscape orientation (pages),
  122-123
leaders, 168, 171
leading, 146, 169
left
  alignment, 30, 145
  indents, 154
  justification, 30
Line Breaks and Fonts as Printed
  check box, 37
lines
  adjusting line spacing, 146-149

placing around paragraphs,
  163-164
selecting in documents, 62-67
list boxes, 14, 18

**M**

Macro dialog box, 300
macros, 289, 295
  automatic, 298
  deleting, 299-300
  recording, 295-298
  renaming, 299-300
  running, 299
mailing labels, creating/printing,
  342-344
main documents, 326
  adding merge fields, 335-337
  linking with data files, 327-331
  merging with data files, 338-341
  removing link to data files,
    341-342
margins
  changing, 237-238
  gutter, 112
  mirror, 112
  setting for documents, 114-119
Maximize/Restore button, 5-6
maximized windows, 5, 314-315
·memory
  conventional, 349
  expanded, 349-350
  extended, 349
  random-access memory (RAM),
    349
Menu bar, 5
menus, 9-14

Edit menu, 9, 68-69
  Copy command, 68-70, 259
  Cut command, 68-72, 259
  Find command, 205-206, 209,
   214
  Glossary command, 69,
   290-294
  Go To command, 42
  Links command, 69
  Object command, 69
  Paste command, 68-70
  Paste Special command, 68
  Repeat command, 68, 77, 293
  Replace command, 68, 78,
   81-83, 205-206, 210-212,
   215-216
  Select All command, 68
  Undo command, 68, 72, 77-78,
   144, 293
File menu, 9, 43
  Find File command, 68, 78-80,
   310-311, 316
  New command, 300-306, 327,
   342
  Open command, 312, 327
  Print command, 58, 188, 241,
   245, 286-287, 294, 346
  Print Merge command,
   327-328, 333-341
  Print Preview command, 34,
   123, 235-236, 346
  Print Setup command, 232-235
  Save command, 45-49, 303,
   333
  Save As command, 45, 304,
   314
  Summary Info command, 103
  Template command, 293, 298

Format menu, 9
  Border command, 160, 163,
   166, 266
  Character command, 178-180,
   191-192, 273, 283
  Columns command, 226-227
  Page Setup command, 112-114
  Paragraph command, 144-146,
   149-152, 156-158, 282
  Section Layout command, 137
  Style command, 274-279, 282,
   306
  Tabs command, 168-172
Help, 9
  Getting Started command, 21
  Learning Word command, 21
Insert, 9
  Break command, 129-130
  Symbol command, 206,
   220-222
pull-down, 8
selecting with keyboard, 16-17
Table, 9
  Column Width, 263-264
  Convert Text to Table, 255, 333
  Delete Cells, 260
  Gridline, 253
  Insert Cells, 260
  Insert Table, 250-251, 332-333
  Merge Cells, 266
  Row Height, 264-265
  Split Cells, 266
Tools, 9
  Bullets, 222-225
  Calculate, 269
  Create Envelope, 344-346
  Grammar, 96-102

Macro, 299-300
Numbering, 222-225
Options, 28, 109-111, 131, 186, 232, 253, 283-284, 320-323, 344
Record Macro, 295-298
Repaginate Now, 131
Sorting, 267-268
Spelling, 86-89
Stop Recorder, 296
Thesaurus, 94-96
View, 9
  Header/Footer command, 124-129
  Normal command, 126
  Page Layout, 228
  Ribbon command, 177
  Zoom, 239-240
Window, 9
  Arrange All, 317
Menus dialog box, 29
merge fields, 326-327
  adding to main documents, 335-337
*Microsoft Word for Windows User's Guide*, 242, 289, 295, 305, 325, 333, 339
Minimize button, 5
  reducing Word to icon, 21
mirror margin, 112
modes, 31-34
monospace fonts, 190-191
mouse, 11-12
  actions, 13
  I-beam/pointer versus insertion point, 11
  navigating documents, 38-41

selecting
  menu commands, 13-14
  text, 62-65
starting Word for Windows, 4
working with dialog boxes, 14-15
moving
  around documents, 38
    with Go To command, 42-43
    with keyboard, 41-42
    with mouse, 38-41
  text, 69-72
  through tables, 254
  windows, 316
multiple windows
  arranging, 317
  navigating/activating, 316

**N**

naming documents, 47
navigation keys, 41
New dialog box, 300
Normal command, 126
Normal mode, 32
NORMAL template, 290
Num Lock key combination, 359
numbered lists, creating, 224-225

**O**

Object command, 69
on-line help facilities, 20-21
on-line lessons, 21
opening
  custom dictionaries, 93
  pull-down menus, 8

option boxes, 14, 18
Options dialog box, 36, 91,
   243-244, 283, 320-323
orphans, 132
Outline mode, 32
Overtype mode, 31


**P-Q**

page breaks
   automatic, 151-152
   controlling, 151-152
   hard, 151-152
   inserting into documents,
      129-130
Page Layout mode, 32
Page Setup dialog box
   for Margins, 112-118
   for Size and Orientation, 119-122
paginating, 131-134
panes, 125
paper size, setting for documents,
   120-122
paragraphs
   formatting, 108, 141-142
      adjusting line spacing, 146-149
      aligning paragraphs, 143-146
      controlling page breaks,
         151-152
      indenting paragraphs, 153-159
      placing borders around,
         160-162
      placing lines around, 163-164
      setting paragraph spacing,
         149-151
      shading, 164-167
      tabs, 168-172

new, creating, 30
   selecting in documents, 64-65
   setting spacing, 149-151
pasting text, 69-72
permanent fonts, 199
PgDn key, 42, 359
PgUp key, 42, 359
point size, 176
   changing, 191-194
pointing, 13
portrait orientation (pages),
   122-123
Print dialog box, 29, 57, 313, 338
Print Merge dialog box, 338
Print Merge Setup dialog box, 327
printer
   drivers, 231
   fonts, 189-194
printers
   common problems, 246-247
   defining active printer, 232-235
printing
   documents, 57-58, 240-241
      previewing, 235-238
      print options, 243-244
      selected parts, 241-243
      to files, 245
   envelopes, 344-346
   form letters, 338-341
   glossary entries, 294
   hidden text, 187-189
   list of styles, 286-287
   mailing labels, 342-344
proportional fonts, 190-191
PrtSc key, 73
pull-down menus, 8

question mark (?) wildcard, 56
quitting Word for Windows, 22

**R**

radio buttons, 18
random-access memory (RAM), 349
Record Macro dialog box, 295-298
recording macros, 295-298
records, sorting in data files, 334
Rename Style dialog box, 286
retrieving documents, 54-56
Ribbon, 6, 19
   aligning paragraphs, 146
   changing fonts/point size, 194
   defining styles, 274-280
   formatting characters, 176-178
   turning on/off, 26-28
right
   alignment, 30, 145
   indents, 154
rivers, 184
rows
   adjusting height, 264
   editing in tables, 261
   indenting/aligning in tables, 265
Ruler, 6, 19
   indenting paragraphs, 155
   setting
      margins, 118-119
      tabs, 171
   turning on/off, 26-28


**S**

sans serif font, 190-191
Save dialog box, 29
Save As dialog box, 314
saving
   documents, 45-49
      Autosave feature, 50-51
      Fast Save feature, 52
   form letters, 341
   text/graphics as glossary entries, 290-292
scalable fonts, 192, 195
screen fonts, 194
scroll bar arrows, 40
search strings, 78-80
searching for files, 310-311
section formatting, 107, 134-138
Section Layout dialog box, 137
selection bar, 7
sentences, selecting in documents, 64
serif fonts, 190-191
shading paragraphs, 164-167
Shift key combinations, 67, 359
shortcut keys, 218
   finding/replacing formats, 216-218
snaking columns, 225-227
soft fonts, 195
software recommendations for Word for Windows, 349-350
sorting
   and displaying documents, 311
   items in tables, 267-268
special characters
   adding, 220-222
   ANSI, 221-222
spell checker, 86-90
Spelling dialog box, 29, 87-88
Spike, 76-77, 290
   versus Clipboard, 72-73
splitting windows, 318
starting Word for Windows, 1-4
statistics on documents, 103

status bar, 7
  indicators, 31
STDUSER.DIC dictionary, 86-90
Style dialog box, 274-276, 280
styles, 273
  adding/merging to templates, 306
  applying, 282-283
  changing, 284-286
  defining, 273-280
    basing on existing styles,
      279-280
    with Format, Style command,
      277-278
    with Ribbon, 274-275
  deleting, 286
  printing list of, 286-287
  renaming, 286
  specifying next style, 280-282
  viewing style names in document
    window, 283-284
superscript/subscripts, 181-182
switching applications, 319
symbols
  finding/replacing, 218-219
  of formatting, 36-37


T

Tab key, 19, 360
tabbed indents, 155
Table menu, 9
  Column Width command,
    263-264
  Convert Text to Table command,
    255, 333
  Delete Cells command, 260
  Gridlines command, 253
  Insert Cells command, 260
  Insert Table command, 250-251,
    332-333

  Merge Cells command, 266
  Row Height command, 264-265
  Split Cells command, 266
tables, 249
  converting text to table format,
    254-257
  creating, 250
  editing, 258
    cells, 259-260
    rows/columns, 261
    selecting text, 258-259
  formatting, 261
    adding borders to tables,
      265-266
    adjusting row height/space
      between columns, 264
    changing column/cell widths,
      261-263
    indenting/aligning rows, 265
    merging/splitting cells, 266
    text in tables, 267
  inserting into documents,
    250-253
  navigating, 253-254
  performing calculations in,
    269-270
  sorting items in, 267-268
tabs, 168-169
  clearing, 172-173
  setting, 169-172
Template dialog box, 293
templates, 116, 289-290, 300
  adding/merging styles to, 306
  assigning/changing templates for
    documents, 305-306
  creating, 303-304
    from documents, 301-302
  editing, 305
  NORMAL, 290

**375**

**376**

text
  aligning, 30
  converting to table format,
    255-257
  copying, 69-70
  cutting, 70-72
  editing in tables, 258-259
  elements of, 35
  finding, 78-80
  formatting text in tables in cells,
    267
  hiding, 185-186
    printing hidden text, 187-189
  justifying, 30
  moving, 69-72
  pasting, 69-72
  replacing, 78, 81-83
  saving as glossary entries,
    291-292
  selecting, 62
    with keyboard, 65-67
    with mouse, 63-65
Text area, 7
text boxes, 14, 18
thumb (scroll bars), 7, 40
title bar, 5
toggle key, 31
Toolbar, 6, 19, 319
  adding buttons to, 320-321
  data file Toolbar buttons, 329-330
  deleting buttons from, 321-322
  reassigning command/macro
    buttons, 323
  turning on/off, 26-28
Toolbar dialog box, 29
Tools menu, 9
  Bullets command, 222-225
  Calculate command, 269-270
  Create Envelope command,
    344-346

Grammar command, 96-102
Macro command, 299-300
Numbering command, 222-225
Options command, 28, 109-111,
  131, 186-189, 232, 253, 283-284,
  320-323, 344
Record Macro command, 295-298
Repaginate Now command, 131
Sorting command, 267-268
Spelling command, 86-87
Stop Recorder command, 296
Thesaurus command, 94-96

U

Undo command, 72, 77-78, 358
units of measurement (in Word),
  109-111
User Info dialog box, 29

V

vertical scroll bars, 39
View dialog box, 28
View menu, 9
  Header/Footer command, 125-127
  Normal command, 126
  Page Layout command, 228
  Page Setup command, 112-114
  Ribbon command, 177
  turning on Ribbon/Ruler/Toolbar,
    26
  Zoom command, 239-240
viewing
  contents of Clipboard, 75-76
  fonts, 196-197
  style names in document
    window, 283-284

## W-Z

widows, 132
wildcard characters, 56, 81, 311
WIN.INI dialog box, 29
Window menu, 9
  Arrange All command, 317
Windows, installing Word for
  Windows from, 352-354
windows
  active, 25
  closing, 317
  document, 25
  full screen, 5
  maximized, 5, 314
    restoring, 315
  moving, 316
  multiple, 316-317
  panes, 125
  resizing, 316
  splitting, 318
Word for Windows
  quitting, 22
  reducing to icon, 21
  starting, 1-4
word wrap, 30
WYSIWYG format, 31

zooming documents, 239-240

**377**

# Sams—Covering The Latest In Computer And Technical Topics!

## Audio

| | |
|---|---|
| Advanced Digital Audio | $39.95 |
| Audio Systems Design and Installation | $59.95 |
| Compact Disc Troubleshooting and Repair | $24.95 |
| Handbook for Sound Engineers: The New Audio Cyclopedia, 2nd Ed. | $99.95 |
| How to Design & Build Loudspeaker & Listening Enclosures | $39.95 |
| Introduction to Professional Recording Techniques | $29.95 |
| The MIDI Manual | $24.95 |
| Modern Recording Techniques, 3rd Ed. | $29.95 |
| OP-AMP Circuits and Principles | $19.95 |
| Principles of Digital Audio, 2nd Ed. | $29.95 |
| Sound Recording Handbook | $49.95 |
| Sound System Engineering, 2nd Ed. | $49.95 |

## Electricity/Electronics

| | |
|---|---|
| Active-Filter Cookbook | $24.95 |
| Basic Electricity and DC Circuits | $29.95 |
| CMOS Cookbook, 2nd Ed. | $24.95 |
| Electrical Wiring | $19.95 |
| Electricity 1-7, Revised 2nd Ed. | $49.95 |
| Electronics 1-7, Revised 2nd Ed. | $49.95 |
| How to Read Schematics, 4th Ed. | $19.95 |
| IC Op-Amp Cookbook, 3rd Ed. | $24.95 |
| IC Timer Cookbook, 2nd Ed. | $24.95 |
| RF Circuit Design | $24.95 |
| Transformers and Motors | $29.95 |
| TTL Cookbook | $24.95 |
| Understanding Digital Troubleshooting, 3rd Ed. | $24.95 |
| Understanding Solid State Electronics, 5th Ed. | $24.95 |

## Games

| | |
|---|---|
| Master SimCity/SimEarth | $19.95 |
| Master Ultima | $16.95 |

## Hardware/Technical

| | |
|---|---|
| First Book of Modem Communications | $16.95 |
| First Book of PS/1 | $16.95 |
| Hard Disk Power with the Jamsa Disk Utilities | $39.95 |
| IBM PC Advanced Troubleshooting & Repair | $24.95 |
| IBM Personal Computer Troubleshooting & Repair | $24.95 |
| Microcomputer Troubleshooting & Repair | $24.95 |
| Understanding Fiber Optics | $24.95 |

## IBM: Business

| | |
|---|---|
| 10 Minute Guide to PC Tools 7 | $9.95 |
| 10 Minute Guide to Q&A 4 | $9.95 |
| First Book of Microsoft Works for the PC | $16.95 |
| First Book of Norton Utilities 6 | $16.95 |
| First Book of PC Tools 7 | $16.95 |
| First Book of Personal Computing, 2nd Ed. | $16.95 |

## IBM: Database

| | |
|---|---|
| 10 Minute Guide to Harvard Graphics 2.3 | $9.95 |
| Best Book of AutoCAD | $34.95 |
| dBASE III Plus Programmer's Reference Guide | $24.95 |
| dBASE IV Version 1.1 for the First-Time User | $24.95 |
| Everyman's Database Primer Featuring dBASE IV Version 1.1 | $24.95 |
| First Book of Paradox 3.5 | $16.95 |
| First Book of PowerPoint for Windows | $16.95 |
| Harvard Graphics 2.3 In Business | $29.95 |

## IBM: Graphics/Desktop Publishing

| | |
|---|---|
| 10 Minute Guide to Lotus 1-2-3 | $9.95 |
| Best Book of Harvard Graphics | $24.95 |
| First Book of Harvard Graphics 2.3 | $16.95 |
| First Book of PC Paintbrush | $16.95 |
| First Book of PFS: First Publisher | $16.95 |

## IBM: Spreadsheets/Financial

| | |
|---|---|
| Best Book of Lotus 1-2-3 Release 3.1 | $27.95 |
| First Book of Excel 3 for Windows | $16.95 |
| First Book of Lotus 1-2-3 Release 2.3 | $16.95 |
| First Book of Quattro Pro 3 | $16.95 |
| First Book of Quicken In Business | $16.95 |
| Lotus 1-2-3 Release 2.3 In Business | $29.95 |
| Lotus 1-2-3: Step-by-Step | $24.95 |
| Quattro Pro In Business | $29.95 |

## IBM: Word Processing

| | |
|---|---|
| Best Book of Microsoft Word 5 | $24.95 |
| Best Book of Microsoft Word for Windows | $24.95 |
| Best Book of WordPerfect 5.1 | $26.95 |
| First Book of Microsoft Word 5.5 | $16.95 |
| First Book of WordPerfect 5.1 | $16.95 |
| WordPerfect 5.1: Step-by-Step | $24.95 |

## Macintosh/Apple

| | |
|---|---|
| First Book of Excel 3 for the Mac | $16.95 |
| First Book of the Mac | $16.95 |

## Operating Systems/Networking

| | |
|---|---|
| 10 Minute Guide to Windows 3 | $9.95 |
| Best Book of DESQview | $24.95 |
| Best Book of Microsoft Windows 3 | $24.95 |
| Best Book of MS-DOS 5 | $24.95 |
| Business Guide to Local Area Networks | $24.95 |
| DOS Batch File Power with the Jamsa Disk Utilities | $39.95 |
| Exploring the UNIX System, 2nd Ed. | $29.95 |
| First Book of DeskMate | $16.95 |
| First Book of Microsoft Windows 3 | $16.95 |
| First Book of MS-DOS 5 | $16.95 |
| First Book of UNIX | $16.95 |
| Interfacing to the IBM Personal Computer, 2nd Ed. | $24.95 |
| The Waite Group's Discovering MS-DOS, 2nd Edition | $19.95 |
| The Waite Group's MS-DOS Bible, 4th Ed. | $29.95 |
| The Waite Group's MS-DOS Developer's Guide, 2nd Ed. | $29.95 |
| The Waite Group's Tricks of the UNIX Masters | $29.95 |
| The Waite Group's Understanding MS-DOS, 2nd Ed. | $19.95 |
| The Waite Group's UNIX Primer Plus, 2nd Ed. | $29.95 |
| The Waite Group's UNIX System V Bible | $29.95 |
| Understanding Local Area Networks, 2nd Ed. | $24.95 |
| UNIX Applications Programming: Mastering the Shell | $29.95 |
| UNIX Networking | $29.95 |
| UNIX Shell Programming, Revised Ed. | $29.95 |
| UNIX: Step-by-Step | $29.95 |
| UNIX System Administration | $29.95 |
| UNIX System Security | $34.95 |
| UNIX Text Processing | $29.95 |

## Professional/Reference

| | |
|---|---|
| Data Communications, Networks, and Systems | $39.95 |
| Handbook of Electronics Tables and Formulas, 6th Ed. | $24.95 |
| ISDN, DECnet, and SNA Communications | $49.95 |
| Modern Dictionary of Electronics, 6th Ed. | $39.95 |
| Reference Data for Engineers: Radio, Electronics, Computer, and Communications, 7th Ed. | $99.95 |

## Programming

| | |
|---|---|
| Advanced C: Tips and Techniques | $29.95 |
| C Programmer's Guide to NetBIOS | $29.95 |
| C Programmer's Guide to Serial Communications | $29.95 |
| Commodore 64 Programmer's Reference Guide | $24.95 |

| | |
|---|---|
| Developing Windows Applications with Microsoft SDK | $29.95 |
| DOS Batch File Power | $39.95 |
| Graphical User Interfaces with Turbo C++ | $29.95 |
| Learning C++ | $39.95 |
| Mastering Turbo Assembler | $29.95 |
| Mastering Turbo Pascal, 4th Ed. | $29.95 |
| Microsoft Macro Assembly Language Programming | $29.95 |
| Microsoft QuickBASIC Programmer's Reference | $29.95 |
| Programming in ANSI C | $29.95 |
| Programming in C, Revised Ed. | $29.95 |
| The Waite Group's BASIC Programming Primer, 2nd Ed. | $24.95 |
| The Waite Group's C Programming Using Turbo C++ | $29.95 |
| The Waite Group's C: Step-by-Step | $29.95 |
| The Waite Group's GW-BASIC Primer Plus | $24.95 |
| The Waite Group's Microsoft C Bible, 2nd Ed. | $29.95 |
| The Waite Group's Microsoft C Programming for the PC, 2nd Ed. | $29.95 |
| The Waite Group's New C Primer Plus | $29.95 |
| The Waite Group's Turbo Assembler Bible | $29.95 |
| The Waite Group's Turbo C Bible | $29.95 |
| The Waite Group's Turbo C Programming for the PC, Revised Ed. | $29.95 |
| The Waite Group's Turbo C++Bible | $29.95 |
| X Window System Programming | $29.95 |

## Radio/Video

| | |
|---|---|
| Camcorder Survival Guide | $14.95 |
| Radio Handbook, 23rd Ed. | $39.95 |
| Radio Operator's License Q&A Manual, 11th Ed. | $24.95 |
| Understanding Fiber Optics | $24.95 |
| Understanding Telephone Electronics, 3rd Ed. | $24.95 |
| VCR Troubleshooting & Repair Guide | $19.95 |
| Video Scrambling & Descrambling for Satellite & Cable TV | $24.95 |

### For More Information, See Your Local Retailer Or Call Toll Free

# 1-800-428-5331

*All prices are subject to change without notice. Non-U.S. prices may be higher. Printed in the U.S.A.*

# Sams' First Books Get You Started Fast!

"The First Book Series ... is intended to get the novice off to a good start, whether with computers in general or with particular programs ...."

**The New York Times**

The First Book of WordPerfect 5.1
*Kate Miller Barnes*
275 pages, 7 3/8 x 9 1/4, $16.95 USA
0-672-27307-1

## Look For These Books In Sams' First Book Series

**The First Book of Excel 3 for the Mac**
*Christopher Van Buren*
320 pages, 7 3/8 x 9 1/4, $16.95 USA
0-672-27328-4

**The First Book of Excel 3 for Windows**
*Christopher Van Buren*
320 pages, 7 3/8 x 9 1/4, $16.95 USA
0-672-27359-4

**The First Book of Harvard Graphics**
*Jack Purdum*
300 pages, 7 3/8 x 9 1/4, $16.95 USA
0-672-27310-1

**The First Book of Lotus 1-2-3 Release 2.3**
*Alan Simpson & Paul Lichtman*
330 pages, 7 3/8 x 9 1/4, $16.95 USA
0-672-27365-9

**The First Book of Microsoft Windows 3**
*Jack Nimersheim*
304 pages, 7 3/8 x 9 1/4, $16.95 USA
0-672-27334-9

**The First Book of Microsoft Word 5.5, Second Edition**
*Brent Heslop & David Angell*
320 pages, 7 3/8 x 9 1/4, $16.95 USA
0-672-27333-0

**The First Book of Microsoft Word for Windows**
*Brent Heslop & David Angell*
304 pages, 7 3/8 x 9 1/4, $16.95 USA
0-672-27332-2

**The First Book of Microsoft Works for the PC**
*Debbie Walkowski*
304 pages, 7 3/8 x 9 1/4, $16.95 USA
0-672-27360-8

**The First Book of MS-DOS**
*Jack Nimersheim*
272 pages, 7 3/8 x 9 1/4, $16.95 USA
0-672-27312-8

**The First Book of Norton Utilities 6**
*Joseph Wikert, Rev. by Lisa Bucki*
275 pages, 7 3/8 x 9 1/4, $16.95 USA
0-672-27384-5

**The First Book of Paradox 3.5**
*Jonathan Kamin*
320 pages, 7 3/8 x 9 1/4, $16.95 USA
0-672-27370-5

**The First Book of PC Paintbrush**
*Deke McClelland*
289 pages, 7 3/8 x 9 1/4, $16.95 USA
0-672-27324-1

**The First Book of PC Tools 7**
*Gordon McComb*
350 pages, 7 3/8 x 9 1/4, $16.95 USA
0-672-27371-3

**The First Book of Personal Computing Second Edition**
*W.E. Wang & Joe Kraynak*
275 pages, 7 3/8 x 9 1/4, $16.95 USA
0-672-27385-3

**The First Book of PFS: First Publisher**
*Karen Brown & Robert Bixby*
308 pages, 7 3/8 x 9 1/4, $16.95 USA
0-672-27326-8

**The First Book of PowerPoint for Windows**
*Douglas Snyder*
330 pages, 7 3/8 x 9 1/4, $16.95 USA
0-672-27356-X

**The First Book of PROCOMM PLUS**
*Jack Nimersheim*
250 pages, 7 3/8 x 9 1/4, $16.95 USA
0-672-27309-8

**The First Book of PS/1**
*Kate Barnes*
300 pages, 7 3/8 x 9 1/4, $16.95 USA
0-672-27346-2

**The First Book of Q&A 4**
*Sandra E. Schnyder*
272 pages, 7 3/8 x 9 1/4, $16.95 USA
0-672-27311-X

**The First Book of Quattro Pro 3**
*Patrick Burns*
300 pages, 7 3/8 x 9 1/4, $16.95 USA
0-672-27367-5

**The First Book of Quicken in Business**
*Gordon McComb*
300 pages, 7 3/8 x 9 1/4, $16.95 USA
0-672-27331-4

**The First Book of the Mac**
*Carla Rose & Jay Rose*
350 pages, 7 3/8 x 9 1/4, $16.95 USA
0-672-27355-1

**The First Book of UNIX**
*Douglas Topham*
300 pages, 7 3/8 x 9 1/4, $16.95 USA
0-672-27299-7

**The First Book of WordPerfect for Windows**
*Kate Barnes*
400 pages, 7 3/8 x 9 1/4, $16.95 USA
0-672-27343-8

## SAMS

**See your local retailer or call 1-800-428-5331.**

# Sams Covers All Your Word Processing Needs

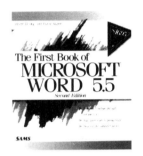

### The First Book of Microsoft Word 5.5, Second Edition

*Brent Heslop & David Angell*

Practical business examples combined with step-by-step instructions offer you a complete overview of Word 5.5! The book discusses advanced features such as macros and file export in an easy-to-follow manner.

320 pages, 7 3/8 x 9 1/4, $16.95 USA
**0-672-27333-0**

### The First Book of Microsoft Word for Windows

*Brent Heslop & David Angell*

Quick Steps tutorials, graphic icons, and an overview of advanced Windows features help you produce professional documents. Written for uninitiated users as well as busy executives who need a clear, concise introduction to Version 1.1.

304 pages, 7 3/8 x 9 1/4, $16.95 USA
**0-672-27332-2**

### SAMS

See your local retailer or call 1-800-428-5331.

# Sams Guarantees Your Success In 10 Minutes!

The *10 Minute Guides* provide a new approach to learning computer programs. Each book teaches you the most often used features of a particular program in 15 to 20 short lessons—all of which can be completed in 10 minutes or less. What's more, the *10 Minute Guides* are simple to use. You won't find any "computer-ese" or technical jargon— just plain English explanations. With straightforward instructions, easy-to-follow steps, and special margin icons to call attention to important tips and definitions, the *10 Minute Guides* make learning a new software program easy and fun!

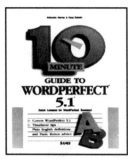

**10 Minute Guide to WordPerfect 5.1**
*Katherine Murray & Doug Sabotin*
160 pages, 51/2 x 81/2, $9.95 USA
**0-672-22808-4**

**10 Minute Guide to MS-DOS 5**
*Jack Nimersheim*
160 pages, 5 1/2 x 81/2, $9.95 USA
**0-672-22807-6**

**10 Minute Guide to Windows 3**
*Katherine Murray & Doug Sabotin*
160 pages, 5 1/2 x 81/2, $9.95 USA
**0-672-22812-2**

**10 Minute Guide to PC Tools 7**
*Joe Kraynak*
160 pages, 5 1/2 x 81/2, $9.95 USA
**0-672-30021-4**

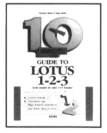

**10 Minute Guide to Lotus 1-2-3**
*Katherine Murray & Doug Sabotin*
160 pages, 51/2 x 8 1/2, $9.95 USA
**0-672-22809-2**

**10 Minute Guide to Q&A 4,
Revised Edition**
*Arlene Azzarello*
160 pages, 51/2 x 81/2, $9.95 USA
**0-672-30035-4**

**10 Minute Guide
to Harvard Graphics 2.3**
*Lisa Bucki*
160 pages, 51/2 x 81/2, $9.95 USA
**0-672-22837-8**

## SAMS

### See your local retailer or call 1-800-428-5331.

# Turn to Sams For Complete
# Hardware and Networking Information

**The Business Guide to Local Area Networks**
*William Stallings*
400 pages, 7 3/8 X 9 1/4, $24.95 USA
**0-672-22728-2**

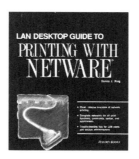

**LAN Desktop Guide to Printing with NetWare**
*Sams*
350 pages, 7 3/8 X 9 1/4, $27.95 USA
**0-672-30084-2**

## More Hardware & Networking Titles

**The First Book of Personal Computing
Second Edition**
*W.E. Wang & Joe Kraynak*
275 pages, 7 3/8 X 9 1/4, $16.95 USA
**0-672-27385-3**

**The First Book of PS/1**
*Kate Barnes*
300 pages, 7 3/8 X 9 1/4, $16.95 USA
**0-672-27346-2**

**IBM PC Advanced Troublshooting &
Repair**
*Robert C. Brenner*
304 pages, 7 3/8 X 9 1/4, $24.95 USA
**0-672-22590-5**

**IBM Personal Computer
Troubleshooting & Repair**
*Robert C. Brenner*
400 pages, 7 3/8 X 9 1/4, $24.95 USA
**0-672-22662-6**

**Interfacing to the IBM Personal
Computer, Second Edition**
*Lewis C. Eggebrecht*
432 pages, 7 3/8 X 9 1/4, $24.95 USA
**0-672-22722-3**

**LAN Desktop Guide to E-mail
with cc:Mail**
*Bruce Fryer*
350 pages, 7 3/8 X 9 1/4, $24.95 USA
**0-672-30243-8**

**Microcomputer Troubleshooting &
Repair**
*John G. Stephenson & Bob Cahill*
368 pages, 7 3/8 X 9 1/4, $24.95 USA
**0-672-22629-4**

**Understanding Local Area Networks,
Second Edition**
*Stan Schatt*
300 pages, 7 3/8 X 9 1/4, $24.95 USA
**0-672-27303-9**

## SAMS

**See your local retailer or call 1-800-428-5331.**

# Look to Sams for THE BEST
# in Computer Information!

**The Best Book of MS-DOS 5**
*Alan Simpson*
650 pages, 73/8 X 91/4, $24.95 USA
**0-672-48499-4**

**The Best Book of Harvard Graphics**
*John Mueller*
400 pages, 73/8 X 91/4, $24.95 USA
**0-672-22740-1**

## Look For These Books In Sams' Best Book Series

**The Best Book of AutoCAD**
*Victor Wright*
800 pages, 73/8 X 91/4, $34.95 USA
**0-672-22725-8**

**The Best Book of Lotus 1-2-3
Release 2.3**
*Alan Simpson*
850 pages, 73/8 X 91/4, $26.95 USA
**0-672-30010-9**

**The Best Book of Lotus 1-2-3
Release 3.1**
*Alan Simpson*
750 pages, 73/8 X 91/4, $27.95 USA
**0-672-22713-4**

**The Best Book of Microsoft Windows 3**
*Carl Townsend*
440 pages, 73/8 X 91/4, $24.95 USA
**0-672-22708-8**

**The Best Book of Microsoft Works
for the PC, Second Edition**
*Ruth K. Witkin*
500 pages, 73/8 X 91/4, $24.95 USA
**0-672-22710-X**

**The Best Book of WordPerfect 5.1**
*Vincent Alfieri, revised by Ralph Blodgett*
800 pages, 73/8 X 91/4, $26.95 USA
**0-672-48467-6**

# SAMS

## See your local retailer or call 1-800-428-5331.

# Reader Feedback Card

Thank you for purchasing this book from SAMS FIRST BOOK series. Our intent with this series is to bring you timely, authoritative information that you can reference quickly and easily. You can help us by taking a minute to complete and return this card. We appreciate your comments and will use the information to better serve your needs.

1. Where did you purchase this book?

☐ Chain bookstore (Walden, B. Dalton)  ☐ Direct mail
☐ Independent bookstore  ☐ Book club
☐ Computer/Software store  ☐ School bookstore
☐ Other _____

2. Why did you choose this book? (Check as many as apply.)

☐ Price  ☐ Appearance of book
☐ Author's reputation  ☐ SAMS' reputation
☐ Quick and easy treatment of subject  ☐ Only book available on subject

3. How do you use this book? (Check as many as apply.)

☐ As a supplement to the product manual  ☐ As a reference
☐ In place of the product manual  ☐ At home
☐ For self-instruction  ☐ At work

4. Please rate this book in the categories below. G = Good; N = Needs improvement; U = Category is unimportant.

☐ Price  ☐ Appearance
☐ Amount of information  ☐ Accuracy
☐ Examples  ☐ Quick Steps
☐ Inside cover reference  ☐ Second color
☐ Table of contents  ☐ Index
☐ Tips and cautions  ☐ Illustrations
☐ Length of book
☐ How can we improve this book?_____
☐ _____

5. How many computer books do you normally buy in a year?

☐ 1–5  ☐ 5–10  ☐ More than 10
☐ I rarely purchase more than one book on a subject.
☐ I may purchase a beginning and an advanced book on the same subject.
☐ I may purchase several books on particular subjects.
☐ (such as _____ )

6. Have your purchased other SAMS or Hayden books in the past year? _____
If yes, how many _____

7. Would you purchase another book in the FIRST BOOK series? _____

8. What are your primary areas of interest in business software? _____

☐ Word processing (particularly _____ )
☐ Spreadsheet (particularly _____ )
☐ Database (particularly _____ )
☐ Graphics (particularly _____ )
☐ Personal finance/accounting (particularly _____ )
☐ Other (please specify _____ )

Other comments on this book or the SAMS' book line: _____
_____

Name _____
Company_____
Address _____
City _____ State _____ Zip_____
Daytime telephone number _____
Title of this book _____

Fold here
- - - - - - - - - - - - - - - - - - - - - - - - - - - - - - - - - - - - - - - - - - - - - - - - -

NO POSTAGE
NECESSARY
IF MAILED
IN THE
UNITED STATES

## BUSINESS REPLY MAIL
FIRST CLASS    PERMIT NO. 336    CARMEL, IN

POSTAGE WILL BE PAID BY ADDRESSEE

### SAMS

11711 N. College Ave.
Suite 141
Carmel, IN 46032–9839